IN SEARCH OF CLIMATE POLITICS

MATTHEW PATERSON
University of Manchester

CAMBRIDGE
UNIVERSITY PRESS

CAMBRIDGE
UNIVERSITY PRESS

University Printing House, Cambridge CB2 8BS, United Kingdom

One Liberty Plaza, 20th Floor, New York, NY 10006, USA

477 Williamstown Road, Port Melbourne, VIC 3207, Australia

314–321, 3rd Floor, Plot 3, Splendor Forum, Jasola District Centre, New Delhi – 110025, India

103 Penang Road, #05–06/07, Visioncrest Commercial, Singapore 238467

Cambridge University Press is part of the University of Cambridge.

It furthers the University's mission by disseminating knowledge in the pursuit of education, learning, and research at the highest international levels of excellence.

www.cambridge.org
Information on this title: www.cambridge.org/9781108838467
DOI: 10.1017/9781108974912

First published 2021

Printed in the United Kingdom by TJ Books Limited, Padstow Cornwall

A catalogue record for this publication is available from the British Library.

ISBN 978-1-108-83846-7 Hardback
ISBN 978-1-108-97141-6 Paperback

IN SEARCH OF CLIMATE POLITICS

In what ways is climate change political? This book addresses this key – but oddly neglected – question. It argues that in order to answer it we need to understand politics in a three-fold way: as a site of authoritative, public decision-making; as a question of power; and as a conflictual phenomenon. Recurring themes centre on de- and repoliticization, and a tension between attempts to simplify climate change to a single problem and its intrinsic complexity. These dynamics are driven by processes of capital accumulation and their associated subjectivities. The book explores these arguments through an analysis of a specific city – Ottawa – which acts as a microcosm of these broader processes. It provides detailed analyses of conflicts over urban planning, transport, and attempts by city government and other institutions to address climate change. The book will be valuable for students and researches looking at the politics of climate change.

MATTHEW PATERSON is Professor of International Politics in the Department of Politics at the University of Manchester. His research focuses on the political economy, global governance, and cultural politics of climate change. His books include *Global Warming and Global Politics* (1996), *Climate Capitalism* (with Peter Newell, Cambridge University Press, 2010), and the prize-winning *Automobile Politics: Ecology and Cultural Political Economy* (Cambridge University Press, 2007). He was a lead author for the 2014 report of the Intergovernmental Panel on Climate Change (IPCC).

Contents

Figures and Tables

Figures

Tables

Contributors

Kofi Agyapong Adomako is a former student in the master's program in Environmental Sustainability at the University of Ottawa, Canada.

Louis Machabée is a former student in the master's program in Environmental Sustainability at the University of Ottawa, Canada.

Merissa Mueller is a former student in the master's program in Environmental Sustainability at the University of Ottawa, Canada.

Xavier P-Laberge is a PhD student in Political Science at the University of Ottawa, Canada.

Bora Plumptre is a climate policy analyst at the Pembina Institute and former student in the master's program in Environmental Sustainability at the University of Ottawa, Canada.

Preface

This book has a slightly odd format that needs a bit of explanation. It is the result of a project within a grant funded by the Social Sciences and Humanities Research Council of Canada, on the 'Cultural Politics of Climate Change'. Within that, one project was to focus on the city of Ottawa. What I decided to do was to map initiatives across the city and then instead of solely hiring graduate students to carry out work as research assistants (although there was some of this), to fund them to do their own work under my supervision on some aspects that we had identified in the mapping process. I had always made explicit to them that, alongside their own pieces of work for their master's program, I would then assemble and develop the various pieces into a book. I was exceptionally lucky to get such a good, enthusiastic group of students.

This book is, among other things, the result of that collaboration. So while the book as a whole is my own project, and the key arguments developed through it are mine, much of the material has been the output of their initial pieces, which I have then reworked. So most of the chapters here have myself plus a co-author, who did, with one exception, do their master's thesis or major research paper on that subject. The extent of re-writing has varied of course for each one (not really because of the quality of the student's original work but more so because of the work needed for the book's narrative), and this is slightly reflected in the author order for each chapter.

Another effect of this is that while several of the chapters rely on interview material, among other sources, there is no standard practice across the book regarding questions of anonymity and attribution. The simplest rule of thumb for reading these is that where the interviewee is named, I carried out the interview, and where it is anonymous, it was carried out by my co-author on that chapter for their master's degree research.

Acknowledgements

When asked what I do for a living (I am very chatty on trains and in queues), I end up joking that I am very lucky as I am never going to be out of a job – I teach politics and I work on climate change. Neither is going away anytime soon. But neither is my dependency on many other people (or anyone else's such dependency of course) who have made a venture like this possible. Thank you to all.

I need first of all to thank my co-authors for their willingness, even enthusiasm, for this way of working on a project. Kofi Agyapong Adomako, Louis Machabée, Merissa Mueller, Xavier P-Laberge, and Bora Plumptre have all been excellent to work with throughout and I hope they have learned as much about academic research and the publishing process as I have about new ways of putting a book project together.

I had a number of other students working with me as research assistants. Xavier P-Laberge (again), René Richard, Benoit Metlej, Josée Provençal, and Benson Westerterp all did excellent work digging up documents for various chapters, and helping me build the database to map climate initiatives across the city, in particular.

Beyond these, the research was funded by a grant entitled 'Cultural Politics of Climate Change', from the Social Science and Humanities Research Council (SSHRC) of Canada. Thank you to the SSHRC for that funding. That grant involved a number of other colleagues that I consulted at various points for this research and have been part of broader conversations about its theoretical discussion. Thanks to Harriet Bulkeley, Simon Dalby, Darren Fleet, Shane Gunster, Matthew Hoffmann, Bob Neubauer, Paul Saurette, and Johannes Stripple. On the Ottawa material, thank you in particular to Caroline Andrew, for various chats over lunch giving me context on Ottawa city politics. While he spent a short time with me as a postdoctoral fellow at the University of Ottawa, Dave Gordon gave very good insights into aspects of city networking and carbon accounting that inform Chapter 4 in particular. Beyond the grant, I have had excellent feedback on presentations of various parts of the book, both empirical chapters and the overall arguments, at the University of East Anglia, Lancaster University, conferences of the Association of American Geographers, the Royal Geographical Society / Institute of British Geographers, Earth Systems Governance, Transition Towns groups in Buxton and Holmfirth, the environment and politics group at Manchester hosted by Tomas Fredriksen, and in particular the participants in a workshop at Manchester hosted and funded by the Sustainable Consumption Institute. That workshop in particular helped me see the wood for the trees and finish the project. Thanks to Joe Blakey, Harriet Bulkeley, Neil Carter, Mike Hodson, Marc Hudson, Sherilyn Macgregor, Andy McMeekin, Magdalene Rodekirchen, Paul Tobin, and Joanna Wilson for helping me see what needed to be done to kick it into shape.

I am also grateful to Ecology Ottawa who have been extremely generous with time over the years and allowed me to see some of the process from the inside of their campaigns and organizing. Thanks in particular to Graham Saul, Trevor Haché, and Robb Barnes. Thank you more broadly also to the various interviewees for the chapters who provided their time and reflections on the various issues at stake. Thank you specifically to Kai Millard for digging out a report from February 1992 and working out how to read it into a modern version of WordPerfect!

A version of Chapter 5 was previously published as Matthew Paterson and Merissa Mueller (2018) Cultural Conflicts and Decarbonization Pathways: Urban Intensification Politics as a Site of Contestation in Ottawa, In Andrés Luque-Ayala, Harriet Bulkeley, and Simon Marvin, eds., *Rethinking Urban Transitions: Politics in the Low Carbon City*. London: Routledge, 203–23. Thank you to the editors and to Routledge for permission to reproduce the chapter here. Thank you also to those who gave permissions to reproduce a number of figures in the book.

At Cambridge University Press, thanks to Matt Lloyd for his enthusiasm about the project overall, Sarah Lambert for her efficient processing of the manuscript, Liz Steel for her admirable copyediting, and the reviewers for both enthusiasm and good critical insight as to what I needed to do to the book.

I have always worked to music but have gotten out of the habit of recording this properly in the acknowledgements. I now find I have three sorts of days in music–work terms. A normal work day focused on writing or teaching is an Underworld day; if I need a bit more of a gentle lift then it is a Cocteau Twins day; while a stress day that needs to calmly work through things when way behind is a King Tubby, dub reggae day. Thankfully this project has not needed many of the latter. All three I find put me in a frame of mind where I can concentrate for much longer than otherwise I would be capable of. Thank you to their varying sorts of brilliance.

Thanks to Jo for sharing my life for what is approaching thirty years now. I am very skeptical of the apparent tradition of male academics thanking their partners for 'suffering' them while they finish a book. No one we share our lives with ought to 'suffer' for the writing of a book: if they do, your priorities are all wrong. I am pretty sure Jo has not made any sacrifices for this book, or any of my others. She will of course tell her many followers on Twitter if I am deluding myself.

This book is for Anice (both of them) and Freya. Anice, my mum, died in 2014, while Anice, my niece, was born in 2015. She and Freya (my daughter) will experience the full gamut of what climate politics has to throw at them. I think they'll throw a lot back at it too.

Acronyms

AQCCMP	Air Quality and Climate Change Management Plan
CaGBC	Canada Green Building Council
CCP	Cities for Climate Protection
CDP	Community Design Plan
CSOC	Community Services and Operations Committee
FCM	Federation of Canadian Municipalities
FIT	feed-in-tariff
FSS	Faculty of Social Sciences (University of Ottawa)
GEGEA	Green Energy and Green Economy Act (Ontario)
GHG	greenhouse gas
GMF	Green Municipal Fund
GND	Green New Deal
ICLEI	International Council for Local Environmental Initiatives
IESO	Independent Electricity System Operator (Ontario)
LEED	Leadership in Energy and Environmental Design
NCENN	National Capital Environmental Nonprofit Network
NCC	National Capital Commission
NGO	Non-Government Organization
OMB	Ontario Municipal Board
OREC	Ottawa Renewable Energy Cooperative
OSEG	Ontario Sports and Entertainment Group
PCP	Partners for Climate Protection program
RE	renewable energy
RMOC	Regional Municipality of Ottawa-Carleton
TMP	Transportation Master Plan
UNFCCC	United Nations Framework Convention on Climate Change
UofO	University of Ottawa
XR	Extinction Rebellion

1

Introduction

In April 2016, the University of Ottawa made a curious decision regarding climate change. The previous couple of years saw campaigning by student groups, supported by some academics, to get the University to divest the holdings in its pension funds and endowments from fossil fuels. This was in common with divestment campaigns on many other university campuses across North America and beyond, as well as in churches and some larger institutional investors. In response, the University announced that it would not divest from fossil fuels but later on in the report making this announcement, it stated that it would take the investments out of the various fossil fuel companies it had holdings in, and shift that money into 'clean energy' investments. In other words, it decided to divest from fossil fuels but would not accept publicly that it was doing this (see Chapter 8 for a longer discussion of this episode).

What is going on here? Why would a public institution such as a large university effectively deny that it was acting on climate change in ways that campaigners had demanded, even while it was in fact acceding to those demands? My aim in this book is to explore in what ways we can think of climate change as *political*. This vignette, which is discussed in more detail in Chapter 8, exemplifies many of the sorts of processes I want to bring to light.

First, it helps us think about some key conceptual questions about politics – is it a site of collective decision-making (the university in this case), is it about the power and authority to generate or resist change, or is it about conflict or consensus? I unpack these three in Chapter 2. With the first, of course, my choice of vignette is question begging – isn't politics as a site restricted to governments? One answer to this question is precisely that if politics is also about power and authority, we have to look for it in many more sites than just national governments. But more importantly, if politics means all three of these, how do they interact? One interpretation of this decision is that the university sought to *depoliticize* climate change, in saying both that it was not really bowing to pressure from student groups, and not really making a public statement that could be regarded as hostile to fossil fuel interests, precisely in order to secure the political *authority* of the university senior management. That is, thinking about the multiple dimensions of politics as a concept helps us understand the nature of the processes by which responses to climate change are generated and justified.

Second, this vignette helps us think about some of the drivers of responses to climate change. What we see in the university's decision is that in explaining why they are divesting (although they refuse the term), they are doing so as a strategy that combines a logic of investment with a logic of public reputation and corporate identity. Their decision was driven by questions of return on investment, combined with a desire to present the university as a progressive, civic-minded institution playing a role in questions of broad social interest: Hence the 'clean energy' frame for the decision. This I call a *cultural political economy* argument. An important implication of this is that climate politics can be everywhere – in all human activities and relations. Climate change is everyday, mundane, implicated in the normal dynamics of our societies (Saurin 1994).

Third, the story helps us focus in on two core dynamics and dilemmas in addressing climate change politically. One of these I call a tension between *purification* vs. *complexity*, while the other is a dynamic between *depoliticization* and *repoliticization*. One powerful logic for campaigners and decision-makers alike is to engage in 'purification' of climate change – to simplify it to a single enemy (the fossil fuel industry), a single policy tool (carbon pricing), or a single magic technology (battery storage), most notably. For campaigners in particular, this enables them to mobilize effectively (as enemies are surely useful, as are simple stories about magic solutions), and to sharpen public attention on climate change itself, the threats it poses, and so on. Divestment campaigns have been one of a number of recent forms of more confrontational politics (alongside anti-pipeline campaigns, the Sunrise Movement, school strikes for climate, and Extinction Rebellion), which have this logic at their heart. They *purify* climate change through a focus on the fossil fuel industry as the enemy. But also, while the university tried to *depoliticize* the divestment decision by emphasizing its technical or managerial character, activists also *repoliticize* it by making the power relations involved in shifting away from fossil fuels apparent, and insisting on collective public decision-making to challenge that power. But on the other hand, climate change also has a powerful logic that stands in stark tension to this desire for purification. It is enormously complex, entailing dealing with almost all social and economic activity, developing and deploying new technologies, shifting social practices in varying ways in systems with very different structures and actors (think electricity vs. transport vs. agriculture and all the nuances within each of those sectors). It is hard to see how purification *on its own* can account for the political dynamics entailed in shifting such an enormous complex system. 'System change not climate change' is a common slogan of these campaigning groups, raising the question of what is the 'system' and how do systems change? Nevertheless, the purification of climate change has been crucial to generating shifts in power relations and dynamics on the issue.

1.1 Why Focus on a City? And on Ottawa?

Chapter 2 develops these three core arguments in more detail, and they provide the arguments I try to develop throughout this book. I do so by exploring climate change within the city of Ottawa. In part, the attempt to theorize climate politics arises out of my own, very minor, role in some of the processes analysed here – including the divestment story above and some work over the years with local non-government organization (NGO) Ecology Ottawa. Studying a place you live in also enables the researcher to follow processes reasonably closely, and pay attention to context and in particular to the structures and practices of daily life through which climate change interventions are generated and upon which those interventions act.

A good deal of recent work on climate change politics has focused on the urban scale, or 'cities and climate change'.[1] While this book is not first and foremost seeking to contribute to these debates specifically, it is the case that the urban scale is where very large proportions of climate change interventions take place, and where the key carbon-generating systems – housing, transport, energy consumption, industry – are located physically, organized techno-economically, and governed politically. The urban scale is where we can bring sharply into focus the mundane character of much of climate politics, as well as the dynamics of what I call in Section 1.2 'implicit' climate politics. Focusing on a single city can be a useful way to explore the key political dynamics of climate change.

But Ottawa is also interesting in relation to the existing research on climate change and cities in that much of that work focuses, for good reasons, on 'pioneer' or 'leader' cities and city networks. We know a lot about Copenhagen, Vancouver, and various other cities that have got serious plans in place for reducing their greenhouse gas emissions and seem to be on track to meet them. And we know a lot about networks such as C40 or the International Council for Local Environmental Initiatives (ICLEI)'s Cities for Climate Protection network, which are, as Kern and Bulkeley (2009) pithily term them, 'networks of pioneers for

---

[1] For a small selection of this literature, see: Bulkeley et al. (2010, 2015), Hodson and Marvin (2010), Bulkeley (2013), and Luque-Ayala et al. (2018). A substantial focus of this literature is on city networks on climate change, see for example: Bulkeley and Betsill (2003), Bouteligier (2012), Gordon (2013, 2016b, 2020), and Lee (2014).

pioneers' (see also Gordon 2016a). But we know less about the 'ordinary' cities that struggle with climate change. These cities take some occasional initiatives, they implement them partially but they suffer political setbacks or bureaucratic inertia. Climate action thus comes in waves and stutters in between, by which time the city's emissions have grown further. They almost certainly fail to overcome basic contradictions between their imperatives for local economic development, combined with cultural norms about transport, housing, and the like, and addressing climate change effectively. These cities are probably the considerable majority of the world's cities. And this certainly characterizes Ottawa – at times in its history, especially during the 1990s, it was seen as a 'pioneer' but it has failed to sustain early momentum that would justify such a label (see Chapters 3 and 4 in particular for more details on this checkered history of the city). As such, there is much to be learned about the character of climate politics from exploring it in a place such as Ottawa.

In short, Ottawa is ordinary. Most cities, or at least their boosters, tell a story as to their uniqueness. But most cities are in fact rather similar in many respects. I hope in what follows that readers, whether they are in Brisbane, Toulouse, Hyderabad, Montevideo, Liverpool, Milwaukee, or Accra, will see dynamics familiar to those in their own settings. Indeed, an additional value in focusing on cities is that these similarities cut across geopolitical fractures in ways that states do not – city politics in the cities mentioned above are much more similar to each other than is the case across the countries in which they are situated. The diversity of cities across the world is not usefully understood in terms of categories of North/ South (Robinson 2006) and in cities across this divide we see: Conflicts over urban planning, transport policy, housing, and commercial buildings; Faltering steps to address climate change stymied by apathy, corporate lobbying, resistance by car drivers but occasionally mobilized in novel and even inspiring ways to create change; or Recurrent dilemmas generated by competing emotional attachments to climate action and to familiar and convenient daily routines.

Nevertheless, to aid such a comparison to your own situation, here are a few specifics about Ottawa. It is a city of a little under a million people. In the 2011 census its official population was 883,390, and its current (2020) population is estimated at around a million. It has a sister city on the other side of the Ottawa river, Gatineau, which if added in, comes to around 1.2m in the 2011 census (City of Ottawa 2016). But a substantial amount of the territory of the city is rural, at least since various previous municipalities were amalgamated into the current City of Ottawa in 2001 (see Chapter 3), meaning the urban population is somewhat lower. This has implications for the balance of urban, suburban, and rural forces in the City Council, which have significant effects on the dynamics of decision-making over sustainability, as we will see both generally (see Chapter 3) and for particular questions such as planning and transport (see Chapters 5 and 6 in particular). This also means that, in territorial terms, it is the largest big city in North America, at 2,790 km^2. Like much of Canada, Ottawa has a climate of extremes – average daily high temperatures in July of around 27°C (with temperatures in the 30s reasonably common) and average daily low temperatures in January of around –15°C (with temperatures in the –20s also commonplace). There is snow on the ground for between four and five months of the year. This has obvious implications for heating, cooling, and transport in the city.

Ottawa is also the capital of Canada, which generates a number of specificities. One is that it is a 'government town' – the federal government dominates employment in the city, especially since the collapse of hi-tech firm Nortel, the principal private sector employer, in 2009. Another is that its median income is relatively high, around 30 per cent higher than the Canadian average. A third is that it has some institutional quirks. One is the aforementioned split of the physical urban area into Ottawa and Gatineau, a split that is also across the provincial boundary between Ontario and Québec, a long legacy of Queen Victoria's decision to locate the capital precisely on the border between francophone and anglophone parts of what was becoming Canada during the nineteenth century. This has effects for coordination of urban decision-making, most notably over public transport infrastructure, which is only very loosely integrated between the two. The other, however, is the presence of a federal jurisdiction, the National Capital Commission (NCC), that straddles both Ottawa and Gatineau, owns significant amounts of land, and has specific rights over planning that is not the case in other cities.

Nevertheless, despite these specifics, Ottawa is, like many other cities, a city whose politics is often dominated by the questions of urban planning, transport, local economic development, and housing. And thus it is dominated by the interests, values, and visions surrounding these – dominant actors such as property developers, local communities defending their neighbourhood, city managers struggling to meet competing demands for low property taxes, efficient transport systems, and so on.

1.2 Why We Need to Search for Climate Politics

But while the book arises out of this research in Ottawa, it also arises out of a realization that while many people such as me teach, talk, write, and think about climate politics, none of us really says what it *is*. That is at least the premise of this book. While there is a vast body of work analysing various aspects of climate change politics, from the United Nations Framework Convention on Climate Change (UNFCCC), to national climate policy, to the politics of specific policies such as carbon markets, there is nevertheless very little which explicitly addresses the question of how we should understand the political character of climate change *per se*. We use all the terms that connote specific aspects of political life – power, authority, conflict, or governance, for example – and there are endless terminological and theoretical debates about the meanings of these but we don't do the same with politics itself, in relation to climate change. What is political about climate change? What sorts of political forces and dynamics drive responses to climate change forward and hold them back? What are the political dynamics and dilemmas for those pushing for adequate responses to climate change?

There are of course also many who decry the political character of climate change. 'If only we could keep the politics out' is a common enough refrain. They think politics is somehow noise, getting in the way of us recognizing our common interests in dealing with climate change. This is most explicitly seen in the argument by James Lovelock that we need to abandon democracy to address climate change (Willis 2020: 1). This is often just a simple misunderstanding: The reflection of how in many societies 'politics' has come in public discourse to have the very narrow meaning of *politicking* – the jockeying for position between different groups of professional *politicians*, the cynical manipulation of citizens and electoral processes to pursue these aims, and so on. Such an account operates as a self-fulling prophecy of course (Hay 2007). But politics has a much longer history and richer, more important set of meanings than this particular expression, and we shouldn't allow it to be captured by such a superficial way of understanding it.

Other people think that climate change is not political but instead an economic or technological question. It is a simple matter of 'getting the prices right' to generate incentives for investors, producers, or consumers to shift behaviour accordingly, or of finding the sorts of technologies that can effectively decarbonize our various economic and social activities that currently spew carbon into the atmosphere at a still increasing rate. The economy and technology are indeed important but it is a mistake to think that they are themselves not political. If we ask how the prices may be made to be 'right', then we are immediately in the conflicts over taxation, emissions trading, and the power relations that will enable or constrain such 'carbon pricing'. Ditto with technology – radically new technology is almost always highly disruptive, and as such is resisted by many forces (economic, cultural, and political) that seek to prevent its emergence, and at the same time it requires huge amounts of effort to produce.

Against those who argue this is just really fundamentally about a technological revolution, and who do so because they believe that people will not voluntarily change their daily practices sufficiently, it is crucial to understand that technical and social change are always closely intertwined. It is simply a false dichotomy to make this contrast between technology and behaviour. The most obvious way to debunk this persistent myth is to think about the emergence and dominance of the automobile in Western societies and then globally (if unevenly across time and space). From 1900 to 1950, the US (a little later elsewhere) underwent a major 'energy transition', where transport systems shifted from rail, horses, cycling, and walking to being dominated by the car. Was this a technical change? To be sure. Was it social change? Definitely. Could these two be separated out from each other? The attempt would be an absurdity. The lives led, the possibilities enabled (and others foreclosed), and the dangers generated were all enabled by the technology of the automobile, and conversely the social, cultural, and political visions created for the car shaped its future (see especially Sachs 1992; Gartman 1994; Paterson 2007). Similar stories could be told for the various other key elements in the energy transitions involved in industrial capitalist development – coal/steam and electricity, in particular.

Building on this, it is really important to underscore how integral fossil energy is to the modern world. Whether or not we believe that the global economy can be disentangled from fossil energy, and whether or not we believe doing so requires us to abandon economic growth as a collective goal, or capitalism as a social system, historically it is not an accident that fossil fuels have been central to the social, economic, and political dynamics of the last 200 years. We can measure this statistically through the exponential rise of both coal consumption and then later on oil and gas, and its correlations with global economic growth. But the nitty-gritty details perhaps demonstrate this deep link more effectively. As Andreas Malm shows, industrialization was proceeding reasonably well in Britain on the basis of water power, and the shift to coal and steam power was only decisive in the mills around Manchester after the 1826 spinners strike, when mill owners decided to automate spinning, which gave a decisive advantage to coal/steam over water as a source of power for mills. Coal/steam was a class strategy to undermine the power of workers in the production process (Malm 2015). But coal was also central to the democratization of Western societies: The forces that mobilized most system-atically and effectively for universal *male* suffrage in the late nineteenth and early twentieth centuries across the West were trade unions, who derived their power from their ability to control the flow and use of coal – dockworkers, railwaymen, steelworkers, and coal miners themselves (Mitchell 2013). Conversely, oil has tended to undermine democracy, as workers were unable to effectively control its flow to generate political reform. And politicians in democratic societies have competed over their abilities to mobilize fossil energy most effectively, and distribute their benefits to citizens smoothly, from Herbert Hoover's 'a chicken in every pot: two cars in every garage' (as quoted in Wernick 1991: 71) to 'Mondeo Man' being one of the key signifiers in the 1997 UK general election (Paterson 2007). Dealing with climate change without 'politics' makes little sense when we understand the depth with which the causes of climate change are integral to our political life.

This also implies that almost anything can be understood as part of climate politics. Climate politics is not analytically reducible to the things that are articulated explicitly in relation to climate change. Anywhere there is political activity (collective authoritative decisions, conflicts and power relations, and the relations between these elements) that entails energy use, we can treat these as questions of climate politics. Even if actors have not yet sought to frame an object as a climate change object, since its qualities and relations will be transformed as we respond to climate change, then we can explore its dynamics to help us think through climate change's politics. We can think for example about meat and dairy: For a long time ignored in the climate change debate, it has erupted in perhaps the last five years as an object of attention, from the methane emissions from cows, sheep, and goats, to the embodied energy of animal feed and mechanized farming. However, it would still have made sense to analyse the politics of meat as a climate change question even though the number of actors that had explicitly made the link in any sort of sustained way was vanishingly small, since it was always the case that any serious response to climate change had to address the meat (or perhaps more precisely and certainly most importantly, the cow/sheep/goat/dairy) question. Much climate politics is thus 'implicit' – logically contained in an activity, decision, initiative, or conflict, even if climate change is not mentioned explicitly. Indeed, there are often reasons to avoid framing an issue as about climate change: Even if explicit 'climate denial' is not in play (and, perhaps surprisingly, it is completely absent from the processes I analyse in this book), the sort of everyday denial that Kari Norgaard (2011) analysed is commonplace. She uses this to refer to the fact that while people are widely aware of climate change, its causes, dangers, and potential catastrophic consequences, they carry on about their daily lives as if ignorant, rarely mentioning it, not connecting it to their daily routines and habits, or to the political setting in which they find themselves.

I proceed therefore with the proposition that climate change is intrinsically political. I also proceed on the basis that, contra those who seek to 'keep politics out', who worry that the politicization of climate change only makes dealing with it more difficult, thinking more carefully about climate change's political qualities will be helpful in advancing responses to climate change. As such I seek to build on those claims emphasizing the need to politicize climate change, not depoliticize it (e.g. Pepermans and Maeseele 2016; Mann and Wainwright 2018; Wall 2020; Willis 2020). As Rebecca Willis (2020, 3) argues, 'the problem is not *too much democracy*, it is *too little*'. For democracy, read politics, and indeed as we will see in Chapter 2, in many ways the two stand in for each other – to make climate change 'more political' is to bring it squarely and explicitly within the realm of fully democratic deliberation, contestation, and decision-making.

I assume readers are familiar with the litany of impacts of climate change, some already well underway, and many more to come or to intensify, and that the stakes are exceptionally high in terms of the effects on human misery and perhaps even civilizational survival. In recent years the stakes have become ever more sharply identified, and barely a week goes by without a new report detailing new evidence of the severity of the likely impacts. If you are not familiar with these, then there are myriad sources of such information: This book is not one of them. I also assume that readers are reasonably familiar with the scale of the challenge, the need in effect to get GHG emissions to more or less zero (and probably also to generate novel forms of 'negative emissions') in a spectacularly rapid timeframe, way beyond any such transformation human societies have ever experienced. But the premise that is perhaps new to many, is that understanding the political drivers of these potential transformations is key to understanding whether or not we can pursue them effectively. Chapter 2 is therefore aimed at elaborating what it means to think about climate change as political.

1.3 How I Explore Climate Change As Political

Chapter 2 develops the conceptual arguments sketched in the opening paragraphs of this introduction in much more detail to provide the core of the argumentative terrain of the book. What the rest of this book is designed to do is to develop an analysis of climate politics that tries to retain all three senses of politics – the arena of collective decision-making, power relations, and the dynamics of agonistic conflict – as well as to demonstrate and explore the cultural political economy drivers of climate action and the tension between purification and complexity. This means that climate politics can be understood in relation to a recurring dynamic of de- and re-politicization, as climate interventions are rendered technical but then repoliticized. But I also seek to keep in play a sense that the politics around climate interventions is never divorced from the material specificities of the intervention: Rebuilding a streetscape, changing planning practices, accounting for carbon, and managing the infrastructure of a large public institution, particular models for investing in renewable energy (to take some of the examples discussed in later chapters), will each have specific political dynamics in part produced by the technical, place-specific, material qualities of the intervention and its contexts.

How then do I seek to develop these arguments? The material for this book draws principally on research on climate change politics within the city of Ottawa, Canada, carried out between 2010 and 2016.

Throughout the book I explore the diverse *sites* of climate politics in the city:
The decision-making processes in the City of Ottawa[2] itself (Chapter 3); how that
site is made by collaborative networks and the spreading of carbon accounting as a
governance tool – that is, as a way of exercising power – to the City (Chapter 4);
within the University of Ottawa (Chapter 8), the Ottawa Renewable Energy
Cooperative (Chapter 9); and in the main non-state carbon accounting initiative,
Carbon 613 (Chapter 4). The book also maps the broad range of climate
governance initiatives across the city (Chapter 7).

The book also demonstrates questions of *power* and *conflict* in climate politics.
It shows how technocratic attempts to govern carbon entail the exercise of
expertise-based power that seeks to become routinized in daily activities – carbon
accounting (Chapter 4) is emblematic here, but the University of Ottawa's very
successful energy management systems also have this quality (Chapter 8), as do
some aspects of the efforts to shift urban infrastructure across the City through
'intensification' (construction within existing urban boundaries rather than out on
the city's edge, Chapter 6) or 'Complete Streets' (rebuilding streets for multiple
users rather than just cars, Chapter 5) as planning philosophies. It also shows
various ways that the power of specific groups and interests shapes the trajectory
of climate change action in the city. The power of property developers in the
planning process is perhaps the most obvious (Chapter 6) but we can also discern it
in the class dynamics of renewable energy development (Chapter 9), the power of
finance and accounting that lurks in stories about carbon accounting (Chapter 4) or
fossil fuel divestment (Chapter 8), and the broad cultural power of a car-centred
transport norm (Chapter 5). It also shows how when such initiatives frame them
through highly consensual, deliberative discourses, such initiatives then efface the
conflicts implicit in them with problematic effects (Chapter 9). Finally, it shows
the dynamics of repoliticization, as various actors contest the power of other actors
and decisions at various sites of climate politics, from students contesting the
University of Ottawa over divestment (Chapter 8), pro-car forces resisting the shift
in urban infrastructure entailed in Complete Streets (Chapter 5), or councillors and
community groups resisting building projects in the city under the banner of
'intensification'. Many of these have the dynamic of de- and re-politicization
developed in Chapter 2.

We also see the *cultural political economy* argument reflected in various ways
throughout the book. It shows how corporate strategies, and relations to the
council, shape the form that climate change action takes in relation to planning and
building development (Chapter 6), remaking street infrastructure (Chapter 5), and

---

[2] A terminological note is in order. Following local convention, when I use 'City of Ottawa', capitalized like
this, or just 'City', capitalized, I refer to the city council. If I just say 'the city', lower case, then I am referring
more broadly to the city as a whole (including but not reduced to the council).

in novel financing arrangements for renewable energy (Chapter 9). It also demonstrates how broad models of corporate governance, notably carbon accounting (Chapter 3) and private ownership of energy resources (Chapter 9), shape climate governance initiatives. It shows the affective or cultural dynamics of this, from how carbon accounting is mobilized through narratives of heroes (Chapter 4), intensification is resisted through attachment to place and particular urban aesthetics at the same time as promoters valorize the aesthetics of tall buildings (Chapter 6), and how car-driving subjectivities shape the conflicts over rebuilding the street infrastructure (Chapter 5).

Finally, the book explores various moments where the tension between the two key dynamics of *purification* and *complexity* erupts. It shows the complexity of climate politics as entailing myriad actions by different actors in different ways, and reducing it to a single site fails to enable us to understand this complexity (Chapter 7). It demonstrates the ways in which patient and increasingly experimental attention to the complexity of large-scale systems of physical infrastructure can produce very significant gains in climate outcomes (Chapter 8). And it shows how opposition to intensification, purified as opposition to property developers, stands uneasily with the complexities of reshaping urban infrastructure to make it low carbon, requiring a more understanding of the cultural complexities of climate change best understood through the notion of ambivalence (Chapter 6). But it also shows how purification can at times work very effectively to shift public debates and generate novel initiatives. While purification regarding intensification (Chapter 6) operates to produce opposition to low carbon shifts even by proponents of climate action, at the University of Ottawa it generated, in the form of the divestment campaign, heightened attention to aspects of climate change previously ignored by the University (Chapter 8).

The cases also show an ongoing dynamic relationship between *depoliticization* and *repoliticization*. In many cases, depoliticization is the dominant dynamic – within the City of Ottawa's processes themselves (Chapter 3), within processes of carbon accounting (Chapter 4), the University of Ottawa's intensive energy management systems (Chapter 8), the activities of the Ottawa Renewable Energy Coop (Chapter 9), and the broad mapping of the initiatives across the city that we present (Chapter 7). As will become clear, it is not that depoliticized management always fails in relation to climate change – while within the City of Ottawa it has perhaps only achieved limited results, within the University of Ottawa it has had very considerable success at managing and reducing the university's emissions. At other times, we show attempts by governing authorities to depoliticize which do not really manage to do so, as in the cases of Complete Streets (Chapter 5) or intensification projects (Chapter 6). Nevertheless, we see relatively few instances of open repoliticization of climate change itself, the most prominent example being the divestment campaign at the University (Chapter 8). Instead, we see multiple small-scale repoliticizations over specific projects or initiatives, the Complete Streets project on Main Street (Chapter 5), and individual building projects legitimized by reference to the overarching norm of intensification (Chapter 6). The closest we get to explicit repoliticization in terms of new democratic practices regards the Ottawa Renewable Energy Coop (Chapter 9), and that is rather timid, perhaps, as a democratic experiment.

These cases analysed are themselves quite heterogeneous, and this choice was deliberate. Exploring diverse sites and processes of climate politics helps identify the key dynamics in play because when we see similar processes in different settings, we know something deeper is going on. They are also heterogeneous in another way, hinted at when I argued that in principle climate politics is going on everywhere, even if the term climate change is not deployed. For the mapping exercise undertaken in Chapter 7, the selection criteria here was that climate change had to be deployed in some way to justify the initiative or action, although it did not need to be the *principal* rationale. In part this was for manageability reasons but there is also something different entailed by exploring the explicit politics of climate change from its implicit politics. But I did want to also explore the latter, and Chapters 5 (on Complete Streets) and especially 6 (on conflicts over intensification) do focus on conflicts and initiatives where climate change plays at best a minor role in the overt political debate. However, these are clearly articulated by some of the actors involved as those necessary to address climate change (to reshape streetscapes away from the automobile, or to increase urban density), and even without their recognition of this, this is nevertheless the case. We can learn a lot about climate politics by looking at interventions that might be consistent with the sorts of transformations responses to climate change entail, even if climate change is not invoked as a primary rationale for those interventions.

Given the heterogeneity of the sites and processes, the research proceeded in a diverse manner also. It entailed archive work in the City of Ottawa archives, media analysis, interviews, some direct observation (of city council meetings, field sites), interviews with key participants in the various processes, and documentary analysis of the various initiatives, qualitatively coded for different aspects of their efforts to govern climate change and occasionally supplemented with simple exercises in network analysis to explore particular patterns. It also entailed working at times with Ecology Ottawa, the key local NGO working on climate change.[3] Finally, the research has proceeded in a highly collaborative relation with a number of graduate

---

[3] I can't claim to have played anything more than a very minor role in their work. However I have produced a number of reports for them over the years (notably Ecology Ottawa 2009; Paterson 2010b), presented at workshops they have organized, and prompted by them acted as an expert witness in an appeal by the property developers to the Ontario Municipal Board (see Chapter 8 on this institution's role in the planning process).

students at the University of Ottawa. Where a chapter has a co-author on it, apart from Chapters 7 and 8, this means that the chapter arose out of a masters' thesis or research paper by the co-author, supervised by me and co-designed in the context of the overall project that funded this research. I have then taken that initial piece of work and turned it into the chapter you see in this book.

A final consequence of this is that the arguments I develop here do not unfold in a neat linear narrative. This is probably obvious from the way the chapters have just been discussed. Each has enabled me to consider the three aspects of the book, and combine them, in specific ways. The structure of the book should be understood as a journey through these arguments via the various empirical narratives, rather than organized to develop the overall argument progressively. But my aim is that the cumulative effect is to persuade you that to understand climate politics is to do so via the interactions between politics as a site of collective decision-making, politics as power, and politics as conflict, to see specific events in climate as driven by the interaction between the contested search for accumulation and the cultural values attached to our daily practices, and to see the dilemmas facing agents in climate politics as ones between seeking to simplify, or purify climate politics to a single cause, struggle, solution, and the inherent complexity of transforming the entire fabric of our societies in the ways we need to.

2

In Search of Climate Politics

To think politically about climate change, we need to elaborate the arguments I sketched out via the University of Ottawa divestment story in Chapter 1. First, we need to conceptualize explicitly what we mean by politics. Second, we need to think about the political drivers of (and obstacles to) climate change action, a question I will suggest can be understood via a notion of cultural political economy. Third, we need to think about the dynamics that arise out of these first two, which I take to be two-fold: On the one hand a recurring dynamic between depoliticization and repoliticization, and on the other hand a tension I characterize as 'purification vs. complexity', between the instinct to want to find simple 'solutions' or enemies to fight, and the multidimensional qualities of the high carbon world that needs to be transformed. To start, however, it is perhaps worth thinking a little about how climate change is commonly conceptualized and framed, in public discourse as well as across various academic disciplines, in order to tease out what the politics of these specific climate change frames are.

2.1 Politics in Existing Framings of Climate Change

There are many such frames and I gloss over lots of nuance here, but I group them into three for the current purposes: System adjustment and maintenance frames, systemic inequalities and contestation frames, and system transformation frames.

2.1.1 System Adjustment and Maintenance Frames

These tend to conceptualize climate change, and propose interventions in relation to it, from within the dominant sets of ideas within the contemporary social order, and aim, implicitly or explicitly, to minimize the impacts of climate policy on that order. At a broad level we can see this in the almost-obsessive focus among policy-makers – in rich and poor countries alike – with what the impacts of any specific

14

climate policy will be on GDP growth. This functions as a fundamental constraint on climate policy and often the decisive criteria against which a policy is judged – if the impacts on growth are too severe, the policy will be rejected, and conversely, if policies that can accelerate growth can be identified, they will be favoured. Within this overall orientation to climate change focused on system maintenance, we can see a few specific ways of framing climate change.

First is the framing of climate change as a simple 'emissions problem'. Here, climate change is understood in relation to the immediate emissions – CO_2, CH_4, CFCs, etc. – but the frame is that the underlying sources of those emissions are not interrogated (an 'emissions fetishism' if you like, see Lohmann 2010). At the same time, the focus is on the departure of emissions levels from the status quo rather than on the end goal of emissions levels. The structure of United Nations Framework Convention on Climate Change (UNFCCC) agreements and national policy processes has tended to reflect this frame, in the UNFCCC's initial goal (see United Nations 1992, articles 4.2a and b) of stabilizing industrialized countries' emissions by 2000 at 1990 levels, the Kyoto Protocol's goal of a 5.2 per cent cut of industrialized countries' emissions by 2008–2012, and many countries' individual targets from their unilateral ones announced in the early 1990s through to their Nationally Determined Contributions (the principal obligation states undertook) under the Paris Agreement.[1] This focus on departure from the status quo makes policymakers think about short- to medium-term cuts of 5, 10, or 20 per cent, neglecting any sense of broad transformations involved in responding to climate change in favour of focusing on specific gains within the existing overall structure.

The second frame is of climate change as a 'market failure' problem. This is the dominant economists' understanding of the problem (see classically Stern 2007). Markets either fail to adequately reflect the 'real' costs of greenhouse gas (GHG) emissions and thus government intervention is needed to 'internalize' these costs (the Pigouvian approach) or alternatively there are inadequately specified property rights that lead to suboptimal resource use (the Coasian approach). Either way, intervention, either through taxation or allocating property rights, is needed to correct these market failures. Intrinsically however, it is not necessary to establish a particular end goal in terms of levels of emissions; rather, once prices adequately reflect real costs, the market will decide the 'optimal' rate of GHG emissions.

Third is a related understanding of climate change as a 'global commons' problem. This is ubiquitous especially in thinking about the global dimensions of climate change as exemplified in the relevant chapter of the last IPCC report (Stavins et al. 2014). Here, the *problématique* of climate is turned into one of

---

[1] The Paris Agreement does supplement this with a collective long-term goal of limiting temperature rises to 2°C, and to aim for 1.5°C, but this only bears a tangential relationship to the national-level targets, generated 'bottom-up' by countries, which remain framed in terms of departures from the status quo.

cooperation: How to get disparate actors with different particular interests but a shared common interest in 'solving the problem' to overcome both their specific differences and the general problem of trust and free-riding seen to be persistent in such collective action problems. This frame is the basis for the vast majority of work on the international dimensions of climate politics in particular, given the lack of a global authority capable of compelling states to act on climate change. As Tom Princen usefully reminds us, however, there can be extensive cooperation that is simultaneously utterly useless in addressing the underlying problem (Princen 2003, 2005).

2.1.2 Systemic Inequalities and Contestation Frames

For many, climate change is understood more in relation to questions of inequality and (in)justice. One of the key early interventions in international climate debates (Agarwal and Narain 1991) argued for the need to think explicitly about the key differences in human circumstances entailed in climate change, that are dangerously elided when we think of climate as a commons or simple emissions problem. They showed that how you account for GHGs matters – if you only count aggregate emissions for each country vs. per capita emissions, you get a greatly different sense of who is responsible for climate change. And if you fail to distinguish between what they called 'luxury' and 'survival' emissions, you compound that injustice. Once you count properly, they argued, it becomes easy to see that climate change is effectively a form of global 'slow violence' (Nixon 2013) where the world's rich, mostly located in the global North, impose the costs and impacts of climate change on the poor and vulnerable, mostly located in the global South.

This generates what is often known as a 'climate justice' frame (e.g. Shue 2014; Ciplet et al. 2015). This sort of a frame motivates many social movements involved in climate politics. Increasingly, these inequalities and injustices in climate change politics are understood as multiple, not simply a North–South question but intersecting with other key social–structural faultlines of gender, race, and class (e.g. Newell 2005; MacGregor 2014; Buckingham and Le Masson 2017; Pearse 2017), and sometimes along more crude lines focused on the way that intensified inequality means that the '1 per cent', or the very rich, have particularly important roles in generating climate change (Kenner 2019).

2.1.3 System Transformation Frames

For system transformation frames, climate change is fundamentally a transformative process, popularized by Naomi Klein's memorable title *This Changes Everything*

(2014). Humanity as a whole has never collectively attempted the sort of profound transformation – at once social, technological, political, and economic – that taking the carbon out of the global economy involves, while dealing with those climate changes already in train (Newell and Paterson 2010, 1). It entails a rapid, radical change in more or less every aspect of the infrastructure of social life: Work, travel, housing (and all the objects in our homes), cooking, farming – all will change, and a good number of specific activities will simply disappear. This transformation will come about either because we decarbonize fully in the next forty years or so or because climate change itself overwhelms the capacity of our institutions to adapt adequately. And it is also those radical, rapid transformations that human societies have undergone – of which industrialization from Britain in the nineteenth century (with its global causes and consequences, most notably in slavery) to China today – have almost always been brutal for more or less everyone who experienced them, and often highly violent affairs.

There are a number of ways that such a transformation has been understood however, with different political implications. First is the discourse of 'decarbonization' (see e.g. http://deepdecarbonization.org/). This discourse, which emerged first around 2000, introduces an important shift, in that it does focus explicitly on the question of transformation of the energy system, and contains within it an explicit end goal (see Paterson 2016 on the logic of 'decarbonization' as a frame). The discourse has certainly been productive in political terms, enabling some countries to imagine more radical policies than a narrower 'emissions problem' frame has. But decarbonization remains quite slippery and highly malleable in that what decarbonization might mean is unclear. It could simply mean that the carbon doesn't get in the atmosphere (via Carbon Capture and Storage, CCS) or even that it does get there but is then removed (via Carbon Dioxide Removal, CDR, technologies). In this case it is perhaps simply a radical version of the emissions problem, enabling an imagination of zero net emissions without necessarily changing the energy system that radically. But decarbonization permits more radical interpretations also, including that of a transition away from fossil fuels.

Second is the 'low carbon transitions' understanding of climate change (e.g. Scrase and Smith 2009; Bulkeley et al. 2010; Geels 2014). The transitions approach has become a dominant frame especially in some northern European countries, and also frames climate change as a question of energy system transformation. This usually has a theoretical underpinning in complex systems theory, which is deployed to understand how large complex systems tend to reproduce themselves over time (via concepts such as path dependence, lock-in, and so on) but also to think about how 'tipping points' might be generated to shift the socio-technical energy system from a high-carbon state to a low- or zero-carbon state. Some of this literature emphasizes how difficult a problem climate change is, referring to it as 'superwicked' (Levin et al. 2012). Compared to the decarbonization frame, it is worth underscoring that it is much more specific in emphasizing the transition as a *socio*-technical one in the energy system (whereas decarbonization focuses principally on the carbon itself) and focuses closely on how transitions in complex systems occur.

Third is the framing of climate change as 'the end of fossil fuels' (Princen et al. 2015; Paterson 2020). This frame has its roots variously in the emergence of the 2°C target during the 2000s, Ecuador's attempt to get industrialized countries to provide money to avoid pumping oil from the Yasuní National Park, the emergence of 'leave it in the ground' storylines of climate justice groups campaigning in the UNFCCC and in relation to mountain top removal mining, fracking, oil pipelines, and then fossil fuel divestment. It was then solidified in the IPCC Fifth Assessment Report in 2013–14 and the Paris Agreement in 2015, both of which expressed clearly that the end game was now 'net zero emissions', which many commentators realized means in practice zero fossil fuel use (and of course also probably 'negative emissions technologies').

Fourth is an explicit anti-capitalist framing of climate change (see e.g. Clark and York 2005; Lohmann 2006; Pelling et al. 2011; Koch 2012; Klein 2014; Malm 2015; Wright and Nyberg 2015; Mann and Wainwright 2018; also, cf. Newell and Paterson 2010). For many activists deploying the 'system change' slogan alluded to in Chapter 1, the system referred to here is capitalism. The transformation entailed in this frame is therefore a transformation, even a revolution, towards a non-capitalist form of society. The key dynamics of capitalism understood within this frame as inimical to dealing with climate change are varied, but the most important are the dependence on and obsession with economic growth / capital accumulation; the dominance of the profit motive in decision-making and the constant desire to externalize social and ecological costs; the intrinsic nature of the link between fossil energy and capitalist development; its persistent inequalities and injustices (hence this articulates closely with the climate justice frame); and the structural power of business within the politics-as-site.

2.2 Thinking Politically about Climate Change

We can see that a substantial number of these frames seek to frame climate change as something to be taken out of the realm of explicit public/democratic decision-making and dealt with by some form of technocratic/expert process – a question of markets, efficiency, and (socio)technological innovation, notably. This is a dynamic of depoliticization, which I spell out more later on. This is very clearly the case with the 'system maintenance' frames idea of climate as an emissions problem, a market failure or a commons problem. Even when they have an implicit notion of conflict – as in the commons frame for example – this is rendered technical through the language of collective action problems and reduced analytically via game theory into a question of incentives, side-payments, optimal solutions, and the like. This is most explicitly seen in the questioning of whether democracy can address climate change adequately, as we saw in Chapter 1. The 'systemic inequalities' frames often foreground power (but not always, as sometimes they become a simple ethical plea or normative vision) but mostly miss the point about transformation. But this is even the case with a good number of the 'system transformation' frames (decarbonization, transitions) that have within them a notion of transformation associated with climate change (see also Blythe et al. 2018). Even the 'end of fossil fuels', while it foregrounds questions of power and is explicitly political in the sense of being focused on the struggle between fossil fuel corporations and the rest of humanity, risks depoliticizing by foreclosing debate through the invocation of a hard end point that constrains the open public debate regarded by many as intrinsic to political life. But to understand these particular points about those frames, we need to go 'back to basics' about what we mean when we use the term *politics*.

2.2.1 Conceptualizing Politics

Politics can be understood in three distinct ways, all of which express something that we mean when we use the term in everyday speech, which political science as an academic discipline has tried to express more precisely.[2]

First is to think about politics as the site(s) of collective authoritative decision-making. This is what is usually contained in the commonplace conflation of politics with parliament, legislation, government, and in the abstraction of this focus in much of contemporary political science via the concept of 'the State'. It is what Leftwich (2004) refers to when he discusses thinking about politics as an 'arena'. But even when we focus, as lots of recent research on climate politics does, on novel arenas for climate change – transnational, multilevel, non-state, public–private hybrids, and so on – what is political about climate is that it entails collective decisions that make rules that bind us, distribute authority and resources, and decide between competing options, interests, and values. To be interested in

---

[2] I am certainly condensing here more than many might feel comfortable with. Colin Hay (2002, 61–62) gives twelve definitions in regular use, for example, although I think many of those collapse into the three I give here. There is one in particular that I leave out here but which is present in some existing work on climate politics. This is where politics is explicitly conceptualized as a question of strategic intervention towards the pursuit of emancipation. Mann and Wainwright (2018) for example think about climate politics mostly this way, as do from various perspectives Connolly (2017), MacGregor (2014), and Wall (2020), although they also at times articulate it as a set of arenas or power struggles.

climate politics is thus to be interested in the dynamics involved in and between these sites. What sorts of decisions get made? How (and how effectively) do the decision-making processes work? How do the decisions become authoritative and bind actors to them?

This way of thinking goes back to the canons of Western political thought. The term itself derives of course from the Greek 'polis', meaning simply the city, and where the very existence of politics is premised on the emergence of urban civilization and expressed in specific institutional arenas – the agora as a site of direct legislative decision-making, combined with election by lot to a governing authority, notably (of course always premised on slavery, and the exclusion of women and foreigners from citizenship) – that give us one important meaning for politics. For some, the conception is more restrictive still: Not only is politics only an arena, and in fact a specific kind of arena. Bernard Crick (among others) most vociferously argued that not all forms of government entail politics: 'politics is simply the activity by which government is made possible when differing interests in an area to be governed grow powerful enough to need to be conciliated' (Crick 2000, 30). For Crick, not all governments entail politics – either because the societies are not complex enough to have many 'differing interests' or, where some groups are able and willing to use sufficient coercion to mean other groups do not have to 'be conciliated', domination or tyranny exists, but not politics.

But this argument by Crick neglects a second way to think about politics, which is through the concept of power. As classically stated by Max Weber,

When a question is said to be a 'political' question, when a cabinet minister or an official is said to be a 'political' official, or when a decision is said to be 'politically' determined, what is always meant is that interests in the distribution, maintenance, or transfer of power are decisive for answering the questions and determining the decision or the official's sphere of activity.

(Weber 2013/1919, 78)

Leftwich (2004) refers to this as thinking about politics as a 'process'. For Hay (2002, 169), 'power is to politics what time is to history', that is, the central organizing concept that is both the focus of attention and also the key process that is assumed to be why studying politics is important. Power is also crucial to a classic definition of politics as 'who gets what, when, how' (Lasswell 1936). Crick, by contrast, regarded this as not fundamental to politics, writing 'why call struggle for power "politics" when it is simply a struggle for power' (Crick 2000, 20).

To think about politics in terms of power is to direct attention less at specific institutions but to a much broader set of social processes. Indeed politics becomes more or less omnipresent in this way of thinking – hence why phrases such as 'the personal is political' become meaningful – this was deployed initially by feminists and then taken up by others to refer to how broader political systems and processes structure personal life (the State regulates marriage, fertility, sexual violence, and so on) but also how power relations are entailed in personal relations themselves and thus those relations can be understood as political. We are thus interested in various diverse questions about the sources of power; who gets power and how; the different ways it operates and produces effects; and how all these aspects of power can change over time. But we are also immediately interested in how power is contested and challenged, since the exertion of power rarely occurs without some resistance.

A third way I want to think about politics is to take sides with those who argue that politics should be understood as fundamentally a conflictual rather than consensual process. There is a tradition of thought that insists that politics is in fact a rather rare occurrence, and only occurs when there are institutions and practices that seek to deliberate collectively, balance competing interests fairly, reason properly about decisions, and seek consensus wherever possible. This is Crick's view very explicitly but it can also be seen in the 'deliberative turn' in democratic theory, most commonly associated with Dryzek (e.g. 2000): The point of politics is to seek some sort of accommodation between competing interests, through a process of deliberation rather than bargaining. In contrast, Mouffe (2005) has provided the most widely read arguments that this insistence on deliberation and consensus is at best a naïve misunderstanding and at worst a dangerous threat to democratic practices. It is naïve in missing what she sees as the fundamentally antagonistic quality of human societies – that we are organized into competing collective identities (classes, nations, etc.), whose constitution depends fundamentally on their articulation in relation to 'others'. 'The political' is thus necessarily antagonistic. Power relations thus are central to this account of politics but the antagonisms are not solely reducible to conflicts over power. But while this is (for her) the misunderstanding of politics made by people such as Crick or Dryzek, Mouffe also argues that to aim for consensus when the underlying logic of politics is conflictual, as many contemporary political parties and leaders have done (in the West, from Mitterand in the 1980s, to Blair and Clinton in the 1990s), is on the one hand to be 'post-political' in the sense of pretending that fundamental conflicts can be wished away, and on the other hand to mean that those conflicts must take on more radical forms, enabling the emergence of anti-democratic forces – theocratic, racist, populist, and so on – to thrive. The challenge of democracy is to transform the intrinsically antagonistic character of politics not into a fake consensus but into an 'agonistic' politics: Turning enemies (who must be eliminated) into opponents (who must be beaten but respected).

Machin (2013) walks us through a narrative of different accounts of climate politics to arrive at one drawing on Mouffe's (2005) agonistic account of politics. That is to say, against a range of political analyses that focus variously on deliberation, and even politics as a consensual activity, Mouffe and Machin insist that politics must be understood, and climate politics with it, as a conflictual process, and the democratic challenge is to contain conflict and political competition effectively – so it becomes 'agonistic' rather than 'antagonistic', that is, tending to collapse into warfare or fascism. The hard distinction between deliberation and conflict is perhaps overplayed: Dryzek (e.g. 1999) situates his arguments for deliberative democracy specifically in relation to ongoing social conflicts, and deliberation is not framed as a means of 'overcoming' those conflicts to produce consensus. And in the climate change context, Willis (2020) shows how citizens' assemblies similarly do not need to be designed to pursue consensus or ignore conflict but precisely to channel and clarify the stakes in dealing with climate change, and often exist precisely in the context of ongoing contestation such as via Extinction Rebellion (XR).

One of Mouffe's (and others') claims is that we currently exist in a 'post-political' world: That is, that political life is being organized institutionally so as to suture over conflicts, to govern on the basis of a claimed consensus over the basic norms and practices of governance. For Mouffe, the rise of both fundamentalisms and authoritarian right-wing politics is intimately connected to this hegemonic centrism: Marginalized groups, having no means of institutionalized expression, turn to extremist politics in response. Swyngedouw (2010) in particular extends this logic to climate politics. He argues that climate politics is being practised in a technocratic and market-centred fashion that presents it as if there are no fundamental conflicts entailed involved in dealing with climate change.

This focus on conflict at the heart of climate politics is an important insight. Of course, we can readily find lots of analyses of specific conflicts in climate politics. There are conflicts over (and extensive academic analysis of): North–South inequalities; between fossil fuel companies and a range of activists; climate denial; between key countries in negotiations; or the injustices and adequacy of carbon markets; and contradictions between government claims about acting on climate while continuing to allow high-carbon development. The ideas of Machin, Swyngedouw, and others provide additional reasons for wanting to think about political conflict as an *inherent* dynamic in climate change politics.

2.2.2 Politics As Multidimensional

We do not need to choose between these three ways of thinking about politics, as we try to conceptualize climate change politically. Rather, since all three contain important elements of how we routinely think about politics, all three need to be kept in play in order to analyse it. For example, if we only think about sites and processes of collective decision-making, as does much of the literature on climate change policy and governance (with some honourable exceptions such as Bulkeley 2016 or Willis 2020), we often end up with rather anodyne, functionalist, 'apolitical' accounts of how such governance may be improved. The vast literature on the UNFCCC, for example, almost all falls into this trap (but for exceptions, see e.g. Paterson 1996; Ciplet et al. 2015), and even where power is taken seriously, the over-riding goal is to use this insight to understand how to make international climate governance 'better' (e.g. Victor 2004, 2011). Even if we understand such sites as intrinsically antagonistic, as does for example Hulme (2010) in his influential *Why We Disagree about Climate Change*, to focus as he does on the sources of these disagreements without honing in also on the question of power relations – how for example we disagree about climate change not only because of different value systems but because climate change in some senses is a form of violence being done by some people against others – is to miss an important component of politics in general but particularly regarding climate change. Conversely, however, if we restrict our analysis to the operations of power, which is less often done but can be found for example in some work using notions of governmentality (Paterson and Stripple 2010, for example, might fall into this trap), we risk reducing climate governance to rather smooth, technical affairs.

Of particular importance to illustrating this point is Harriet Bulkeley's (2016) book *Accomplishing Climate Governance*. As Bulkeley states, there is plenty of work about climate change's politics but 'for the most part, climate change is treated as an object, a biophysical condition, to which various social entities – actors, institutions, policies – respond'. Instead, we need to shift our 'attention . . . to the ways in which climate change comes to be made political and how, in turn, political conditions are made in relation to climate change' (Bulkeley 2016: 2–3).

Bulkeley, however, shifts attention quickly to the question of governance. She concedes that there are other 'sets of political conditions to which climate change gives rise' such as 'violence, security and conflict' (2016: 3) but nevertheless this focus on governance risks limiting the account of the ways in which climate change is political. In focusing the attention on how governance is 'accomplished', which Bulkeley does through an interrogation of different modes of authorization, or how authority is generated through the activity of attempting to govern climate change, the principal effect is to privilege analytically the process of the 'orchestration of distinct modes of power', that is the activity of those seeking to govern, make rules, allocate resources, and so on. It is not that other dimensions of politics (conflict, notably, to take her point above) are ignored in the analysis but they are treated as secondary to the primary focus on governing.

There has been a recent spate of interest in emphasizing the political qualities of climate change, focused on how it is structured as a conflict of interest and power between organized groups seeking to affect public policy (Breetz et al. 2018;

Sovacool and Brisbois 2019; Colgan et al. 2020; Mildenberger 2020; Stokes 2020). This literature combines the three elements of politics articulated in Section 2.2.1, roughly by assuming (although rarely expressed this explicitly) that politics is a power struggle between organized groups seeking to influence authoritative decision-making by the state. In addition, the playing field is understood as skewed in favour of incumbent, fossil fuel interests. These provide excellent insights and keep all three elements in how we think about politics in play. Nevertheless, these accounts are highly actor-focused, and can be usefully extended by considering not only the actors and their agential power (incumbent groups vs. others) but also by thinking about the overall structure within which they operate – capitalism – and the cultural dimensions which enable their power. Put differently, they have unnecessarily limited the account of the political to that of the authoritative decision-making forum of the state (at various levels) and the attempts to seek that. In Section 2.2.5 I develop this point by introducing cultural political economy as a way to include these sorts of analyses but go beyond them in a way that will become clear in the empirical analyses.

2.2.3 Depoliticization and Repoliticization

Two things flow from how I have developed the notion of climate politics so far. The first of these are the notions of *depoliticization* and *repoliticization*. These are important processes in climate politics that we will see at various points throughout the book. They can be usefully understood as logically entailed in the three-fold account of politics developed so far. Barry's (2002) 'The Anti-Political Economy' is particularly useful. In this context, depoliticization refers then to the way in which actors manage to take decisions out of the realm of collective decisions being made within deliberative, public processes. The 'politics' in depoliticization is politics-as-arena. In the context of climate policy and politics, that usually means to take them in a technical and/or economistic setting, where experts decide on appropriate means of governing a problem. This sort of depoliticization normally therefore entails a rhetoric that climate change is a technical question, that climate policy will benefit everyone, and that ignores questions of power and conflict.[3] That is, depoliticization is a political strategy in terms of politics-as-power. It is a strategy of those seeking to maintain or change the distribution of power within society. Conversely, repoliticization is in part a reversal – it seeks explicitly to bring climate change squarely into the realm of democratic decision-making – but

---

[3] Of course such depoliticization could occur in other ways, for example when theocratic authorities are able to regulate on the basis of some claim to enacting God's will, or in the recurrent appeals in environmental discourse to 'nature' as a source of authority. Such a move can clearly be seen as a strategy of power to take decisions out of a public, political arena.

it almost always also entails emphasizing that power relations are important, that incumbent forces need to be challenged, and understands conflict as central to climate change action.

It is not however simply that depoliticization is 'bad' and repoliticization is 'good'. It is more that we should assume that there is a dialectic between the two. Depoliticization is central to the arguments in climate policy debates to seek 'climate policy stability' (e.g. Rosenbloom et al. 2019), i.e. to think about policy and institutional dynamics that make policy reversibility difficult. This may indeed be a valuable part of promoting climate action. Nevertheless, even if climate advocates may reasonably seek to depoliticize, Barry (2002) argues that depoliticization, over time at least, usually fails. In one of the examples he discusses, air pollution from vehicle exhausts has been dealt with by a series of technical regulatory fixes – banning lead from petrol, catalytic converters, annual emission inspections, and so on – but actors end up being able to repoliticize questions of air quality and car exhausts, because despite all these technical fixes, air quality remains very poor. The dynamics of climate change seem to me frequently to have this sort of quality, so this conceptualization of politics is particularly fruitful. We will see this dynamic unfold in a number of contexts throughout this book.

2.2.4 Tensions in the Politics of Climate Change: Purification vs. Complexity

The second arises out a desire to identify a singular 'solution' to climate change. As I hinted in Chapter 1, you don't have to delve too hard in climate change to find propositions that simplify the question of climate change to a single cause, characteristic, and corresponding solution. For some economists, 'getting a price on carbon' will magically solve it. For some engineers or techno-enthusiasts, a specific technology, be it wind, nuclear, energy efficiency, battery storage, thorium, or something else, will do the job. For misanthropic Malthusians, get human numbers down, and problem solved. I call these approaches 'purifications' rather than simplifications because it seems to me they not only are over-simplistic (even though they are) but they rely on the specific reduction of a hugely complex set of questions surrounding climate change into a singular solution – they purify it of its complexities.[4]

---

[4] 'I recognize that 'purification' has all sorts of other connotations – religious, racist, etc. – and I absolutely do not seek to attach these associations to those I critique here, although, to be fair, lots of Malthusians focused on human population are at least implicitly racist, and sometimes explicitly, as in the famous case of Garrett Hardin (see Mildenberger 2019). I struggled for the right word to capture what I am describing here. Conversely, 'simplification' doesn't really capture the process of abstracting from complexity I think is going on when people seek their preferred silver bullet to solve climate change. And it is somewhat too dismissive: There can be strategic value in some forms of purification.

These examples – technology, prices, population – are all purifications that are depoliticizing. They can often be seen precisely to arise out of the cultural political economy dynamics discussed in Section 2.2.5. Economists proposing that 'getting the prices right' will solve the climate problem reflect the hegemonic ideology of neoliberal capitalism fairly evidently. They share with technology-boosters the (mostly unacknowledged) recognition of the stickiness of daily practices and the difficulty of such social change combined with the unquestioned normative value of unrestrained capital accumulation, and seek simple 'silver bullet' solutions as a work-around. Population fetishists rarely explicitly share Malthus' open hostility to the poor but nevertheless simplify the problem to one of poor people having too many children, and depoliticize in the process.

But not all purifications are depoliticizing. The accounts of climate politics as agonistic are themselves forms of purification, or at the very least risk it. A number of scholars have started to analyse climate change politics by insisting on its agonistic character, and indeed at times insist on the necessity of taking sides in the struggle that entails. They have attempted to make arguments seeking to repoliticize climate change (e.g. Goeminne 2013; Kenis and Mathijs 2014; Pepermans and Maeseele 2016). Mann and Wainwright are perhaps the most explicit in this regard: 'our goal is to make climate *more* political' (Mann and Wainwright 2018: xii). Agreed. In doing so they articulate more explicitly than any other literature on climate change what they mean by the term politics (see notably Swyngedouw 2010; Machin 2013; MacGregor 2014; Rice 2016; Connolly 2017; Mann and Wainwright 2018). Often, this narrative is married to an explicitly anti-capitalist vision (e.g. Wall 2020).

Following this logic, many climate justice movements, such as for divestment or in XR, purify climate change to a Manichaean struggle between 'fossil fuels and humanity', often relying explicitly on a war metaphor to sustain this narrative (Mangat et al. 2018). In climate movements, a slogan often circulates, a quote from the American anarchist Utah Phillips: 'The earth is not dying, it is being killed, and those who are killing it have names and addresses' (see e.g. Climate and Capitalism 2009). And a good deal of the literature on the relationship between capitalism and climate change poses the question as a stark 'capitalism vs. the climate' question, or in Malm's pithy phrase, 'the enemy is fossil capital' (Malm 2020, 15). Capitalism is framed in these approaches variously as the cause of climate change, needing to be transcended to address climate change but there is also often a sense that once we have eco-socialism or something like it, solving climate change will become immediately easier: At the very least this is the case implicitly, in that such writers don't really discuss explicitly why the structure of such societies might actually enable them to decarbonize effectively.

My point is not that these arguments are 'wrong', and indeed it is precisely that they contain a very important set of insights. Rather that there seems to me to be a recurrent tension in climate politics between these attempts to repoliticize climate change, to frame it as a power struggle between various opposing forces (fossil fuels vs. humanity, neoliberalism vs. democracy, rich higher emitters vs. climate vulnerable, and so on), and the messy complexity of the high-carbon world as a socio-technical system (e.g. Hoffmann 2011; Levin et al. 2012; Bernstein and Hoffmann 2018). Machin (2013) and Swyngedouw (2010) seem to me to ignore this latter dynamic, which involves thinking about the concrete interventions involved in the pursuit of decarbonization occurring at myriad scales, by diverse actors with their own logics, in ways that make identification of an 'enemy' or a single effective site of struggle, rather difficult. The political logic of climate change understood in terms of complexity is, in Harriet Bulkeley's (2016) words, one of 'accomplishing' – patient, inventive, experimental, determined, anything but 'heroic'. I call this a 'purification vs. complexity' argument.

Insisting on the agonistic qualities of climate politics is a useful counterpoint to Bulkeley's account of climate governance as something that is 'accomplished' (as opposed perhaps to say 'implemented'). Her account reminds us usefully that paying attention to how power is mobilized and effected (not just 'who has it') in climate politics is important. In her words, for at least some aspects of climate politics: 'this is not the politics of vested interests and decision points, but a slow burning, unfolding, enveloping and ongoing form of the working of power' (Bulkeley 2019, 14). But there does not need to be the choice that she presents here – rather, it is *both* the 'politics of vested interests . . .' *and* the 'slow burning, unfolding . . .' that help us understand the dynamics. Purification *and* complexity, not *or*: We do not need to choose between them but rather to consider how we keep both in play. Purification has clearly been highly important in mobilizing movements around specific aspects of the climate problem, and sharpens our focus on some of the key actors blocking change. And focusing on the complex and messy dynamics of decarbonizing the food system, or concrete, without considering the power relations and conflicts of interest, risks being a more complex form of depoliticizing technocratic governance.

2.2.5 Shaping Climate Change Action: Cultural Political Economy

These dynamics of depoliticization and repoliticization, purification and complexity, remain rather abstractly understood. We need also to ask questions of the sorts of specific forces that drive forwards and block climate action. If we do so, then my response is the following: Low carbon transitions and the conflicts they generate are driven by the interrelated dynamics of capital accumulation on the one hand and the subjectivities that generate desires for the objects and practices that generate that accumulation on the other. In other words, in terms of the way I would use the term cultural political economy (see Paterson 2007; cf. Best and Paterson 2010; Sum and Jessop 2013). This is perhaps easiest to see in relation to forces *opposing* low carbon transitions: Incumbent economic interests such as coal and oil companies seeking to shore up their assets and business models to enable continued capital accumulation on the one hand, and powerful emotional forces around practices such as driving, flying, meat-eating, or air conditioning that produce cultural resistance to low carbon transitions. These are not reducible to each other, and thus arguments focused solely on corporate power and strategy (e.g. Mildenberger 2020; Stokes 2020) only address half the problem. But these same types of forces drive forward climate policy, whether relatively minor (in the 'emissions' frame) or more transformational: Those climate policies that have gained traction have done so because sufficient numbers of businesses have seen an investment opportunity to support them, and because of cultural valuing of those novel directions for society. Part of this cultural valuing for some people may be because they value addressing climate change *per se*, but climate-related motivations are rarely if ever sufficient to drive responses forward, and at least they need to be articulated with an excitement for specific low carbon practices and the sort of social change they enable. The final thing to say about this cultural political economy perspective is that it implies that there are always profound legitimacy challenges for decarbonization. The processes and politics of accumulation are themselves always contested (this is intrinsic to power relations in capitalist society), and this is the case with capital-centred responses to climate change. This means that there are often similarities in the way that low carbon projects and high-carbon projects are contested. Carbon markets have been subject to acute legitimacy challenges for precisely these reasons and are perhaps the most crudely 'capitalist' responses to climate change, creating new, financial commodities whose relation to actual processes of decarbonization is tenuous at best (Newell and Paterson 2010; Paterson 2010a). But even more substantive low carbon trajectories have similar political dynamics: Objections to wind turbines and objections to fracking by social movements frequently take more or less the same form, and adopt the same rhetoric, and this is largely because those projects are driven by the pursuit of private capital accumulation.

Another way to understand this is to think of it in terms of the framework of 'devices, desires and dissent' that Harriet Bulkeley, Johannes Stripple, and I developed (Bulkeley et al. 2016). That is, climate politics can be seen in the complex relations between: The devices we use in daily life, the complex systems those devices make up, and the devices by which we are governed; the desires for those devices as well as in relation to climate change itself; and the dissent that

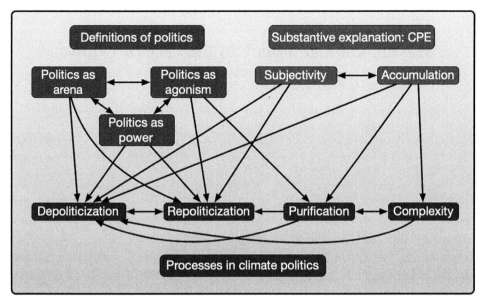

Figure 2.1 Processes in climate politics

generates mobilization over climate change but also over the attempts to shift our use of specific devices in low carbon directions.

The conclusion takes up the implications of these various arguments, especially in relation to anti-capitalist arguments about climate politics. In the meantime, we will encounter it playing out in various moments in the empirical story of climate politics in Ottawa as it unfolds.

2.3 A Summary

For the visually minded, Figure 2.1 summarizes these various elements in the arguments I develop across the book. As mentioned in Chapter 1, they are inter-related in complicated ways and the book doesn't map them out in a linear way. But nevertheless, the lines indicate the principal ways I see the arguments connecting. Some lines have arrows only one way, implying a causal process, for example how the dynamics of accumulation explain why some actors seek to purify and depoliticize climate change, while others have arrows at both ends, implying basic features or processes that mutually constitute or shape each other. Some arrows are missing, implying I don't see important connections: You may get to the end of the book of course and disagree with me on this!

3

Making Climate Policy in the City of Ottawa

MATTHEW PATERSON AND KOFI AGYAPONG ADOMAKO

Like many cities, the City of Ottawa got interested in climate change early on. It set ambitious targets, only to realize they were extremely demanding if not impossible to meet. It thus scaled back its ambition, and the history of its response at the overall level of the City Council can be characterized in two ways. On the one hand, it responded to the emergence of city networks on climate change to do enough to report to the network of Canadian cities – the Partnership for Climate Protection – and meet its expectations. But these expectations have throughout been minimal – to create inventories of emissions, develop plans for them, and monitor progress. On the other hand, the City has, episodically, generated moments of enthusiasm for action on climate change, developing more overarching plans and a variety of specific initiatives. These bursts of energy occurred around 1991, 2004, and 2012–13. But in none of them did the burst of energy turn into sustained attention. We focus our analysis on the period through to 2014 when the Air Quality and Climate Change Management Plan (AQCCMP) was adopted.[1] In part this is because the main patterns are easily identified up to this date, and in part because Chapters 5 and 6 discuss two particular aspects of the more recent politics (Complete Streets, and intensification) in more detail.

This chapter therefore analyses the dynamics of this aspect of climate politics. It shows, as outlined in Chapter 2, that this is only a very small part of where we might find climate politics. If we restricted our analysis of climate politics to this official politics of setting targets and making formal policies where climate change is explicitly the object of governance, we would not have very much to say. As will become clear in later chapters, these targets and policies are rather abstracted from the everyday politics of the city as it affects climate change – the politics of

---

[1] We recognize that lots has happened since then in Ottawa, with the completion of the light rail project, the ongoing campaigns by Ecology Ottawa and others, and various new initiatives. Apologies to those in Ottawa seeking commentary on the latest developments, but they will have to fill in the gaps. The patterns nevertheless seem to us to be clear.

urban planning, transportation, and buildings notably. They have tended as a consequence to pursue a depoliticizing strategy to address climate change by focusing in a managerial way on a particular set of programmes – which became less ambitious and more limited over time compared to initial lofty goals and have only very rarely engaged in large scale public debate.

3.1 From the Toronto Conference to Amalgamation: Climate Leadership in Ottawa

In the aftermath of the 'Conference on the Changing Atmosphere' in Toronto in 1988, which was the high-profile conference that was highly significant in launching climate change onto the international political agenda in that year (see Boyle and Ardill 1989; Paterson 1996), various municipalities in Canada took up the challenge to reduce their CO_2 emissions (Torrie 2015). These early initiatives mostly took the character of overall GHG emissions targets without much by way of detailed plans for implementation. The City of Ottawa was an early leader in that regard.[2] The process within the City was driven by two processes: Opportunistic but shallow engagement by City politicians who established targets on emissions with little sense of the work involved; and a small, underfunded but entrepreneurial unit within the City's administration that developed various initiatives, notably in carbon accounting, buildings efficiency, and inter-city networking (see Chapter 3 on this), connected to attempts to meet these targets.

They also had the character of an informal sort of accountability among peers, operating via challenges by mayors to each other. On 19 February 1990, Mayor Arthur C. Eggleton of Toronto sent a letter to Mayor Jim Durrell in Ottawa challenging the City to take a stand on greenhouse gas emissions, similar to commitments Toronto had announced. Toronto had already engaged in an extensive process, producing a long report entitled 'The Changing Atmosphere: A Call to Action', the title echoing that of the 1988 Toronto Conference, which detailed the nature of climate change as an issue, and the nature of appropriate action at city level (City of Toronto 1989). Mayor Eggleton included this report in his challenge to Mayor Durrell.

Ottawa's Environmental Advisory Committee made a series of proposals to the City's Community Services and Operations Committee (CSOC). These focused on the adoption of a commitment to 'a 20% or greater reduction of the 1988 levels of

---

[2] As will become clear later, the City of Ottawa refers to two different entities across the time period of the historical survey provided in this chapter. Prior to 2001 what is now the City of Ottawa was organized into 11 municipal governments, one of which was called the City of Ottawa (and which covered the current city centre and most of the inner suburbs, at least west of the Rideau River), and a second tier across the whole of the region, the Regional Municipality of Ottawa–Carleton, or RMOC. For the purposes of this analysis, we only focus on the City of Ottawa in this earlier period.

carbon emissions into the atmosphere within the City of Ottawa by the year 2005'
(City of Ottawa 1990a, 143). This is more or less identical to the target
recommended by the Toronto Conference in 1988 (Toronto Conference 1989),
although that recommendation focused on CO_2 emissions specifically – whether
'carbon' emissions was intended to mean the same thing is unclear. The
Environmental Advisory Committee also recommended some specific actions to
explore to start working on this commitment. Some of these involved establishing
new administrative arrangements in the City, to be able to coordinate progress
across departments, and the use of an existing consultative process with citizens
known as the Central Area Forum to discuss ways to reduce CO_2 emissions.

In terms of sources of emissions, it proposed establishing an Energy Efficiency
Office, but most strongly framed the challenge specifically in relation to the
question of transport, mentioning the need to contain urban sprawl, proposing a
'Kick the Car' campaign, to investigate the possibility of testing vehicles for
emissions, and to use parking fees as a strategy 'to encourage public transit use'
(City of Ottawa 1990a, 145). The Community Services and Operations Committee
(on 13 June 1990), and then the City Council as a whole (on 20 June), approved
the proposals by the Environmental Advisory Committee, except that it decided to
increase the commitment to a 50 per cent reduction in carbon emissions by 2005
(City of Ottawa 1990a, 143). This decision was made without any reflection by
councillors on what it entailed to achieve such a target (Spears 1992; interview
with Paul McDonald, 2017).

Between 1990 and 1992 the City concentrated its efforts on building the new
administrative arrangements and developing the knowledge base for future
actions. It established a position of Environmental Manager within the
Engineering and Works Department. This position, taken by Paul McDonald,
formerly of Transport Canada, had very little budget and encountered
considerable resistance from existing City engineers and planners. McDonald
however had significant connections in the federal government, saw the
opportunity to join the International Council for Local Environmental Initiatives
(ICLEI)'s Cities for Climate Protection campaign (see more in Section 4.1) to
gain access to their resources and ideas, and used these to develop initiatives on
climate over the coming years (interview with Paul McDonald, 2017). He brought
in around $2 million[3] in the next few years from these sources. He also built links
with private consultant Ralph Torrie who was developing models for monitoring
and planning CO_2 emissions, which became the basis for the City's first carbon
accounting efforts, and initiated the first informal network of Canadian cities
working on climate change, which developed later into the Federation of

[3] Figures refer to Canadian dollars, unless otherwise specified.

Table 3.1. *Ottawa CO$_2$ emissions, 1990*

	Total Carbon Dioxide Emissions from Energy Use – In Ottawa in Kilotonnes (1990)			
	Natural Gas	Electricity	Oil Products	Totals
Residential	289.5	455.4	158.1	903.0	23%
Commercial	454.2	686.8	60.4	1,210.1	31%
Industrial	58.6	76.2	244.3	379.1	10%
Transportation	1.5	0.0	1,408.5	1,410.0	36%
Totals	803.7	1,227.0	1,871.4	3,902.1	
	21%	31%	48%		

Source: Redrawn from City of Ottawa (1992b, 160).

Canadian Municipalities' (FCM) Partners for Climate Protection programme (PCP) (see Section 4.1).[4]

The City built in mention of the need to tackle GHG emissions in its 1991 Official Plan (Torrie Smith Associates 1994, 33), and repeated the 50 per cent cut target (Spears 1992). It commissioned Friends of the Earth to produce an inventory of emissions in the city, the first effort to account for CO$_2$ emissions in the city (Millyard 1992). This inventory covered CO$_2$ emissions for both corporate (i.e. from City Council direct operations) and community emissions (i.e. from the city's population as a whole) (City of Ottawa 1992a, 417), and drew out policy implications, mostly focused on pursuing energy efficiency (Millyard 1992, 1).[5] This inventory identified the transportation and buildings sectors as the largest sources of emissions (see Table 3.1).

In the summer of 1992 (shortly after the United Nations Conference on Environment and Development in Rio de Janeiro and the signing of the UNFCCC), at meetings in July and August, on the basis of this preparatory work, the City developed a more concrete set of commitments and plans. The overall ambition of a 50 per cent target was scaled back by the City, to 20 per cent by 2005, and 50 per cent by 2020 (City of Ottawa 1992b, 158–59), and the underlying report illustrated the increased attention to the complexity of reducing emissions drove this scaled-back target.[6] The initial proposal by the Environmental Advisory

---

[4] The other cities involved, according to McDonald, were Vancouver, Calgary, Edmonton, Regina, Toronto, Montreal, and perhaps Halifax. Interview with Paul McDonald (2017).

[5] In the earlier documents this distinction is not made, although implicitly (given for example that they discuss questions of urban sprawl and promoting transit) it is clear that they intend to cover both corporate and community emissions.

[6] The other shift, less important, was that the baseline for cuts becomes 1990 rather than 1988, falling in line with the various national targets announced and implicitly incorporated into the UNFCCC.

Committee was that this be simply reduced to 20 per cent, but the CSOC, and then the full Council, amended this to read a 'minimum' 20 per cent cut. So at this point the councillors' instincts were still to increase the ambition proposed by the City's officials and advisors. Nevertheless, the City had clearly engaged in considerable work to think through the logic of the target it had set. It reasoned that 'the Toronto target is not an easy one' (City of Ottawa 1992b, 161), and emphasized the need for multilevel cooperation with the province of Ontario and the federal government. They stated that Friends of the Earth supported the revised target. But this shift in Ottawa's case was contextualized in relation to emerging collaboration among municipal authorities. The explanation for the decision in August 1992 mentions the adoption of the Toronto target by other 'cities in Canada (Toronto, Victoria, Vancouver, Regina and Ottawa)', the formation of ICLEI 'of which the City of Ottawa is a member', and specifically its 'Urban CO_2 Project', in which Ottawa was one of only twelve cities globally to participate at that point (City of Ottawa 1992b, 161).[7]

Compared to the 1990 proposal, the 1992 one was clearly made on the basis of a much more thorough process of evaluation and planning. Alongside the inventory and the work by council officers, there was a consultative process, with submissions from community groups such as Citizens for Safe Cycling, a well-established cycling lobby in the city. This produced the scaled back target. But it also produced a withdrawal from identifying the particular sectors or strategies to reduce emissions (no mention of urban sprawl, for example), in favour of establishing particular processes for proceeding. The issue was gradually becoming depoliticized and incorporated into normal council planning processes. The Department of Engineering and Works was established as the lead department within the City's organizational structure (as it had already been done for environmental policy more generally – see City of Ottawa 1990b), which was charged with establishing a 'Special Taskforce on the Atmosphere' to come up with advice about actions the City could take to reach the target (City of Ottawa 1992b, 158).

The Taskforce first met in January 1994. It was chaired by Mayor Jacquelin Holzman and comprised various city officials but also two senior civil servants in the federal government (including Gordon McBean, one of the organizers of the Toronto Conference). It divided its work into the development of an 'action plan' and an 'implementation plan' (City of Ottawa 1994b, 5). The former was to be focused on three key areas: 'residential buildings; commercial buildings; and transportation/urban form', and lists of specific actions that could be undertaken in

---

[7] The others were Toronto; Ankara; Copenhagen; Dade County, Florida; Denver; Hannover; Helsinki; Minneapolis/St Paul; Portland, Oregon; Saarbrucken; and San Jose, California.

these areas were developed (Torrie Smith Associates 1994, annex B). The key element in the latter was contained in its first proposal, made in June 1994, specifically the creation of a '20% Club', where a broad range of organizations could sign up voluntarily to commit themselves to reducing CO_2 emissions within the timeframe of the City's target. Members of the club would be required to make a public commitment to a 'specific CO_2 reduction target', compile an inventory of emissions and use this to monitor progress towards the target, and produce a 'Corporate Action Plan' detailing how they intended to meet the targets set (City of Ottawa 1994a, 115). These three elements (targets, inventories, action plans) mirrored the approach to be developed by the City itself. The proposal also suggests that participants focus on energy efficiency in their buildings and vehicle fleets, and behaviour change in their 'employees and clients' to reduce energy consumption (City of Ottawa 1994a, 114).

The taskforce produced its proposed strategy in 1995 *Opportunities for Energy Efficiency: A Call to Action* (City of Ottawa 1995a). This constituted the first strategy document on climate change since the development of interest in the subject at City level in 1990, and outlined eleven main elements pursued as separate programmes to cut emissions in residential, commercial, and transportation sectors. This was approved by the City Council (City of Ottawa 1995b) and thus became the first GHG strategy the City adopted (and the taskforce was disbanded in the process).

As hinted in the name, at the core of this strategy was a focus on energy efficiency, combined with establishing a routinized system for monitoring and reporting on GHG emissions in the city, and monitoring the implementation of the strategy and tracking its progress towards the overall 20 per cent cut to which the City had committed itself. The strategy started to take on familiar elements: The ongoing development of GHG inventories and monitoring, and the methodological issues surrounding that; a series of partnerships with other institutions, especially private sector organizations (construction companies, energy service companies), to spread information about energy efficiency; the development of building-level GHG rating systems; improvements to public transit in the city; and the pioneering of alternative fuel vehicles, especially in the City's fleet (City of Ottawa 1995b, 56). The discourse justifying the project was firmly focused on the economic benefits of energy efficiency – cost-savings to householders, businesses, and the city government itself, with a secondary focus on improvements to urban air quality (City of Ottawa 1995b, 56).

We can also, however, see a disjuncture (also familiar) between the framing of energy efficiency overall and its operationalization. The framing is broad, thinking about energy efficiency not only in terms of specific objects (houses, cars) but also of the overall urban system:

Better efficiencies can be found in our buildings, in our equipment, our appliances, and our vehicles. Improving the efficiency of our systems (reducing the number of energy-requiring steps rather than maximizing the efficiency of each step) can also pay big dividends, especially in the transportation and industrial production sectors. Intensifying development, increasing the opportunities for shared use of resources, improving the percentage of public transit and alternative transport ... trips ... can also achieve substantial reductions in greenhouse gas emissions. Another opportunity for greenhouse gas reduction lies in fuel switching.

(City of Ottawa 1995a, 70)

We can thus see an implicit notion of a switch from thinking about energy efficiency to thinking about carbon efficiency (although this sort of explicit frame was not really articulated anywhere in 1995). But the actions to be undertaken only focused on the first of these – improving the energy efficiency of buildings and vehicles – and in a very limited way the third – trialling alternative fuel vehicles. The shopping list of possible actions (from Torrie Smith Associates 1994) is reproduced (City of Ottawa 1995a, 79–85), which includes things such as 'urban planning to reduce origin–destination distance for major trip modes' (83), and some of the submissions from the Environmental Action Committee emphasize these more structural or cultural questions, including a sub-section on 'Canadian culture and the automobile', and the 'dependence on fossil fuels' (125–29). But elements such as these are avoided in the final list of eleven specific actions to be undertaken.

For a few years from 1996 onwards, the City had a regular reporting process on progress regarding this action plan. Reports were released in 1996, 1997, and 1999 (City of Ottawa 1996, 1997, 1999). Two things are worth highlighting from these reports.

First is that they showed significant reductions from corporate emissions (i.e. the emissions from the City Council's own facilities and vehicle fleets), and modest cuts for city-wide emissions, although the reports note that data for city-wide emissions are not as reliable as for corporate emissions. Between 1990 and 1998, the city's corporate emissions declined by 19 per cent, while community emissions declined by about 5 per cent. The reductions in the corporate emissions came somewhat as a surprise to the council, which framed the 20 per cent cut as an 'ambitious' goal (e.g. City of Ottawa 1996, 1). Nevertheless what became clear early on was that around half of the emissions cuts were produced by changes in the electricity system at provincial level, specifically the rise of nuclear generation in the province. This change stalled around 1996–97 (as several nuclear power stations were shut down during 1997, see City of Ottawa 1997, 19; 1999, 51), and Ottawa's emissions (corporate and, to a lesser extent, community) increased again as a result. By 1996, the city's corporate emissions were down 29 per cent compared to 1990 levels, but by 1998 they were only 19 per cent down on 1990 levels. This effect was even more marked for community emissions, where the entirety of the modest cuts noted in 1997 were due to this fuel switching (City of Ottawa 1998, 167). The rest of the cuts were produced by fuel switching in city buildings from electricity and oil to natural gas, modernization of the streetlighting system, and to a lesser extent fuel switching and energy efficiency improvements in the City's vehicle fleet (see City of Ottawa 1997, 18, table 2). In the streetlighting system, however, we can see clearly that a one-off investment to improve the efficiency of streetlights only had a short-term effect, in the emissions for 1996. By 1998 they were almost back to 1990 levels, due to the expansion in the amount of streetlighting provision in the city (see City of Ottawa 1999, 53), and notably, by this point the City started reporting the success of this initiative in terms of avoided CO_2 emissions rather than absolute emissions cuts.

Second is that the City was clearly very active in this period, developing numerous programmes to address GHG emissions, both corporate and community. Within the City's own operations, these focused on the following: Building retrofits to improve energy efficiency; energy reductions in vehicles; 'employee involvement programmes'; 'employer-led transportation demand management'; and ongoing monitoring and evaluation of the GHG targets (City of Ottawa 1997, 3). In the first of these, they developed an operating principle to retrofit energy building with a payback of seven years or better. The second involved mostly shifts of a number of vehicles to using ethanol-blended fuels, and also, in some areas (e.g. parking enforcement officials), shifting to using bicycles instead of cars. For community emissions, the two most active areas were in the CO_2 Corporate Challenge and in developing a range of information systems for citizens, especially through the 'Ottawa Green Information Line' (City of Ottawa 1998, 181), which aimed to provide information on the best investments to improve energy efficiency in homes and businesses, and in the development of transport demand management systems. By 1998 this had developed into a system of supporting (via an intermediary organization, EnviroCentre, and in partnership with NRCAN) home energy audits. In the Corporate Challenge, a number of organizations had signed up by 1997, including the Civic Hospital, the Mountain Equipment Co-op, Natural Resources Canada, and the University of Ottawa. In 1998 this was redesigned into the Commercial Building Efficiency Partnership (City of Ottawa 2000, 46–47), where the City aimed at acting as an entrepreneur between owners of commercial buildings and energy service companies working on building energy management and retrofits aimed at energy efficiency. But the city was also investigating more system-wide possibilities such as district heating (City of Ottawa 2000, 47–48).

3.2 Amalgamation and the Stalling of Climate Policy in Ottawa

By 1998 Ottawa was recognized as a leading city in climate change action, within Canada at least. It had done so via the largely depoliticized strategies detailed in Section 3.1, avoiding significant conflict or open debate about either the value or the details of the strategy. While a good chunk of its emissions cuts came from benefits of changes in provincial electricity policy, it nevertheless had developed a number of programmes that had direct effects on emissions, and had an active system of monitoring progress and identifying means of developing policy and action further. Ottawa was the only municipality in Canada to gain a 'gold' status under the federal government's Voluntary Challenge Registry (City of Ottawa 1999, 60; Spears 2000), and received similar accolades from the PCP network.

But two developments were to occur that caused the City's efforts to stall. First, a number of key officials in the City who had been responsible for the City's climate initiatives left their positions in 1998 or 1999 (interview with Paul McDonald, 2017). This resulted in a halt in some of the activities connected to the action plan and the progress report was delayed until the City of Ottawa recruited new people to fill the positions.

Second, shortly afterwards, the amalgamation of the Regional Municipality of Ottawa–Carleton (RMOC) and eleven other municipalities in 2001 to form the new City of Ottawa affected climate policy development negatively for a number of years, as the new administration focused on core administrative and other logistical issues (City of Ottawa 2003). While many environmental commentators do assume that consolidation of city-regions into a single tier of government ought to make it easier to control sprawl and enact various other environmental improvements (e.g. Reese 2004, 595; Jimenez and Hendrick 2010), the driver for the amalgamation into a single municipality was a transparently ideological focus on reducing costs to taxpayers, exemplified in the name of the provincial legislation that enabled it, the 'Fewer Municipal Politicians Act' of 1999. City amalgamation was pursued by the provincial Conservative government of Mike Harris as part of a range of neoliberal reforms such as privatization of various province-owned industries, education reforms modelled on the Thatcher government's reforms in the UK in the 1980s, and downloading services from the provincial government to municipalities (Graham et al. 2001; Andrew 2007; Leffers 2015b), and in the case of urban amalgamation, was carried out in the name of cost reductions for citizens (framed of course as 'taxpayers') without regard to evidence as to whether or not amalgamation would in fact do this.[8] Improved urban planning was not integral therefore to the rationale for amalgamation in Ontario, let alone the pursuance of the climate policy that the old City of Ottawa had pursued.

---

[8] Later analyses suggested it either did not reduce such costs, or perhaps even increased them. See Reese (2004).

Nevertheless, the approach to climate policy adopted was vulnerable to the large scale institutional–political change imposed by the province.

On one level, amalgamation involved simply a massive reorganization of the provision of a city's services, integrating departments from the old municipalities into a single structure, dealing with differing union contracts, working out which policies from each municipality will become those of the new city, and so on, and Ottawa was mired in these for several years (see especially Rosenfeld and Reese 2003, 2004). This occurred in a particularly short period of time, with the provincial legislation to create the new political structure being passed in December 1999 and the new City to start operating from January 2001, creating a massive workload for the reorganization and significant legacy issues to be resolved. But on another level amalgamation also entailed significant political issues to be resolved, of which the two most contentious were the question of how to deal with the different debt levels of each municipality and whether or not the new city would be officially bilingual (Graham et al. 2001). The former of these had more direct impacts on the development of climate policy, affecting the fiscal basis for investments in new infrastructure or energy efficiency programmes. The key issue was that the former City of Ottawa had much greater debts than the suburban municipalities, which suburban councillors and residents did not want to pay for, but urban councillors argued were the result of the old City paying for services that suburban residents used (roads, hospitals, etc.,) but not vice versa.[9]

It thus took a number of years before attention to climate change in the city returned, with a new environmental strategy adopted in October 2003 as part of the Ottawa 20/20 Growth Strategy which focused less on greenhouse gas reduction (City of Ottawa 2003), and a year later, with a new 'Air Quality and Climate Change Management Plan' (AQCCMP) (City of Ottawa 2004).

The development of a new climate plan began in 2004, three years after amalgamation, and was finalized and approved by the City Council on 12 January 2005. The 2005 AQCCMP framed climate change specifically in relation to air quality and health, both because mitigating climate change will have health benefits and because reducing GHGs will also reduce many other air pollutants.

Like the earlier plans of the old City of Ottawa and the RMOC, the new plans set targets for 20 per cent cuts in GHG emissions, over 1990 levels. However, the deadlines for meeting these targets were pushed back, to 2007 for corporate emissions and 2012 for community emissions (City of Ottawa 2004). This

[9] Regarding the question of bilingualism, hotly contested at various sites in Canadian politics, the RMOC, the old City of Ottawa, and two other of the older municipalities were officially bilingual (meaning that they provided services to citizens in both French and English, and city council business would be conducted in both languages), but not the rest. The province decided not to make the new City bilingual, in response to some suburban councils and a significant anti-francophone strain among Conservatives (Graham et al. 2001, 266), but allowed it to set its own language policy. The new council did decide to become officially bilingual.

apparent backsliding can in part be explained by amalgamation, in two ways. The first is that amalgamation distracted attention and, while the old City of Ottawa had been developing significant efforts to reduce both corporate and community emissions, from 1998 onwards, and during the amalgamation process, these efforts drifted or were abandoned. Reporting on progress in relation to the old targets stopped. Indeed, the 2005 plan itself hints at this dynamic, stating that 'now that the City has stabilized the majority of its facilities and programs after amalgamation ...', it will be in a position to produce a new inventory during 2005, suggesting that even emissions inventories ceased production in the interim period (City of Ottawa 2004, 32).[10]

The second reason, however, is because what was being added to the old City through the amalgamation was all the suburban areas of the broad city-region. And here, as the report makes clear, emissions were still going up rapidly. Recall that in the old City of Ottawa, corporate emissions had declined by 19 per cent by 1998 and community emissions had declined by 5 per cent. Corporate emissions also declined in the RMOC, and this produced an overall decline in corporate emissions across the new City of 12 per cent.[11] But community emissions in the other municipalities outside the old City of Ottawa had increased by 43 per cent in the same period (City of Ottawa 2004, 31).[12] This was the result of adding in newer suburban areas, growing more rapidly than the urban core, with larger houses and a more car-dependent character, to the city. As a consequence, while the old city may well have met its 20 per cent by the original target date of 2005, reaching it across the new City now looked impossible. And on top of this shift, by incorporating suburbs with higher per capita emissions, more car dependence, and so on, this had a political effect: The new City of Ottawa saw a shift in balance of power between urban and suburban councillors with important effects on the preferences for the investments and regulatory changes necessary to address the city's emissions (see Chapter 6 in particular on this), and also helped bring about the election of a conservative populist mayor, Larry O'Brien, in 2006, who was hostile to a range of environmentally oriented programmes in the city, most (in)famously blocking the original plan for a light rail scheme and setting that initiative back by about a decade.

---

[10] However, later in the report, an inventory produced in 2002 is referenced (Whitford 2002), although this looks like it only covers the transport and waste sectors. We have not been able to source a copy of this inventory to check.

[11] City of Ottawa (2004, 31). As the report notes, however, the other old municipalities had not constructed inventories of their corporate emissions, so a full account of total corporate emissions was impossible to construct. This figure is the combined reductions in RMOC and old City of Ottawa corporate emissions, which they estimate to be around 80 per cent of total corporate emissions.

[12] We are not totally clear how they arrived at this figure. Community emissions grew from 6,028 to 9,026 tCO_2e (tonnes of carbon dioxide equivalent), which I make to be a 49 per cent increase not 43 per cent. Whichever figure is correct, this creates a dramatically different situation for the new city in moving forward.

Nevertheless, the new target for community emissions still looked pretty ambitious. Achieving 20 per cent cuts over 1990 levels by 2012 while emissions had increased by 43 per cent through to 1998 looked extremely demanding, implying in effect a 44 per cent cut in community emissions from 1998 to 2012.[13]

The 2005 plan was full of programmes and initiatives. It has detailed lists of policies across the transport, buildings, waste management, alternative energy, and land use planning areas to address GHG emissions. In some of these, notably transport, there are already ancillary quantitative targets (increases in walking as a percentage of trips, for example), while in others there are descriptions of a series of initiatives, some already in existence (the Better Buildings Partnership, for example, which has antecedents in some of the old City of Ottawa's initiatives), and others more speculative. A pattern of many ideas, but few of them being attached to budget lines or followed up, was emerging.

However, when the implementation stages of the 2005 AQCCMP ended in 2012, the City had failed to meet its emissions reduction targets once again and had rather achieved 6 per cent and 12 per cent emission reductions for the corporate and community sectors, respectively (City of Ottawa 2014d). Nonetheless, the FCM recognized Ottawa in 2012 as having completed all the five milestones in the PCP programme (Federation of Canadian Municipalities 2013).[14]

Around 2010–11, the political climate in the City changed, which created new space for climate policy in the City. In 2010, Jim Watson was elected mayor, a centrist politician replacing the conservative populist Larry O'Brien. Watson was a long-time Ottawa politician, having been mayor of the pre-amalgamation city in 1997–2000 also. He was later re-elected as mayor in both 2014 and 2018. While not advancing climate change action directly in his campaigning, he was nevertheless significantly less hostile than O'Brien, and widely regarded in the city as a cautious but opportunist politician, looking for good reputational initiatives to attach to as long as the political risks are not too high. He was joined in 2010 by the election of David Chernushenko as councillor for Capital Ward, replacing Clive Doucet. Chernushenko had a long reputation as an environmental activist, standing in the federal election in Ottawa Centre for the Green Party in 2004, and being involved in particular in a range of energy efficiency and renewable energy projects.

Behind this shift, the City had been involved in a three-way process with the City of Gatineau (Ottawa's partner city on the Québec side of the river) and the

---

[13] This mirrors the dynamic of emissions cuts politics at the national level in Canada during this period, if anything more dramatically.

[14] This got the City back to where the old City had been in 1996, when it had reached those milestones (interview with Paul McDonald, 2017).

National Capital Commission (NCC), entitled 'Choosing Our Future'.[15] This started in 2004 and ran through to 2011, producing a series of reports out of its deliberations. The process was not focused on decision-making but rather building consensus and a knowledge base for pursuing sustainability, including climate change, across the city. Nevertheless, it produced a shift in focus across the city and meant that when the immediate political environment changed around 2010, a range of actors were able to mobilize around messages from the Choosing our Future reports, for example around questions of urban density (City of Ottawa 2011b, 16–20; Zeemering 2016, 221; see also Chapter 6).

In relation to climate change, the outcome of Choosing our Future and of the changed political dynamics in the City, combined with the requirement to produce a new AQCCMP in 2014 with pressure for enhanced ambition and action, was a new focus on deliberative efforts to generate new ideas and debate across the city about climate change. Central to this was a major 'Greenhouse Gas Roundtable' organized in March 2013. This was a large public event at City Hall designed to operate as a participative forum. It combined presentations by a range of city officials and councillors, Mayor Watson, and NGO and community groups, with a series of smaller workshops on particular issues in the development of climate policy in the city. The roundtable was attended by around 300 people, way more than city politicians and officials anticipated, and was deployed by groups such as Ecology Ottawa to mobilize support for climate policy.[16] The event was also characterized by an attempt to depoliticize the forum by constraining it to address a specific set of technical questions about low cost emissions reductions generated by a financial framing generated by the well-known (in climate policy circles) McKinsey & Co GHG abatement cost curves (McKinsey & Co 2009; City of Ottawa 2013c), and a refusal by citizens to be limited to these questions and economistic framing.

These discussions, alongside work by City officials, generated the adoption of the updated AQCCMP in May 2014, a new target date of 2024 for 20 per cent per capita emission reductions from 2012 levels (City of Ottawa 2014d). The implementation of this plan has nevertheless been very slow: In the first year of its implementation, only one of five key measures was actually budgeted for, and that was for urban afforestation rather than more transformative measures in the energy/transport areas.

At the same time, during the 2014 election campaign, Chernushenko ran with a campaign for Ottawa to become a '100% renewable energy city'. He was

---

[15] For a brief history of the process, see City of Ottawa (2009). For the reports produced during the process, see the archive collated at Greenspace Alliance of Canada's Capital (n.d.), and especially City of Ottawa (2011b).

[16] See an account of the roundtable, including a link to a full video of the presentations part of the event, at Climate Ottawa (2013).

supported in this by a range of local community groups and NGOs. The strategy was to get the City to increase its level of ambition. But it also entailed a re-framing – Chernushenko felt that climate change as a frame had run its course and was difficult to make inspiring, while the pursuit of local, renewable energy (RE), had a positive framing around which enthusiasm might be more readily generated, partly through a 'clean energy' storyline but also allied to a job creation narrative (interview with Chernushenko, 2017). As chair of the environment committee after the 2014 election, he proposed this as a strategic initiative. The initiative was also prompted by the weak budget allocations to the AQCCMP, suggesting those pushing for climate action in the City try a different approach. While there was some pushback from the Mayor and City officials, the approach was nevertheless approved by council, in modified form. As with the GHG Roundtable, the process was augmented by extensive public meetings developing support for the initiative. At one point in the process, it looked like the process would be stymied by a reorganization and a loss of key personnel (as with the amalgamation process and the loss of key people in the 1990s), combined with relative indifference by the Mayor, but the political momentum generated by these public meetings and Chernushenko's leadership got City employees attached to the initiative to make it happen. The City now has a 'renewable energy transition strategy', known as Energy Evolution (City of Ottawa 2017) – it is weaker than the original 100 per cent renewable proposal, focusing in the first instance only on electricity generation across the city, and relegating building energy use and transport to a second phase. It was also awarded only a third of the $1.5 million initially proposed at a fractious City council meeting (Chianello 2017), and widely panned by critics (e.g. Beer 2018) as inadequate. Nevertheless, the initiative has generated significant additional momentum since around 2015 in climate action by the City, with multiple RE generation projects being funded. But the significant weakening of the strategy also meant that campaign groups such as Ecology Ottawa realized the limits of a strategy to persuade Mayor Watson, and switched to a more combative, politicized engagement with the City as a result (interview with Robb Barnes, 2017). This repoliticization of climate change was also reflected in Clive Doucet returning to city politics by standing, unsuccessfully, against Jim Watson in the City council elections in late 2018, making climate change a significant part of his platform (Porter 2018).

3.3 Conclusions

In this chapter we have elaborated starting from the notion of politics as a site, but also as a single site of collective, public, democratic decision-making and governance: The notion of politics that Crick (2000) for example argued should be the only conception of politics. The exercise demonstrates in part the limited ability of this conception of politics to understand the dynamics, since the drivers of changes in the City's activity on climate change frequently come from elsewhere than the debates within the City Council – from entrepreneurial bureaucrats, from the reorganization of municipal boundaries by the Ontario provincial government, and from the funding relationships between property developers and city politicians, in particular.

The chapter also shows the dangers of depoliticization, in the sense of making things technical, outside of public debate, for climate politics. For the most part, climate policy in the City has remained a technical, managerial matter. Even at the outset, when City councillors decided to increase the ambition of the target from the Toronto target to a 50 per cent cut, this was done without any reference to the political challenges of implementing such a target. We could say there were rhetorical politics going on – competition between the mayors of Ottawa and Toronto, for example – but there was no serious public debate, and the politics of governing climate via the notion of a target for a percentage cut in emissions had already been framed technocratically, from the Toronto conference onwards in 1988. Much of the effort by City officials was then to implement targets in as smooth a bureaucratic process as possible. But this meant that the climate strategy of the City was relatively vulnerable to external shocks, notably amalgamation in 2001 and the election of Larry O'Brien as Mayor in 2006, both of which caused climate policy to stall or go backwards. Conversely, climate policy in the City has been aided by its explicit politicization, as the various mobilizations over climate change in the City since the early 2010s have shown, many led by Ecology Ottawa as well as activist councillors such as Chernushenko. This was intensified by a strategy of organizing large public events to discuss and deliberate on climate policy, as in the GHG roundtable and then over the 100 per cent RE strategy. These events can usefully be understood to be deliberative events that operate agonistically – heightening conflicts in productive ways – similarly to how Willis (2020) discusses the ways that citizens' climate assemblies can channel and shape conflicts over climate change, rather than simply be about 'producing consensus'. We return to some of these specific conflicts later on, notably in Chapters 5 and 6. This chapter thus supports arguments that making climate change political, in the sense of highlighting the conflicts of interest and power explicitly, can be positive for shifting the dynamics in the City.

But it also shows the limits of focusing on politics as a site without also thinking about how it is shaped by what I called implicit climate politics in Chapter 1. There are numerous hints in this chapter about how the ability of City officials or progressive politicians to achieve change was undermined by the well-established dominance of a particular vision of what city life is and should be, with low-density, car-dominated transport and housing systems more or less unquestioned. There were mentions in some policy documents of the need to encourage shifts from cars to transit but even those focused on new transit provision, as in the light rail initiative, or in better cycle provision, assuming that this only complements, not undermines, the centrality of the car and the suburb. But what is interesting is that the City has, at the same time, although largely disconnected from its explicit climate politics, been engaged in initiatives that do seek to disturb this dominant urban vision. I explore two of these initiatives – Complete Streets and intensification – in Chapters 5 and 6, as instances precisely of implicit climate politics.

4

Networked Governance and Carbon Accounting in Ottawa

MATTHEW PATERSON AND KOFI AGYAPONG ADOMAKO

In Chapter 2 we saw the limits of thinking about climate politics only through the notion of politics as a site or arena. There are two main aspects to this argument. One is that we miss lots of what ought to be regarded as political activity on climate change with this sort of one-dimensional account of politics. But the other is that the site itself becomes thought of as static, simply 'there'. But political sites are historical creations, and are constantly, if often subtly, being remade. This chapter focuses on two, intertwined aspects of how Ottawa as a city is being made and remade as a political arena through climate change politics. The first of these is the entanglement of the City in a set of networks of municipalities, both generally and specifically on climate change. The second is through the principal governance strategy of these networks, carbon accounting, a strategy that is widely understood as depoliticizing. Both of these have structured how the City has dealt with climate change in specific ways, explored throughout the chapter.

But focusing on carbon accounting also leads us to think about other sites of climate politics. The organizations developing carbon accounting are both themselves sites of political decision-making, exerting authority across a range of other organizations, and are organizations enabling other agents to engage in climate governance through their own carbon accounting exercises. The second half of the chapter focuses on the key carbon accounting organization in the city, Carbon 613.[1] Carbon 613 promotes business action on climate change with carbon accounting and footprinting as its key techniques. In both Carbon 613 and the City itself, the depoliticizing qualities of carbon accounting are evident. In Carbon 613, however, we find the accounting approach allied interestingly to an attempt to mobilize a strong set of narratives around the agency of the companies, reflecting the cultural political economy argument sketched in Chapter 2 – companies are encouraged both to see carbon accounting as enabling the more effective pursuit of a range of

---

[1] 613 is the telephone code for Ottawa and Eastern Ontario.

business opportunities, and to articulate this with an emotionally powerful low carbon corporate identity. Carbon accounting is about routine, but it does also need the production of desire to work well (Descheneau and Paterson 2011).

4.1 The Partners for Climate Protection Programme and Municipal Climate Governance in Ottawa

The story of climate politics in Ottawa is intertwined with the story of city networks on climate change. In Ottawa's case this is to the Partners for Climate Protection programme (PCP). This is a network of municipalities across Canada focused on climate change. The PCP programme has provided a platform for municipalities in Canada to adopt climate governance in the face of limited support from upper levels of government and barriers including inadequate technical and financial capacity, and the constitutional situation of municipalities as 'creatures of the provinces', that is, only existing because of provincial legislation rather than as having a constitutional basis for their existence (Gore 2010). As such, it reflects Zeemering's (2016, 206) point that cities in such a system need to 'form governance relationships that work outside the traditional channels of federalism and intergovernmental relations'.

The PCP programme was created in 1994 after the 20% Club, a city-to-city network run by the Federation of Canadian Municipalities (FCM), within which Ottawa's 20 per cent target at that point was framed (see Chapter 3), merged with the Canadian version of the Cities for Climate Protection (CCP) programme run by the International Council for Local Environmental Initiatives (ICLEI)– Local Governments for Sustainability (Federation of Canadian Municipalities 2016a). Currently the FCM runs the policy direction and daily operations of the PCP programme whilst the ICLEI provides the technical support and the international linkages on best practices in municipal climate action from across the world (Gordon 2016a; ICLEI–Local Governments for Sustainability 2016). The staff responsible for operations and outreach for the PCP programme are based at the FCM secretariat in Ottawa (Federation of Canadian Municipalities 2016a). The PCP receives financial support for its programmes from the Green Municipal Fund (GMF) which is a \$550 million federal government supported fund administered by the FCM (Gore 2010; Gordon 2016a). Its 2015 annual report highlighted emissions reductions of over 1.8 billion tonnes of CO_2 annually as a result of actions from members and investments of \$2.3 billion in over 800 projects to cut emissions across Canada since the programme began in 1994 (Federation of Canadian Municipalities 2015, 4).

Local governments who committed themselves to the PCP programme agreed to cut emissions from their operations by 20 per cent below 1994 levels and 6 per cent below 1994 levels for community–wide emissions (Gore 2010). Munici-palities must first pass a motion at City Council level to join the PCP programme and are required to adopt the five-stage milestone process that the PCP uses for its municipal climate actions.

The five-stage milestone (Federation of Canadian Municipalities 2016a) includes the following steps:

1. Municipalities must create a baseline emissions inventory and forecast,
2. Set emissions reduction targets,
3. Develop a local action plan,
4. Implement the local action plan, and
5. Monitor progress and report results.

The PCP also encourages its members to develop separate programmes to tackle emissions from the local governments' operations and services from community-wide emissions. As of 2015, the PCP had over 280 members across all the provinces and territories in Canada, with over 65 per cent of the Canadian popula-tion living in a PCP member community (Federation of Canadian Municipalities 2016b). The FCM has been releasing the National Measures Report, an annual progress report on the PCP programme, since 2008 to compile actions and pro-grammes by its members and highlight achievements made by municipalities across Canada (Federation of Canadian Municipalities 2016c). The FCM secretar-iat sends out data collection forms every year to all member municipalities within Canada to compile this report.

The FCM makes use of three main governance mechanisms (information and knowledge sharing, capacity building in the form of financial support for projects, and rule setting and recognition) to exert authority over municipalities through the PCP (Kern and Bulkeley 2009; Gordon 2016a). In terms of information and communication, the FCM shares its greenhouse gas (GHG) inventory tools and software with PCP member communities to maintain standardized emission calculations across the board. Also, the FCM secretariat shares with the various members research on the latest municipal climate change mitigation and adaptation practices from across the world through its website, and also organizes the annual Sustainable Communities Conference to enable members to interact and upgrade their knowledge base.

Through the GMF, the PCP programme has been able govern municipalities by offering financial support in the form of loans and grants to help communities to conduct studies and audits for their GHG emission reduction plans (Federation of Canadian Municipalities 2016d). The last form of governance used by the FCM to exert its influence over the PCP network is using soft power in the form of norm setting and recognition (Andonova et al. 2009). The PCP requires its members to tackle their emissions through its five-step programme of action and also highlights and recognizes the achievements of well performing municipalities.

Even though the PCP has been able to promote climate action within Canadian municipal circles, it has failed to engage dormant members who make up the majority of its membership across Canada due to challenges it faces in its operations (Gore 2010; Gordon 2016a). Gordon (2016a), in his study on the influence of the PCP programme on Canadian municipal climate change governance, attributed the failure of the PCP to engage its inactive members to the material incapacity of the network. He found that the PCP programme had been unable to provide the needed technical and financial support to some of its members to undertake GHG reduction initiatives. In his study on climate governance in Toronto and Winnipeg, he noted that the PCP was massively underfunded to fulfil its mission as a network with a national scope. Gore (2010) had earlier shown that the PCP had an operating budget of $150,000 and a staff of one in 2008, whilst the Australian version of the Cities for Climate Protection (CCP) programme had a $3 million operating budget. The CCP programme enabled by the Australian federal government had a staff of 15 people to help it achieve its community outreach programmes around the same period. This lack of adequate financial resources has made it difficult for the PCP network to organize study tours and workshops for its members that other transnational networks such as Energie-Cités in Europe use to actively engage local governments and highlight the actions embarked on by the active members in its fold.

Gore (2010) attributed the inability of the PCP programme to engage its inactive members more to the organizational structure of the programme. The FCM runs the PCP programme as one of the numerous programmes under its wide scope and currently does not have regional or field offices across Canada. It also lacks a support team at the FCM Secretariat that is dedicated and able to move from one community to another to assess the actions of its members and provide members with any form of technical assistance.

4.2 The PCP and the City of Ottawa

Nevertheless, despite these weaknesses and limits of the PCP, in relation to Ottawa, climate policy and politics in the City has clearly been shaped by participation in the network. Ottawa joined the Partners for Climate Protection programme of the FCM in February 1997 (City of Ottawa 2000, 31). It achieved milestone five for both its corporate and community climate plans in 2012, the old city prior to amalgamation having already achieved this in 1996. We now explore the ways in which the PCP has shaped climate action in Ottawa, and how Ottawa is thus accountable for its climate actions to city networks, through the analysis of three main indicators of influence identified from studies on sub-national networks, specifically: Information sharing and knowledge dissemination; capacity building in the form of financial support for the development of some climate plans; and the adoption of PCP norms and rules for climate policies in Ottawa.

Regarding information sharing, the City of Ottawa incorporated aspects of the PCP's research on climate policies for its 2003 Environmental Strategy for the newly amalgamated City of Ottawa. Also, the FCM and ICLEI shared its software and tools with the City of Ottawa in 2004 to conduct its first GHG inventory after amalgamation (City of Ottawa 2014d). These were also used in the City's 2008 and 2012 greenhouse gas inventories.

The City also used studies and research on municipal climate governance provided by the PCP network in the formulation of policies under both the 2005 and 2014 Air Quality and Climate Change Management Plans (AQCCMPs) (City of Ottawa 2014d). When discussions began for the update of the 2005 climate plan in 2012, Ottawa reviewed the climate action plans from other PCP members in Canada. This review included climate plans from Calgary, Toronto, the Waterloo Region, and Vancouver (City of Ottawa 2014d).

The information sharing partnership within the PCP programme enabled Ottawa to have access to this information and other climate plans from cities across the world through the PCPs' connection to the more global ICLEI network. Since Ottawa is not a direct member of transnational climate networks such as C40, the influence is more indirect.

The information and knowledge sharing connection existing between the two bodies has also been in the reverse direction, with Ottawa providing information on its GHG reduction activities on a consistent basis to the PCP network. Ottawa has been recognized on a consistent basis as one of a select group of communities within the over 280-member network to have shared information on its climate action plans with other PCP members in all the available FCM reports since 2008 (Federation of Canadian Municipalities 2012, 23). Various programmes under the 2005 AQCCMP, including the purchase of 202 diesel–electric buses for OC Transpo (the City's public transport agency) featured in both the 2009 and 2011 editions of the report. Ottawa again provided information on two initiatives, namely the Trail Road Landfill Generating facility and the Energy Management and Investment Strategy, in the 2013 edition of the National Measures Report of the FCM (Federation of Canadian Municipalities 2013, 22–23).

Regarding capacity building, the City received financial support from the PCP programme in the form of loans and grants to enable the Ottawa conduct energy audits in its facilities after amalgamation in 2001. The first evidence of financial enabling provided by the PCP network to support climate change mitigation in Ottawa was a grant of $100,000 in 2001 for the Comprehensive Facility Audit and

Retrofit Strategy across twenty-six city facilities (Federation of Canadian Municipalities 2016d). The grant from the Green Municipal Fund partly funded this project, which identified renewable energy and other energy efficiency opportunities within the facilities audited under the project. The project, which ran until 2003, enabled Ottawa to undertake upgrades in the facilities including city hall, which led to emissions reduction and also enabled it to meet its PCP milestones (Federation of Canadian Municipalities 2016d).

In 2006, the City of Ottawa again received a grant of $35,000 that covered half of the total project cost for its community and corporate greenhouse gas inventory (Federation of Canadian Municipalities 2016d). Through the funds provided, the City conducted an emissions inventory in all the thirteen community districts that made up the City of Ottawa in 2007. Ottawa received this funding through the energy management strategy of the PCP programme. Most of the financial backing Ottawa received from the PCP has been to support programmes targeting corporate GHG emissions rather than on community level emissions.

The third and final way in which the PCP network has played a role in Ottawa's climate policy development is the manner in which the City has adopted the PCP networks' norms and rules in the formulation of its climate change action plans. Ottawa has structured and followed the PCP's norms in its climate policies by conducting GHG inventories for all its new climate initiatives, incorporating strong monitoring and reporting tools for all the actions implemented to cut GHG emissions. It has also had separate programmes to target corporate and community emissions in all its climate plans. All the eighteen individual action plans in the 2005 AQCCMP were aligned to follow the PCP milestone process and therefore consisted of routinely monitoring and reporting on aspects of the project, resulting in the update of the corporate emission plan in 2008. The release of progress reports for both its past corporate and community climate plans also enabled Ottawa to update some programmes under the 2005 AQCCMP.

The PCP's role in climate policy development in Ottawa has enabled the City to undertake its climate change mitigation strategies, especially plans targeting corporate emissions. Ottawa mayor, Jim Watson, confirmed this assertion in both the 2014 AQCCMP final document and 2013 FCM Measures Report (Federation of Canadian Municipalities 2013, 23; City of Ottawa 2014d). The City of Ottawa has been able to commit itself to climate action consistently, mainly through its knowledge sharing partnership with the PCP although it has not achieved the needed emission cuts, especially at the community level.

Ottawa can be described as an active PCP member based on its information sharing practices with the PCP and the manner in which it has adopted PCP norms and rules in its climate governance regime, and therefore falls into the category of municipalities that led Gordon (2016a, 539–40) to describe the PCP as a network 'of and for pioneers'. According to Gordon (2016a), the PCP network consists of two distinct group of municipalities – early leaders in municipal climate governance, such as Ottawa, and another set of municipalities made up of relatively inactive cities that have barely changed their behaviour since becoming members of the PCP network. Ottawa's active participation in the network was recognized in 2012, with the PCP network declaring Ottawa's purchase of diesel electric buses as one of the top ten GHG reduction measures across Canada in 2011 (Federation of Canadian Municipalities 2012, 9). A special feature on Ottawa's climate change initiatives appeared in the 2013 edition of the FCM *Measures* report, focused on the City's achievement of the fifth Milestone in the PCP process in 2012.

Ottawa as a site of climate politics has thus in part been, and continues to be, made by a set of horizontal network relations as well as multilevel government relations. A key aspect of how this has been achieved has been through the development of carbon accounting. Through its involvement in city networks, carbon accounting has both become a core technique for governing climate change in the City, but also a way by which the City has become accountable to those city networks. As in Chapter 3, this represents very effectively a depoliticized approach, specifically a technocratic, managerial one focused on accounting for emissions and generating programmes to address them, without significant public debate and assuming there is little conflict entailed in dealing with climate change.

4.3 Carbon Accounting beyond City Government: Carbon 613

Carbon accounting has been integral to climate governance in many contexts, not just official government processes (e.g. Kolk et al. 2008; Lövbrand and Stripple 2011; Lovell and MacKenzie 2011; Thistlethwaite and Paterson 2016). And it has been central to many initiatives within cities and city networks on climate change (Gordon 2016b). Often deploying the slogan (even cliché) of 'you cannot manage what you do not measure', it proceeds on the basis of getting organizations (or even individuals) to measure and track their GHG emissions as a precursor to designing strategies to reduce them. In terms of the arguments we have been exploring, it functions as a depoliticizing strategy, reducing the complex socio-technical and political-economic processes through which GHG emissions are generated to an abstract number – tonnes of carbon. The conflicts, trade-offs, and dilemmas entailed in any particular effort to reduce emissions (such as those detailed in later chapters) are effaced. All sorts of technical processes and decisions go into the production of the carbon account – how to commensurate different GHGs to each other, where to set the boundaries of what emissions you count and which you don't, and so on.

The conflicts involved in these processes are also erased in the focus on the output – the tCO_2e (tonnes of carbon dioxide equivalent).

In Chapter 7 we map climate change initiatives across the city. A number of these initiatives operate using carbon accounting as an important part of their attempts at governing climate change. These include Bullfrog Power, the Ottawa Renewable Energy Cooperative (OREC) (see also Chapter 9), the radio station Live88.5, the National Capital Commission (NCC), and the Delphi Group. Most of these deploy carbon accounting internally, as with the City, to manage their own emissions. Their practices vary in terms of how they account for carbon, which tools they use, whether they get emissions certified, whether they connect the accounting tool to setting targets, and so on. But one initiative – Carbon 613 – operates as a governance initiative to attempt to get a range of organizations across the city (and recently including the City Council itself) to account for their carbon and connect that to strategies to cut emissions.

Carbon 613 arose as part of a broader network of similar initiatives across Ontario, originally called the Sustainability CoLab, now renamed Green Economy Canada (Green Economy Canada n.d.). Mike Morrice established this in 2014 out of his experience with the flagship programme of the Sustainable Waterloo Region, the Regional Carbon Initiative, upon which the CoLab model is based). Members (termed 'Hubs') of the Green Economy Canada network are all community organizations involved in sustainability programmes centred on target-setting.[2] Michael Murr of Ottawa's EnviroCentre (a well-established environmental organization in the city best known for working on energy efficiency promotion in low-income housing, and providing household energy audits to citizens) decided to join the CoLab network and establish Carbon 613 as a more business-focused arm of the EnviroCentre. Carbon 613 was formally launched in September 2015, with three member organizations (interview with Stu Campana, 2016). Like the programmes run by other organizations in the network (in different regions of the province), Carbon 613 is a collaboration specifically aimed at local businesses. They frame it as an initiative focused on helping businesses set and achieve sustainability-related targets, but in practice these are exclusively focused on carbon, i.e. GHG emissions. Carbon 613 provides tools and knowledge to track and reduce businesses' carbon footprints. By providing a means for businesses to evince an interest in mitigating climate change, it is also implicitly promoted as a kind of marketing effort for those businesses. It is not the only programme or service run through the EnviroCentre, but it is one of its most prominent. In February 2016, the Ontario Ministry of the Environment and Climate Change

---

[2] The other participants in the network are Kitchener-Waterloo, Durham, Kingston, Hamilton-Burlington, and Sudbury. Niagara has also participated but is not, at the time of writing, a participant.

announced $1 million, drawn from the $325 million Green Investment Fund, in new funding for Sustainability CoLab.

Carbon 613 works as a membership organization for interested businesses. Potential members are approached by the organization. Carbon 613 aims to get members from a range of types of business and economic sectors (although they recognize difficulties in getting some key sectors to join, interview with Stu Campana, 2017), and is in part designed also to generate a sense of broad business support for climate action to increase pressure on the City Council itself (Stu Campana, personal communication, 2019). It has for example members from large retail businesses (IKEA), finance (TD, Your Credit Union), consulting firms (Earnscliffe, Delphi Group), community housing (Communityworks, Unity Housing, Coopérative d'Habitation Voisins), hospitality (Angela's B&B, Alt Hotels), and more recently, public organizations such as the Canadian Museum of Nature or the Ottawa-Carleton District School Board and from June 2016 the City of Ottawa itself (Carbon 613 n.d. b), the latter in part in response to Carbon 613's success in demonstrating business interest. Once a member, a business works with the programme to set a carbon-reduction target for the firm's operations. Members commit themselves to a process, including: setting an emissions baseline and a GHG reduction target (within 3 years of joining); making a plan to reduce emissions; and tracking and publicly disclosing emissions annually. Members gain access to a range of services, including: A network of like-minded local businesses committed to sustainability and carbon reduction; a carbon accounting tool and training to assist in setting and achieving sustainability goals; a comprehensive education programme including Carbon 613 'Labs' (highlighting sustainability best practices) and 'Seminars' (presenting current trends and challenges in achieving sustainability in business); and a free subscription to *Corporate Knights Magazine*, a Canadian business sustainability magazine (Carbon 613 n.d. a).

But while carbon accounting and footprinting is central to Carbon 613's work, it works as a sort of underpinning technical infrastructure. Carbon 613's employees spend most of their time working with the organization's members, helping them devise initiatives to reduce GHG emissions, change practices within their organization, learn from each other, and so on. In particular, they look for things that 'provide a good narrative' to both motivate the member's own staff and provide for often visually clear messages that the organization is interested in GHG emissions reductions: 'upgrading lighting, providing electric car charging stations' (interview with Stu Campana, 2017). They connect this back to the carbon accounting picture, to enable members to see the impacts, however small, of their actions on emissions, but the focus of the work done is on the activities and the learning process.

This approach is then as much about both recognizing the members' varied motivations and providing ideas that will motivate them to undertake additional actions. Members are motivated to participate in Carbon 613 in a variety of ways, and usually have mixed motives (interview with Stu Campana, 2017). For most, being active on climate change is one of their motivations. Many will, however, be as motivated by a desire to cut costs, through savings in energy consumption in particular. Some companies (Campana mentioned local financial institution Your Credit Union) may be forced to be particularly responsive to members to justify investments in relation to the bottom line. Others may be more interested in building their reputation with their clients or in specific markets (either specifically as a climate leader or more generally as a good corporate citizen or progressive company). Carbon 613 cultivates this motivation by generating recognition and publicity for their members' efforts. It aims to enable member businesses to become 'revered environmental leaders in Ottawa' (Carr 2017). Others may simply want to learn about innovative ways of organizing their business, or to engage in networking with other like-minded businesses across the city. Carbon 613's goal, to become an organization that local businesses feel they would be actively losing out by not engaging with, reflects this motivation.

Carbon 613's overall approach is therefore to use carbon accounting as part of a thoroughgoing attempt to construct low carbon subjectivities in participating organizations. Alongside members, it enables some other organizations to act as 'catalysers' and 'collaborators' (Carbon 613 n.d. b). Most notable, however, is the framing in its 2016 annual report. This contains a series of 'hero stories' and 'climate quests', its cover has a participant tearing off his shirt to reveal the Carbon 613 logo in place of a Superman S (see Figure 4.1), and there is a sequence of allusions to Roy Lichtenstein's pop art imagery with 'wow' and 'super thank you' slogans. The report starts: 'I can't wait until they finally make a climate change superhero movie. Our hero will always carpool to the scene of the crime, installing LED light bulbs at the speed of, uh, light'. However, Carbon 613 members 'aren't waiting for anyone else to save the day': they are getting on with the job themselves. And they are doing so together, as 'if climate change is the villain threatening our planet, teamwork is its Achilles heel' (Carbon 613 2016, 1). The heroes we encounter in the story are engaged in various initiatives: a B&B providing free bikes to residents; a School board retrofitting buildings with energy efficient lighting and integrating carbon literacy into its curricula; a small office firm reorganizing its entire work process to minimize paper usage; and a group of members collaborating to improve lighting efficiency and then share their experience across the network of Carbon 613 members. Each member in the report is given a superpower befitting a superhero (Carbon 613 2016).

Figure 4.1 Carbon 613 report front cover

This focus on heroes and narratives designed to motivate and inspire is not accidental. In part it is precisely because of the small scale of many of the initiatives and the recognition of their small impact on overall emissions. For Carbon 613's Stu Campana, this was because

we have a lot of SMEs, and many are tenants,[3] so their footprint (or at least the footprint they have any control over) is quite small. We want them to feel important, and do this by showing how it can be done, by 'leading the way' . . . to engage smaller organizations where then numbers may be small but the symbolism and inspiration can be large.

(interview with Stu Campana, 2017)

This is connected to the focus on small but visually obvious and symbolically important activities discussed in the previous paragraph.

This intertwining of routine and desire – creating powerful narratives through which actors can see themselves 'becoming low carbon' over time, and which motivate them, combined with a set of familiar managerial techniques that enable them to integrate low carbon shifts into daily routines, is a common combination in the cultural political economy drivers of climate politics. We can see it in carbon markets (Descheneau and Paterson 2011), but we can see them intertwining in a number of other contexts (see especially Bulkeley et al. 2016). Such an account of climate politics does tend towards depoliticization – in the sense introduced in

---

[3] This is relevant as they then don't control some of the key sources of GHGs, notably to do with the building envelope and insulation, and the heating and cooling system.

Chapter 2 that it imagines decarbonization as a process of learning, networking, (socio)technical innovation. But it nevertheless entails operations of power in the subtle processes of reconstitution of subjectivities as businesses shift towards low carbon practices, and in the generation of political authority for organizations, such as Carbon 613, that are able to coordinate others' activities through the infrastructure of carbon accounting.

4.4 Conclusions

In this chapter we have seen that, even when we think about politics as a site or arena, we have to consider how any specific political arena is constituted. We have seen that political arenas are constantly being made by the networks and relations they are enmeshed in. Some of these entail formal constitutional arrangements, but others are more fluid, as in the PCP programme of the FCM and the way it has shaped climate politics in Ottawa. Principal among these means have been through the spread both of carbon accounting as a governance tool in general but also of specific ways of doing carbon accounting.

But we also saw that such carbon accounting is a diffuse way of doing climate politics, not restricted to formal political arenas but being deployed by a range of actors to exert authority (that is, to enact politics-as-power) in relation to climate change. Carbon accounting thus reflects the dynamic of depoliticization of the issue in terms of rendering it technical, taking it out of deliberative political decision-making processes, but that are nevertheless political in terms of both reflecting strategies of power and generating new forms of power and authority (Barry 2002).

At the same time, carbon accounting operates as a means for certain types of organizations to pursue their business strategies – not only the carbon accounting organizations but the motives of companies to join initiatives such as Carbon 613, seeking new customers or operational efficiencies. But mobilizing such business strategies in the case of Carbon 613 entailed, among other things, rhetorical strategies focused on 'heroes', that is attempts to cultivate not only the sense that carbon accounting was rational and made good business sense, but that it was affectively powerful – to be *desired*.

What we don't see here however is much of a sense of climate politics as contestation. There are no voices of opposition to either carbon accounting or to networks such as the PCP. This aspect of climate politics remains in the sphere and mode of technocratic actors seeking to shift the huge complex system of the high carbon world, without challenging the power of dominant actors or otherwise contesting the terrain of action. In Chapters 5 and 6, however, we shift focus to processes where such contestation is core to what we see.

5

Complete Streets and Its Discontents

LOUIS MACHABÉE AND MATTHEW PATERSON

While the City was developing climate policy in fits and starts, as shown in Chapter 2, there was plenty going on in the City that shaped the patterns of greenhouse gas (GHG) emissions across the city, reflecting what we talked about in Chapter 1 as 'implicit climate politics'. At the same time, while much of the explicit climate politics in the city reflected relatively low levels of political conflict, operationalized for example through the smooth technical arena of carbon accounting, the conflict dimension of politics has been much more central regarding questions of transport and planning.

Central to this type of climate politics in the city are questions of transport, housing, and planning. In this domain, important implicit climate initiatives emerged around the banner of Complete Streets – initiatives to rebuild streets for multiple users rather than just cars. In the case of Complete Streets, the focus of this chapter, the NGO (Ecology Ottawa) that pushed successfully for the adoption of Complete Streets was strongly motivated by climate change concerns, but rarely mentioned it explicitly in their campaign material. The City Council hardly mentioned it at all, even though the policy was being adopted at the same time as the 2014 Air Quality and Climate Change Management Plan (AQCCMP), to which it could plausibly have contributed significantly as a part of the strategy. Nevertheless, climate change played an important role in the development and contestation of Complete Streets, in ways explored in this chapter. We argue in particular here that it functions as a background shaper, an increasing implicit recognition of the trajectory that investments in urban infrastructure need to follow, a side-constraint within which urban initiatives have to operate, if you like.

This chapter and Chapter 6 develop these points through analyses of two moments of conflict in the City's climate politics, over Complete Streets and over planning shifts understood via the frame of 'intensification'. In this chapter, focused on Complete Streets, we see many of the cultural political economy dynamics we saw regarding Carbon 613, but here questions of accumulation and subjectivity are deployed rather differently – as often to oppose low carbon initiatives as to promote them. We also see these questions articulated as competing visions about city life – about what a street is for, how it connects to the lives of people in the city, and the shape of the city's economy, in particular. Finally, we also see the dynamics of de- and re-politicization, with the City's managers seeking to defuse political conflict and debate through resort to technical analyses and expertise, and opponents of Complete Streets initiatives refusing these strategies of the City.

One of the questions this sort of case raises is whether making climate change central to these sorts of initiatives would actually help promote low carbon initiatives: If proponents of Complete Streets had focused on the carbon savings, would opponents have been able to use that to show that carbon savings could be achieved through other means, such as more aggressive promotion of electric vehicles? Instead, the debate was centred on competing social visions for the city and competing interests of different city neighbourhoods, and was rather effective in enabling shifts towards Complete Streets.

We start with an account of how Complete Streets got onto the agenda and became so rapidly adopted by the City Council as a principle for street re-design. We show how it occurred through the interconnections between effective NGO mobilizations, shifts in technocratic planning norms, the timing of policy windows at the City Council, and the dynamics of a specific project – Main Street in Old Ottawa East – that occurred simultaneously with the broader initiative. We then explore in detail the character and dynamics of the conflict over Main Street, showing that it is rooted in competing visions of urban life, and the desires surrounding specific practices associated with those visions.

5.1 Mobilizing for Complete Streets

From 2012 to 2015 a rapid shift in the City's approach to reconstructing its streetscapes occurred. In three years, it shifted to a plan that wherever it was investing in upgrading or renewing infrastructure, it would do so according to a 'Complete Streets' approach. Previously, it would have used the need to upgrade, for example, a sewer or storm drain, to do other improvements, but largely within the context of maintaining the priority of car-based movement around the city within the street's design. In Complete Streets, the streets instead were redesigned to improve use by buses, cyclists, and pedestrians, as well as to provide non-transport uses in terms of seating areas and increased tree cover within the area. Complete Streets was a framing for more socio-environmentally oriented forms of urban development that emerged across North America during the 2000s,

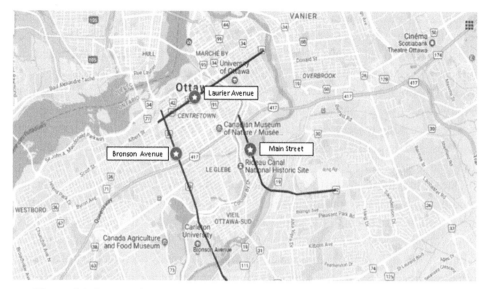

Figure 5.1 Ottawa city centre map, showing Bronson Avenue, Laurier Avenue, and Main Street.
Source: Google Maps, with overlay drawn by Louis Machabée

following on the heels of other such framings as 'new urbanism', 'smart growth', and so on (Moreland-Russell et al. 2013; Zavestoski and Agyeman 2015).

Complete Streets in Ottawa emerged out of an initiative to revitalize Bronson Street (one of the main arterial streets from the city centre to the South, see Figure 5.1). The prompt for the initiative was the need to replace a water main that dated back to the late nineteenth century (Furey 2011). In November 2011, a public meeting was held to present a project, and two competing visions for the purposes of the road were debated, between the vision of Bronson as an arterial road, vs. as a traditional main street, as a locus for neighbourhood activity. There was considerable history in this conflict, going back to the 1980s when Bronson going South (off the map shown) was widened to three lanes each way as an express commuter route to the South end of the city and to its airport, for many destroying the community uses of the street in the city centre (Doucet 2007, 50; Scott 2010). The earlier developments however had, from the perspective of commuter car traffic, left a bottleneck – an area north of Carling Avenue where the street was not wide enough to have both two lanes each way and on-street parking. The proposal on the table from the city was therefore to widen the road, losing sidewalk space, some front gardens, and on-street parking (Furey 2011).

But what was novel in this instance was that a new concept in urban planning was introduced into the debate: Complete Streets. In this instance, it was introduced critically by the journalist covering the public meeting (Furey 2011), but it had clearly emerged into the public discourse on how to frame thinking about urban infrastructure and the uses of streets.

Over the next year or so, Complete Streets started to pop up in other contexts. In May 2012, the City opened a grade-separated cycle lane on Laurier Avenue, one of the main East–West streets in the city centre, and critics of this initiative framed it, as in the Bronson instance, as a problem of Complete Streets.

Complete Streets integrating bike lanes is a flawed model of urban planning ... That's the view that every mode of transportation should be crammed onto a few select streets ... The truth is this has never been about what's best for cyclists and for the city as a whole. It's about special interest groups demanding they have money and attention thrown their way.

(Ottawa Sun 2012, 18)

The same year, the term cropped up as part of the recommendations of an Ontario provincial panel led by the Chief Coroner, reflecting on deaths to cyclists on the province's roads, although obscured by a controversy over the proposal to make the wearing of helmets compulsory for cyclists (Adam 2012). The connection to cyclist and pedestrian safety was picked up later that year by councillor David Chernushenko, recently elected councillor for Capital ward (the ward to the east of Bronson, south of the highway passing through the city, the 417 – the major east–west road in Figure 5.1), who noted the Chief Coroners' panel and picked up in particular on the Complete Streets recommendation (Cockburn 2012).

But the term took off in Ottawa during 2013–14. In these two years, a number of elements combined to produce the shift. The first of these was that the initiative for a Complete Streets project on Main Street became a high-profile controversy, raising the profile of Complete Streets overall. We devote the second part of this chapter to the Main Street conflict, but, briefly, this became high profile because it is one of the arterial roads (such as Bronson Avenue) into the city centre, that is at the same time a main street for its community. Notably, another Complete Streets project was developed at the same time, on Churchill Avenue in the city's west end (off the map in Figure 5.1, about five kilometres west of Bronson Ave), but was developed with little controversy and a section opened in November 2014 (Willems 2014; City of Ottawa 2014a). There were one or two other proposals, notably to make the cycle lane established on Laurier Avenue permanent, and to turn the Byward market area (a busy area of mostly shops, restaurants, and bars on the north-east side of the city centre) into a Complete Streets area (Bernstein and Fleury 2013; Willing 2013),[1] but the vast majority of public attention was on Main Street.

---

[1] This was a guest column: Mathieu Fleury was councillor for the ward covering the Byward market (Rideau-Vanier), while Liz Bernstein was Vice-President of the Lowertown Community Association, the association for the area, as well as a co-founder of Ecology Ottawa.

Second, Ecology Ottawa, the principal environmental NGO focused on action at city level, took it up as a campaign. The City was required by the province to update its Transportation Master Plan (TMP) during 2013, and Ecology Ottawa recognized this as a window for generating new ideas and policy shifts. In March 2013, Ecology Ottawa launched the 'Complete Streets for Ottawa' campaign at a meeting at the University of Ottawa, and launched a petition to make Complete Streets 'an integral part of the planning process for the construction, retrofitting, and maintenance of all roadways' (Jenkins 2013). The meeting brought in speakers from the Toronto Centre for Active Transportation and from Ottawa Public Health, and City Councillor Keith Egli, chair of the transportation committee. Ecology Ottawa had already started the process of building support from a wide range of organizations for the approach – the meeting was supported variously by the Council on Ageing in Ottawa, Ottawa Public Health, Heart and Stroke Foundation, Walk Ottawa, Green Communities Canada, Citizens for Safe Cycling, Student Federation of the University of Ottawa's Bike Co-op, EnviroCentre, Vanier Community Association, and CU (Carleton University) Cycling (see Ecology Ottawa 2015). Ecology Ottawa worked successfully during 2013 to gain support from a wide range of other organizations (including notably financial backing from the Heart and Stroke Foundation, a large national health charity), and gained 2,600 signatures for its petition, which it presented to the Council shortly before the decision on the TMP. The key arguments deployed in the campaign focused on safety and health (see e.g. Spalding 2013a).

After the TMP was approved, Ecology Ottawa switched rapidly to campaigning to ensure its implementation. They organized a Complete Streets Strategy Forum in March 2014, inviting a number of key councillors, as well as citizens and other organizations (Yogaretnam 2014), and produced a lengthy report aimed mostly at community organizers as to how to get Complete Streets initiatives adopted in their neighbourhoods, but also with an eye on shifting the incentives for candidates in the upcoming elections to support Complete Streets (Ecology Ottawa 2014b). This strategy report is one of the few places where climate change gets an explicit and telling mention. At the end of the introduction, after noting that both the Main Street project and the TMP had been approved by City Council, the report states:

But our work is not done yet. The decisions we make today will determine whether we will be able to enjoy increased rates of walking, cycling, and transit-use in the future, or whether we will pave the way for increasing traffic congestion, infrastructure costs, and greenhouse gas emissions.

(Ecology Ottawa 2014b, 4)

In other words, while most campaigning for Complete Streets is focused on questions of safety (especially for cyclists and pedestrians) and health (through the promotion of active transport), it is central to an overall decision about the trajectory of the city in relation to large-scale questions of climate change.

Third, the city's process for developing its TMP gained its own momentum in institutionalizing Complete Streets. Alongside the political pressure from Ecology Ottawa, the city had hired consultants Delcan to produce a report detailing options for the city centre core. The report involved extensive public consultations and research during 2011–13, and contained highly detailed accounts of options, where Complete Streets principles were integrated throughout (Delcan 2013). The City's Transportation Committee approved their report on 27 March 2013, and the TMP incorporated key elements of its conclusions. The Plan itself was approved at a meeting of the Transportation Committee on 7 October 2013 and the full council on 26 November 2013 (City of Ottawa 2013a), with Complete Streets an integral part of the plan (Spalding 2013b).

Fourth, during 2014, as the City was developing an implementation plan for the Complete Streets part of the TMP, there were also city elections, and Complete Streets became an election issue, especially in city centre wards where the proposed initiatives would be concentrated. In Somerset ward, which covers the bulk of the city centre, a number of candidates competed actively to promote Complete Streets, including all three leading candidates (who gained 73 per cent of the vote between them, see City of Ottawa election results at City of Ottawa 2014b), and Catherine McKenney, once she won the seat, promoted Complete Streets very actively. One of the other two, Jeff Morrison, stated at an Ecology Ottawa-organized meeting in June 2014 that city staff should prove why 'a street shouldn't be rebuilt as a complete street, which would make that the default format' (as paraphrased in Mueller 2014b). Candidates in other key inner wards, such as Jeff Leiper, who won in Kitchissippi ward (to the west of the city centre, and includes Churchill Ave), and David Chernushenko in Capital ward, promoted Complete Streets during the election campaign. Ecology Ottawa kept up its campaign to ensure that all work on city streets was done within a Complete Streets philosophy. In the election campaign, they surveyed all candidates in the elections and published the results to enable voters to choose accordingly, reporting that candidates overwhelmingly supported Complete Streets principles (Ecology Ottawa 2014a). Another very active and long-standing NGO in the city, Citizens for Safe Cycling, added its voice to the Complete Streets campaign with the slogan 'I bike, I vote' (Pearson 2014).

5.2 'Three Extra Minutes': Conflicts over the Main Street Complete Street Project

Much of the conflict during the development of the Complete Streets policy in Ottawa centred on the proposed project on Main Street, in Old Ottawa East (see Figures 5.1 and 5.2). As with the Bronson Avenue conflict, this initiative started with a proposal, also in 2012, to replace the outdated sewer and water outlets under Main Street. At that moment, no specific aspiration for the physical infrastructure above the street existed (Interviewee D),[2] and Main Street's existing layout as a four-lane road would be reproduced. Things changed quickly, however, when a group of well-organized residents, supported by their local councillor, lobbied and asked to rebuild a calmer street. Following a detailed process of planning and consultation, their aspirations were in the end satisfied. The City amended the original street plan reconstruction and incorporated several features of the Complete Streets approach in its proposal for the reconstruction of Main Street in June 2013 (City of Ottawa 2013b).

Old Ottawa East is a well-defined community nestled between the Rideau Canal and the Rideau River (see Figure 5.2). Before its amalgamation with the City of Ottawa in 1907, it was a village organized around a unifying main street, along which commercial and social activities took place (City of Ottawa 2011a). A central part of the community has been shaped by the religious order the Oblates of Mary Immaculate, who purchased twenty-eight acres of land in 1863, and established St. Paul University, a Catholic High School, and a Convent within the neighbourhood, as well as the University of Ottawa to the north (Jackson 2015).

As in many such neighbourhoods and the cities they are part of across the industrialized world, the dynamic of the neighbourhood started to change considerably in the mid-twentieth century, through the development of suburban areas further out from the city centre whose design was premised on widespread and expanding car ownership and use. The area south of Old Ottawa East, on the other side of the Rideau River, was a site of significant suburban development – the Alta Vista neighbourhood - and in this case also including the site of a major hospital development. A new bridge, the George McIlraith Bridge (marked MC Bridge in Figure 5.2), was opened in 1966, which connected these new neighbourhoods to the city centre via Old Ottawa East. Main Street was reconstructed to enable this traffic to reach the city centre quickly. From its traditional two-car lane width, the street was expanded to four car lanes, allowing a higher volume of traffic to commute during rush hour (Chernushenko 2013; Chianello 2013).

This is a story familiar to students of urban development, with familiar results. The growing number of cars, their speed, the noise, and the ambient pollution caused local residents to stop frequenting Main Street (Interviewees A and B). The

---

[2] Interviews in this chapter were carried out by Machabée. Seven semi-structured interviews were carried out in total, with representatives of the local community association, councillors, City staff, or private consultants.

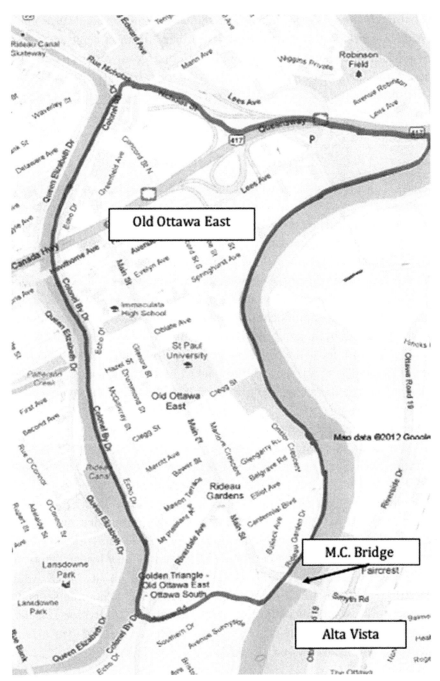

Figure 5.2 Old Ottawa East map. Main Street is the road (marked 72) running North–South through the neighbourhood. The park in the centre is the location of St. Paul University and the Oblate Convent.
Source: Google Maps, with overlay drawn by Louis Machabée

traditional main street was no longer a friendly environment to stroll, shop, and meet people. It became an arterial road, its primary function dedicated to traffic flow. As Main Street became increasingly deserted, local retailers went out of business. Gradually, residents became deprived of most services that typically build the foundation of a community: Grocery stores, boutiques, restaurants, and places to meet.

5.2.1 Revisioning Old Ottawa East

Concerned with the degradation of Main Street and its collateral effects on the neighbourhood, a group of local residents actively involved in the local community association started to take action. In 2005, they organized two public workshops designed to capture the community's vision and expectations for the neighbour-hood (City of Ottawa 2011a). At this point in time, Ottawa was developing new forms of participative planning exercises, through the drawing up of Community Design Plans (CDPs) that would guide the planning process. Old Ottawa East took advantage of this process, producing a vision statement, including related drawings and plans designed by a group of volunteer professionals, and articulating an integrated vision of local development guided by sustainability considerations, ecological principles, and democratic values. After five years of intensive consultations and deliberations, the final version of the CDP was approved by the City Council in August 2011 (City of Ottawa 2011a).

In preparing this document, local residents, religious groups, and business owners were aware that Old Ottawa East was about to undergo significant changes. Three factors were involved. First, the average age of the Oblate Fathers and the Sisters of the Sacred Hearth was increasing and the number of new recruits was experiencing a sharp decline (Duggal 2011). In the near future, this meant that both communities would have to leave their house, sell their properties, and move into nursing homes. Purchased and redeveloped by real estate developers, their properties would be likely to add a significant amount of new housing units in the neighbourhood, potentially doubling the number of residents in Old Ottawa East (Brady 2014a). Second, the City of Ottawa also stated its intention to support any policies heading toward intensification (City of Ottawa 2011b; see Chapter 6). Third, the sewer and water outlets under Main Street had reached their maximum lifetime utility and needed to be replaced.

5.2.2 Transforming the City's Reconstruction Project

In preparation for these works, the City launched a competitive bidding process. The engineering firm to whom the City awarded the contract was required to conduct the design and reconstruction of the street. At the beginning of the process, no specific expectation existed with regard to the street's reconstruction, according to the company's lead consultant. The street had to be rebuilt 'as a four-lane street with narrow sidewalks. That was how the project was scoped' (Interviewee D). Things changed quickly however, a few weeks later, when the City undertook the Environmental Assessment process of the street. Conducted in five steps, the exercise aimed to work out alternative designs and to propose an option suited to local conditions. Carried out by a group of City staff, in partnership with the private consultant (Delcan, the consulting firm that had also produced the report for the city on the city centre, discussed in Section 5.1), the process also benefitted from the advice and guidance of a working group, comprised of representatives from several City branches, businesses, residents, and community organizations.

The first step of the assessment process aimed to identify the local problems and solutions. The second one aimed at doing an inventory of the natural, social, and economic environment (City of Ottawa 2013a). Early on, the local community association involved in these steps saw an opportunity to voice its aspirations for the street renewal. With the recent Community Design Plan in mind, which captured the community's vision and expectations for the neighbourhood, its representatives advocated streetscape improvements that could enhance significantly the street liveability. Currently, explained one interviewee, the level of service provided to pedestrians and cyclists was fairly limited. In many critical locations, sidewalks were narrow and cycling 'was confined to the sidewalk area, given the volume and speed of traffic' (Interviewee D). In addition to requiring improved pedestrians and cyclists' facilities, the local community association also asked for traffic calming measures and better street lighting. Eager to improve the quality of living in their neighbourhood, their representatives wanted to bring back some of the street's original character.[3]

After several working group meetings, stakeholders involved in the Environmental Assessment process came out with five alternative designs and a series of evaluation criteria. The planning of the street renewal was entering into its third phase of preparation. Following a detailed process of examination, one proposal was selected. The preferred preliminary design for the Main Street reconstruction appeared to combine several features of the Complete Streets approach:[4]

---

[3] Although they weren't formulated in terms of 'Complete Streets', their requests had all the attributes of this approach to street design. Back then, as explained by an interviewee, other terms referring to the same idea (that all modes of transportation should be accommodated) were used: 'Prior to CS, we talked about things like "road diet" or "green street" or "healthy street" or "contact-sensitive solutions"' (Interviewee D).

[4] When asked about the extent to which the Main Street conversion corresponds to the original requests, one member of the community association answered this: 'what's being implemented is what we were arguing for … We're pretty comfortable with it' (Interviewee B).

Standard-width sidewalks, safer pedestrian crossings, segregated bike lanes, recessed on-street parking areas, and streetscaping elements such as street lighting, street furniture, public art, trees, and plantings.

In June 2013, the City of Ottawa organized three open houses to inform residents about the reconstruction work and to get public input on the preliminary street designs. In addition to unveiling the preferred option, details were also provided with regard to the street design impacts (City of Ottawa 2013a). Improved cycling and pedestrian facilities meant that room traditionally dedicated to motorists should be narrowed down. From four lanes width, Main Street had to be contracted to two lanes, except at key intersections with turning lanes. Instead of accommodating 1,200 motor vehicles per hour at rush hour, the street's peak capacity was going to be reduced to 900 vehicles (Reevely 2013a). To make up for the loss of vehicle carrying capacity, a combination of suggestions were provided to residents living in and out of the community: Shifting from car use to walking, cycling, and transit use, travelling outside of the peak hours, relying on telecommuting, carpooling, and flexible hours, and taking alternative routes.

If residents of Old Ottawa East were generally pleased with the choice of the preliminary street design, those living to the south were in contrast less enthusiastic. During the weeks before and after the City's open houses, the proposal of reconfigure Main Street into a Complete Street generated strong reactions. In the City staff's offices, at the Transportation Committee, in the local newspapers, and within the local community organizations, there were strongly contrasting views about the 'right' way of laying out Main Street. Broadly construed, two representations of the function of the street were at stake: The current four lane arterial road that maintained the street carrying capacity and traffic flow (for cars), and a Complete Streets approach, which aimed to diversify the transport modes the street would serve and enhance non-transport uses of the street. Tensions between these two contrasting views were mounting as two statutory votes on the future of Main Street were approaching.

On 5 July 2013, councillors sitting on the Transportation Committee voted on a plan to narrow down the driving lanes of Main Street, from four to two. Six councillors voted for and four against (Reevely 2013b). Another decisive moment occurred on 17 July 2013, when the full City Council met to vote on the proposal. Given the fact that the Transportation Committee vote was very close, the stakes were high. Nothing guaranteed that the project could go forward.

As brought up by one interviewee, Mayor Jim Watson, who was in favour of the street's conversion, doesn't like to lose votes. As the day of the vote was approaching, he wanted to know 'how exactly the votes [were] going to go' (Interviewee C). At this moment in time, he considered this exercise as a referendum on the future of the Complete Streets approach. Losing a vote was going to impose a setback to the whole Complete Streets policy. Determined not to lose, the Mayor met with the councillors who advocated the Main Street redevelopment during the past months. He addressed the possibility 'to water down the Main Street proposal' (Interviewee C). The response the councillors provided to the Mayor was unequivocal:

There really isn't a watered-down version that works. In the end, it's either four lanes or it's two lanes. It's either two lanes with cycle tracks or it's four lanes with no cycle tracks.

(Interviewee C)

Strongly motivated to defend the project as initially planned and designed, the councillors asked the Mayor for 'time to lobby and to see where the votes were' (Interviewee C). The approach used to convince the undecided councillors was personalized and strategic:

I went one by one with the help of chair ... We made our list of everyone we thought was supportive, or could be supportive. In the end, we talked to everyone.

(Interviewee C)

The councillors finally won their fight. After a lively discussion at City Hall, the recommended approach of conversion of Main Street into a Complete Street was finally approved. The vote was eighteen to six. The proposal could move ahead. The whole reconstruction was supposed to be completed by the summer of 2016.

The Main Street Complete Street project was thus the outcome of a number of processes: The emergence of participative community planning; the strong affective attachment and mobilization around notions of community by citizens; the shift in technocratic planning norms towards Complete Streets and multi-use street planning; and the strategic calculations of local politicians. But as it was being approved, opponents rapidly repoliticized the project.

5.2.3 Opposition to Main Street as a Complete Street

The proposition to eliminate two vehicle lanes in favour of wider sidewalks and a bicycle path didn't please everyone however. At City Hall, among City staff, in the newspapers and within community organizations, people argued for different views about the right way to design Main Street. Reconfiguring the street promised to have significant impacts on the daily lives of its users.

Opposition to the reconstruction of Main Street was expressed principally in relation to the interests and habits of car drivers using Main Street as a commuter route into the city centre. This opposition was expressed most vociferously by councillors representing wards to the south of Old Ottawa East, especially Diane Deans, Councillor for Gloucester-Southgate. At its heart was the attachment to existing practices and resistance to the threats to those practices. Since 1966, when the City of Ottawa inaugurated the George McIlraith Bridge, residents living south of the community had taken Main Street to drive into the city centre quickly. Main Street had become over the years a key part of the infrastructure of their daily routine. Knowing how long it takes to drive along it, they had learned how to plan and schedule many other activities accordingly. Any alteration slowing down the traffic flow could have a domino effect on other interconnected activities. Part of a larger set of amenities upon which people build their daily habits and routines, Main Street had become embedded within a set of routines and practices that resisted being dislodged.

Early on, the proposition of retracting one vehicle lane in each direction raised concerns with many City's staff, councillors, journalists, and residents living south of Old Ottawa East:

The biggest problem was, is always going to be, will it still flow? Will it still work? Yes, great, wider sidewalks, bike lanes, that's all very nice, but will it still flow?

(Interviewee C)

Challenged to demonstrate that the conversion of Main Street into a Complete Street would not end up in 'complete gridlock' (Interviewee A), the City's traffic engineers commissioned an independent analysis. They sought in effect to depoliticize the question via a technical strategy (Barry 2002). In their mandate, the consultants reviewed different scenarios of street conversion. They assessed the time each scenario added to Main Street commute and provided a recommendation. As reported by one interviewee, 'we were anxious' (Interviewee A). Different scenarios of Main Street redevelopment had already been identified during the Environmental Assessment process (2012–13). After investing so much time and energy in designing these alternatives, several questions emerged: Were the study's results going to endorse or undermine the scenario that had already been labelled as the favourite? Was this scenario evaluated properly in the first place? Would the fears of annoying people in the community to the south intervene in favour of the status quo (four vehicle lanes)? Several stakeholders expressed their discomfort these questions raised for them:

My fingers crossed because I couldn't say to my consultants 'go forward and come up with the report it proves it works'.

(Interviewee C)

The results of the study, that were supposed to be communicated within a relatively short period of time, finally took longer than anticipated:

We were supposed to get the decision after a month, and it got dragged on, dragged on. We didn't know what was happening.

(Interviewee A)

In the end, results showed that, in the best scenario design, the conversion of Main Street into a Complete Street added three extra minutes for travelling through the corridor, between the Rideau River and Rideau Canal, at rush hours. The promoters of the project declared this reasonable. However, to the extent this was an effort to depoliticize the question of time, it largely failed. Councillor Diane Deans stated the result was 'bogus data' (Reevely 2013b), and also asked rhetorically 'Where do all these 300 cars go?', when the results of the traffic calculation came out suggesting the intended design would accommodate only 900 vehicles instead of 1,200 (Chianello 2013). Indeed, the traffic calculations were based upon the current population who used to drive up and down Main Street. They didn't take into account the residents that were about to join the community once the new housing developments were completed (Interviewee B).

While the technicalities of how much time would be lost to drivers was one way that opposition was expressed and managed by the city's planners, the deeper objection concerned a basic question of the purpose of streets. Briefly summarized, it argued that a Complete Streets design is a good design as long as it doesn't interfere with the vehicle carrying capacity of a street. This is why the approach shouldn't be applied to arterial roads and focus essentially on secondary streets:

That depends on the use of the street. If it's a main road that moves cars, then it shouldn't be a Complete Street, because we want the car to go as quickly as possible and safely as possible, so that they move in and out of the communities.

(Interviewee F)

In this philosophy, car lanes, bus lanes, bike lanes, and sidewalks can hardly occupy the same territory. As an *Ottawa Sun* editorial expressed it, this 'view that every mode of transportation should be crammed onto a few select streets' is flawed. Besides provoking culture wars, 'it doesn't take into consideration all of the many non-arterial roads available to us' (*Ottawa Sun* 2012). Therefore, this philosophy rests upon an idea of land division where some streets should be dedicated mainly to cars moving fast while others are more appropriate for mixed uses. When both car drivers and cyclists share the same arterial road, one interviewee contended, safety issues emerge. Travelling on arterial roads with reduced vehicles carrying capacity, drivers are tempted to drive 'in the side streets'. Therefore, says the interviewee, 'the residential streets where people used to play and enjoy their front yard' become hazardous. This is why, he concludes, arterial roads are safer 'if you keep bikes off the road so that cars can go faster' (Interviewee F).

In the case of Main Street (and certainly in contrast to opposition to intensification projects, see Chapter 6), this opposition was relatively weak. No broad movement of commuters was organized to oppose the reduction of the street to two lanes. Transportation committee chair, Keith Egli, noted at the meeting approving the design in July 2013 that, despite the attempt by Deans to prevent the proposal from going through, 'not one of her constituents showed up to tell the committee not to approve the plan ... in contrast to several Old Ottawa East residents who begged the committee to implement it' (as paraphrased in Reevely 2013b).

5.2.4 Community and Place in Old Ottawa East

Conversely, affective mobilization in favour of the plan was very strong. Speed and vehicle carrying capacity were similarly ciphers for those organizing within Old Ottawa East but with the opposite signification: Vehicle speed entailed danger to community residents and, combined with too many cars on Main Street, was precisely what killed the street and the community it ought to be the heart of. In Main Street, the affective power of community and place for those in Old Ottawa East trumped that of speed and convenience for those driving through it. If some residents feared the disruptions it could cause to their routines, others couldn't wait to see the new practices that were going to arise.

The historical background of the shift in Main Street from community street to arterial road framed the orientation of many within Old Ottawa East to the Complete Streets initiative. Several interviewees recall the impacts of this change on the kids and parents' living habits:

It was a horrible street to walk along. It was miserable. People would not bike on it because it was too dangerous and the City kind of let it go crack.

(Interviewee A)

Parents were very nervous of walking with their kids to Lady Evelyn Alternative School in the morning rush hours because the sidewalks were very narrow.

(Interviewee B)

It was too fast. It was not a happy street to be on ... Children at 10 or 11 years old were forbidden to walk alone on it. Even cyclists completely avoid it.

(Interviewee C)

Not surprisingly, when a group of residents held a series of consultations for designing the Community Design Plan, between 2006 and 2011, the first request expressed was about enabling measures to mitigate the street traffic and speed. If, for opponents, speed was what they wanted to avoid giving up, for residents, the speed of cars was precisely the threat. Many felt that the heart of their community was taken over by those living to their south:

It was our street that we walked on. They were making our life more uncomfortable and degrading our quality of life with their commute ... The problem in the community was that this road was being used as a highway.

(Interviewee B)

The aspirations for a calmer street, repeatedly expressed by community members before, during, and after the design of the CDP, was also the first concern addressed during the Main Street designing and planning process in 2012. The engineer consultant in charge of the assignment, in partnership with the City's staff, recalls in these words the expectations of residents:

Their focus was more on the quality of the urban development beside the street. The CDP focused on land use. However, they did have a general aspiration for a more calm street, more traffic calm street, maybe more liveable, and less of an . . . arterial road.

(Interviewee D)

Many saw getting better control over the traffic flow of Main Street as an important first step of action. A calmer street would create suitable conditions for further changes, they thought. People would modify their driving habits, making the neighbourhood a more pleasant and safer place to live in:

We [will] have a slower and more pleasant arterial than it was before. I think it will shape people's habits because, as I said, more people will think about driving a different way, maybe taking a different mode of transportation. Maybe they will want to live closer to the centre.

(Interviewee A)

In the same line of thought, others speculated that a calmer street, with safer sidewalks and secure bike paths, would successively generate an attractive environment for business. As more components that typically fashion a living community are brought together, people would start investing again in the community, contributing to revive its commercial viability:

We will see more people walking in the corridor because the sidewalks are now separated from the fast moving traffic by landscaping and the cycle track . . . We are also certain to see more investment in the community in Real estate developments, where there has been almost no investment over a thirty-year period in the corridor. We will see people investing in their homes and filling new building and more commercial services and shops in the community.

(Interviewee D)

If underlying the opponents' arguments was a philosophy of the street as a place of unrestrained motorized mobility, proponents assumed that streets do not belong to any particular user. Moving beyond an idea of spatial segregation, the arguments of proponents contended that motorists, cyclists, pedestrians, and public transit users have equal rights and deserve an equal level of service. This is the philosophy behind the Complete Streets approach. One interviewee interestingly summarized it in this way:

I think it was Enrique Peñalosa, the mayor of Bogota, who said cities that build good infrastructures, safe for bike lanes, tell its citizens that you are valued, whether you own a

30$ bike or a 30,000$ car. I think that's what Complete Streets does tell us, everyone
is valued.

(Interviewee E)

Instead of focusing on the motor vehicle capacity of the road, said another
interviewee, this philosophy pays attention to the person capacity of the corridor
itself. It is not so much about the carrying capacity than it is about 'accessibility and
mobility' (Interviewee G). Instead of moving people quickly in and out, as valued
by the current culture, streets should be considered as places to live:

[On] traditional main streets, you might have a school, you might have a community centre,
you might have businesses that people walk to, you got churches, you got all sorts of public
institutions that people walk to and gather around, and the culture has not been to
recognize that.

(Interviewee E)

The positive value of reducing the numbers of cars, and their speed, on Main Street
threatened to be derailed by a concurrent development in the area, to do with the
redevelopment of former Oblate land, revealing internal tensions within the attempt
to frame Complete Streets in relation to revitalized notions of community. When
the Oblate Fathers sold their prime piece of real estate along Main Street in 2013,
they wanted to get the fair market value for their property. With one vehicle lane
less in each direction, Main Street was however representing a downside to
their ambitions.

   Even before he bought the piece of property, the real estate developer
announced its intention to build 900 housing units. Similar to other project
developments, he considered that buyers would own a car and appreciate the
possibility of going in and out of the community quickly. Was a downsized Main
Street going to offer them this guarantee? Were people going to buy a house or a
condominium on a piece of property where the only street access promised to
accommodate less cars, at a lower speed? From all accounts, the conversion of
Main Street into a Complete Street was creating unsettling sale conditions. With
less vehicle carrying capacity, the restored Main Street was not only limiting the
number of housing units that could be built on the property, but also downgrading
the price of the land that the Oblate Fathers could get. Interestingly, the issue was
resolved in two ways:

   First, the Oblate Fathers asked the City of Ottawa for a guarantee that the street
redevelopment would not impair the building capacity of the site. Through the
intermediary of their planning lawyers:

The City had to come up with a declaration that in no way, as Complete Streets, these redo
lanes [would] result in having to downsize the number of units that can be built.

(Interviewee A)

At the same time, adds the interviewee, 'I was really pissed off' (Interviewee A). Because it was downsized, providing equal services to all street users, Main Street was at the forefront of sustainability initiatives in the City. It was offering a more attractive place to live. The Oblate Fathers however didn't see the street philosophy from the same eye: 'we don't want it if we're going to have fewer units' (Interviewee A). The City did adapt to the demands of the Oblates, acknowledging this building project and the potential impacts on traffic, although not in ways that fundamentally changed the design of Main Street (see City of Ottawa 2014c). Reflecting later, Chernushenko argued that this was a particularly effective process and the oblate land redevelopment has contributed to the revitalization of Main Street and the development of support for both Complete Streets and intensification (interview, January 2017).

Second, the developer was encouraged to bank on the distinctiveness of Main Street. This approach was suggested by a group of representatives of the local community association. They argued that Main Street had a unique character. Its Complete Streets treatment should be sold as a marketable tool, targeting buyers looking for a community spirit, sensitive to sustainable development. Used as a trademark to boost the attractiveness of the housing project, this strategy was praised as compatible with the developer's expectations on financial returns.

5.3 Conclusions

The redevelopment of Main Street and the broader success at developing Complete Streets within the city was more than simply a shift 'back' from car-centred development focused on arterial roads into a traditional mixed-use main street. It also entailed a self-conscious politics of attempting to shift practices and the desires associated with those practices – driven in effect by the forces of cultural political economy. One group of people were being asked to reconsider the role played by the street in their own interrelated daily routines and habits, so that another group could reinsert the street into their day-to-day practices and therefore restore their own relationship to it. More than replacing the old underground infrastructure, the biggest challenge of this project was to reconfigure people's daily practices and conventions. In this respect, resistance toward the new street design was more than a reaction toward the 'unknown' or the annoyance of losing some of the 'privilege' previously enjoyed by car drivers from the suburbs.[5]

---

[5] These interpretations were provided by one interviewee and a journalist. They were phrased as follows: 'A lot of people don't like change, the fear of change. Well, we're use to what's out there. It may not be as good as it could be, but some people don't like change' (Interviewee A). 'Cars enjoy such special status that any attempt to increase fairness will be felt as an imposition, an attack, on car culture. This is what happens when privilege is challenged' (McLeod 2013, B6).

Conversely, for proponents, the restructuring of physical infrastructure was understood to reinstate Main Street at the heart of a whole ensemble of daily routines, part of a larger living and dynamic system. Citizens were able to mobilize powerful affective desires for community where they recognized that restructuring street infrastructures will engender novel practices. Because the street will be safer, many argued, residents from all ages and conditions will start biking on it: 'We will see some shifts in cycling' (Interviewee D). In this respect, Main Street will provide a 'broader opportunity for an active lifestyle' (Interviewee B). People will want to come to it, to 'sit down to at a patio or spend time to meet' (Interviewee G). It will be 'an area that people would like to walk on' (Interviewee B). With a greater attendance, Main Street will attract new investments: 'We will see people investing in their homes and filling new buildings and more commercial services and shops' (Interviewee D). In brief 'we will have a lively vibrant street' (Interviewee E).

Did the various efforts to depoliticize the initiative by the City – principally through technical studies (notably over how much time car commuters would lose) and consultation exercises work to undermine the anticipated fears of disruption that mobilized opposition? In the end, the answer to this must be no. Councillors representing wards to the south of Old Ottawa East voted against the initiative, and also argued (if less strongly on the question of principle) against the Complete Streets initiatives being built into the TMP. Fears of congestion and delays were invoked throughout the debate. The expertise of the planners was routinely contested and undermined. In the earlier episode centred on Bronson Avenue, one of the objectors to the transport planners 'dramatically accused the presenting engineer of "hiding under the cloak of your expertise"' (quoted in Furey 2011). So Complete Streets remained and remains fundamentally political – about conflicts of interest between those in a particular area and those who move through it, and about associated conflicts over basic philosophies of the principles on which cities should be organized, and about how those differences of interest and vision were articulated within the political system.

Nevertheless, in this instance, at least for the moment, this opposition was overcome. Complete Streets succeeded because of the interaction of various factors, notably:

- the technocratic machinery of City decision-making;
- the mobilization by those in Old Ottawa East, their activist Councillor (David Chernushenko) articulating their views forcefully;
- recent shifts in planning cultures in the Community Design Plans which meant that mobilization worked within the city's structures; and
- the timing in terms of the relationship between the Main Street initiative and the broader development of the TMP, and the way Ecology Ottawa was effective at inserting Complete Streets as an overall approach into that process.

But this win also seems to have had a more generative effect for Complete Streets across the city. The design philosophy for street reconstruction has become 'normalized', in the sense of having become routine across the city, albeit adapted to specific circumstances, and even councillors who objected initially to it have since embraced such projects in their own wards (interviews with Chernushenko and Haché, January 2017).

As we have seen, while the motivations of some actors (especially Ecology Ottawa, but also some councillors, notably Chernushenko) for projects such as Complete Streets did include climate change, and the desire to rebuild the city toward low carbon futures, this never figured in the public pronouncements for or against the initiatives. It was very definitely an implicit climate politics. Three brief observations are worthwhile in relation to this to conclude. First is to reiterate that these are the sorts of projects that are plausibly consistent with low carbon transitions – they challenge the hegemony of high-carbon practices, the social systems they are part of and the physical infrastructures that enable them. So we can learn much about climate politics by studying them. Second is to suggest that this 'implicit' character of climate politics that we have seen regarding Complete Streets is quite representative of how low carbon transitions are being managed in practice across large numbers of sites. Third is to ask, if speculatively, a counterfactual question: What if climate change had been a major part of the public debate about Complete Streets, either in general or in relation to Main Street? It is not obvious that it would have helped – would there have been such effective mobilization, or would opposition have been able to more effectively voice its objection if it could portray the projects as technocratic, 'top-down' efforts by environmentalists to shape practices rather than as an effort at a community's self-defence by street design? Also, it could have succumbed to the problem of carbonification (Stephan 2012; Mert 2013), where if the issue gets reduced to one of carbon emissions, it becomes rather abstracted from the messy social conditions within which those emissions arise, and enables strategies focused only on the carbon question. In the case of Complete Streets, in other words, an explicit climate politics might have opened the door for people to propose electric cars as the solution.

6

Intensifying Conflicts

Agonism and the Politics of Urban Spatial Transformations

MATTHEW PATERSON AND MERISSA MUELLER

6.1 Introduction

Complete Streets represent conscious attempts to remake place-specific urban infrastructures in ways to enable low carbon pathways. But they help us understand at the same time that the production of carbon pathways – high or low – has the patterns of urban development at their heart. How we make space available for specific types of mobility, including whether we enable people to access daily resources and amenities without needing to travel large distances, is key to the carbon trajectories of cities. Attempts to shift these sorts of mobilities have, as was seen in Chapter 5, generated powerful conflicts. In this chapter, we see that these conflicts over how we move about, and the infrastructures that enable that movement, have parallels in conflicts over where we live, and the decisions about where new buildings go up, what types of buildings go up, and who gets to make those planning decisions. In Ottawa, as in many North American cities, these conflicts have been over the term 'intensification', a specific bit of planning language, loosely focused on increasing urban density, around which much contestation has occurred (see also Leffers and Ballamingie 2013; Leffers 2015a, 2015b).

As with Complete Streets, the conflicts over intensification are forms of implicit climate politics: Sites where patterns of greenhouse gas (GHG) emissions are set in train by everyday decisions by municipal governments – where to allow what kinds of buildings to be built – whether or not such decisions are explicitly discussed regarding their climate impacts. Generally, the principal justification given for intensification is not explicitly in relation to climate change strategies or low carbon urban transitions (although such references are growing in official rationales) but rather with respect to social cohesion and urban liveability, the fiscal costs of low-density development (costs that are mostly to do with service provision), enabling transit to work effectively, or 'smart' economic development.

Such interventions are nevertheless part of climate politics: Much of this politics goes on in hidden, subtle ways, and does not need to be articulated explicitly in relation to climate change in order for us to consider it as part of urban climate politics.

In many cities, the politics of urban density is becoming increasingly intertwined with strategies for dealing with climate change. While it has long been known among urban climate change advocates as well as others working for cities that are 'smart', 'liveable', 'sustainable', or some other byword for meaning less car-dependent, that urban density is one of the key determinants of GHG emissions, climate action in most cities has shied away from tackling this question head-on. This aspect of urban climate politics is particularly challenging in North American and Australian cities where the pattern of urban development since the late nineteenth century has produced particularly low-density urban forms that are highly car-dependent – 'sprawl' (e.g. Newman and Kenworthy 1999). Tackling low-density sprawl is thus crucial for pursuing low carbon urban development (e.g. VandeWeghe and Kennedy 2007; Bart 2010; Glaeser and Kahn 2010; Hoornweg et al. 2011; Ala-Mantila et al. 2013), and is a recognized part of urban sustainability governance in Canada (Zeemering 2016, 214–15).

At the same time, since the 1990s, many cities in North America have been attempting to tackle the density question for different reasons. Sprawl generates a number of other social, economic, and environmental costs, in terms of the reduced access to services for those without access to a car, health effects associated to the lack of physical mobility, fiscal costs to municipalities in terms of provision of services (water, sewer, electricity, schools, etc.), and urban air pollution. The recognition of these costs has generated a range of initiatives designed to reorient development back towards inner-urban areas, from changing zoning rules and imposing extra costs on developers for building on the urban fringe, to partnership arrangements for inner-urban construction projects. In many contexts, this process is framed as a question of 'intensification', a frame that has become institutionalized in the municipal planning process. This chapter focuses on one such site, the city of Ottawa – within the province of Ontario, where the planning basic rules are set out within which municipalities such as Ottawa have to operate – where intensification has become an integral part of the language of planners and local politicians.

Focusing on intensification helps us explore ongoing contradictions between existing cultural identities and practices (and the political economic processes they are closely connected to) on the one hand and attempts to generate low carbon transitions on the other. That is, at the same time as various actors and institutions are developing various plans, projects, and experiments to stimulate low carbon development, they are at the same time doing other things that go in the opposite high-carbon direction. As a result, routine high-carbon decisions and the cultures that underpin them undermine explicit attempts to shift cities towards low carbon futures. As a consequence, the political dynamics that make such normality difficult to shift ought also to attain significant attention, since such entrenched regimes also need to be shifted. Urban planning is one such site, certainly in North America. While it is the case that many cities across the continent have developed all sorts of innovations in climate policy, they nevertheless have struggled for the most part to shift the entrenched urban development dynamic centred on road and housing construction, combined with a series of contestations over urban sprawl and site-specific contestations over particular projects (see also Campbell 1996).

Exploring the politics of urban intensification underscores in particular the cultural political economy dynamics of climate politics, as well as of course its agonistic character. That is, we see a number of conflicts that are simultaneously about deep questions of subjectivity and identity and about the overall urban strategy and relations between key economic actors (especially property developers) and the local state. These two intertwined dynamics shape conflicts over intensification, which calls into question the meanings of what Luque-Ayala et al. (2018) refer to as 'everyday and mundane infrastructures' – roads, buildings, sidewalks, and the like.

At the same time, intensification illustrates well the purification vs. complexity tension outlined in Chapter 2. Both proponents and opponents of intensification projects express this through simplifying the politics to one of 'developers vs. community', or conversely through high modernist aesthetic arguments about the value of tall buildings. Both thus abstract from the complex processes of shifting a large system such as the city towards low carbon futures. In particular, the analysis complicates these purifying narratives through drawing out the ambivalence felt towards intensification by a range of actors.

6.2 Density, Intensification, and Low Carbon Transitions

We know in general that increasing urban density is crucial to improving the overall GHG performance of a city (e.g. Hoornweg et al. 2011). Low-density cities have structurally higher emissions than denser ones, primarily due to increased automobile dependence, and secondarily to increased home size and thus heating/cooling bills. European cities tend to have below half the GHG emissions per capita than North American cities as a consequence. In the Ontario context, electricity is highly decarbonized through a mix of hydroelectricity (22 per cent) and nuclear (57 per cent), having entirely eliminated coal-fired generation in 2014, and with rapid growth in wind and solar since the introduction of a feed-in tariff in 2009.[1] This means that transport emissions and direct energy use in buildings (natural gas, mostly, with some propane in rural areas) are extremely important in Ontario's GHG emissions, accounting for 34 per cent and 17 per cent, respectively (Ontario Ministry of the Environment and Climate Change 2015, 30). Therefore, central to decarbonization is the transformation of the transport sector, and thus to understand the causes of automobile dependence – the patterns of urban development. Low carbon transitions involve remaking the urban flows integral to life in cities.

Most North American cities have in place, going back to the 1990s, policies that are at least ostensibly aimed at increasing urban density. This is increasingly articulated in relation to climate change, but was originally driven by a combination of fears about the decline of urban cores, the fiscal costs of low-density sprawl, the social contestation over city form, and urban air quality concerns – many of the forces that generated pushes for the Complete Streets initiatives we saw in Chapter 5. These rationales still dominate official arguments for intensification. The push for increased urban density arises in effect out of a series of internal contradictions within the political economy of urban development arising in particular out of the costs of car-dominated low-density development.

Increasing urban density has been pursued, at least in the Ontario context, through the notion of 'intensification' as a planning tool. In technical bureaucratic language, it refers to the percentage of new residential buildings that must be built inside the existing built-up area. Municipal councils in Ontario are required by the province to set targets in their strategic planning documents. At the same time, however, they are also required to have enough land outside that boundary zoned for residential development equivalent to their projected demand for residential housing over the next 17 years. The pursuit of intensification is therefore structured within the existing urban political economy of development – a particular set of relations between the City Council, property developers, and community groups, as well as relations among councillors (notably between urban and suburban councillors, a relation shaped by the amalgamation of the City in 2001, as shown in Chapter 3), enforced via the jurisdictional subordination of municipalities to the province.

Addressing climate change has only recently become stated as an explicit goal of intensification in Ontario (although it was articulated earlier with notions of 'sustainable development', see Leffers 2015b, 335–36). Intensification was first declared as a goal in the Provincial Policy Statement (the Ontario document that guides municipal planning) in 1996. At this point there was no mention of climate

---

[1] This is also the case for most of Canada. Ontario does still use a little coal-generated electricity, imported from the US. As we saw in Chapter 3, the significant shift during the 1980s and 1990s was towards nuclear power, which helped the City to reduce its GHG emissions during the 1990s.

change at all: Intensification had principally an economic or fiscal rationale, to reduce the costs of infrastructure provision by municipalities. Leffers (2015b) shows that this economic rationale predominated in city councillors' rationales for intensification, at least in the 2000s when he carried out his research. In the revised statement in 2005, climate change is mentioned but only tangentially in a section on 'settlement areas', stating that they should be done so as to 'minimize negative impacts to air quality and climate change' (Ontario Ministry of Municipal Affairs and Housing 2005, section 1.1.3.3). Only in the 2014 statement does addressing climate change become an explicit goal guiding municipal planning, and thus all aspects of the intensification process (see Ontario Ministry of Municipal Affairs and Housing 1996, 2005, 2014). Mentions of climate change are peppered throughout the report, both regarding the implications of planning policy for climate change and its opposite, the latter via the notion of resilience. Planning authorities are instructed via the 2014 policy statement to support land use and development patterns which promote climate change mitigation and adaptation. Climate change as a goal is represented in planning by compact form (intensification), active transportation, focusing on travel-intensive employment and commercial activities in regions well-served by transit, maximizing renewable energy opportunities, increasing vegetation where possible, and pursuing energy conservation and efficiency in the design and construction of buildings. But neither 'carbon' nor 'transitions' are ever mentioned. For most of this period, studying intensification is therefore best understood as a heuristic for the sorts of conflicts that can be expected as cities engage in low carbon transitions rather than direct observations about such transitions.

6.3 Studying Intensification in Ottawa

To explore the politics of intensification in Ottawa, we collected media reports of the public discussions of intensification.[2] We collected all news media documents from local media in Ottawa between 2001 and 2014 where the keyword 'intensification' appeared. This gave 506 articles, all of which (a happy accident, rare in research!) used intensification in the context we were interested in. Of these, the vast majority reported on specific intensification projects: There were basically none that reported on intensification within the overall city planning process, and only a handful that focused in a broader way, usually via an extended interview with a key local politician or developer. Furthermore, most of the coverage focused

---

[2] There are obviously limits and biases in media reports, as in any data source, specifically in the way that they privilege formal political actors more than others, and may have specific editorial agendas that are pursued in the stories. Leffers (2015a, 2015b) however provides analyses largely consistent with the one we provide here, based mostly on participant observation and archive methods.

specifically on the conflicts involved over these projects. Much of the coverage was focused on public meetings that were either formal consultation meetings organized by the city or developers, or as community-organized meetings around specific projects. As such, and despite the limits of media as a source, it is a useful way to explore the character of the conflicts over intensification projects. And reflecting the point above, very few of our sources mention climate change or GHGs at all; climate change is tangential to the explicit politics of intensification. To be specific, climate change appears in only six of our 506 articles, almost all simply invoking the general claim that pursuing higher urban density is important to deal with climate change, and 'carbon' only appears twice, both simply stating that intensification enables a lower 'carbon footprint' for the city. Neither climate change nor carbon are invoked explicitly in any of the specific conflicts we discuss.

We analysed these sources in a number of ways. We looked at some of the basic demographics to identify the main patterns. The projects were geo-coded and analysed using Geographical Information System software (ArcGIS) to see the basic spatial patterns (notably, to see if the conflicts were principally over inner-urban or suburban projects), we used it to identify some of the key actors who recur across a range of projects, and we coded the principal discursive themes, for a subset of the projects which were heavily discussed in the media reports (and thus a source of relatively rich data).

At least, as represented in media reports, the significant majority of the projects discussed were in the urban core. That is, intensification focuses in Ottawa on large projects in inner-urban wards. Figures 6.1 and 6.2 show this graphically. They show that 68 per cent of all projects mentioned are located in one of four wards – Somerset (which includes the city centre), Capital (the ward directly to its South), Kitchissippi (to its West), and Rideau-Vanier (to its immediate East).

We turn now to exploring three elements in the narratives in these reports that we argue are key to understanding the political dynamics of intensification.[3] For each, we develop the general narrative but then illustrate it specifically regarding conflicts over one specific construction project (for a summary description of these projects, see Table 6.1).

6.4 Political Economy: Intensification As Spatial Fix

The first is that the dynamics of intensification do not mark a significant break from traditional political–economic dynamics of urban growth in North American

---

[3] Leffers (2015a, 129–31) highlights different but closely related themes in his analysis of opposition to intensification, that he characterizes as: 'failure in execution', 'loss of 'space', and 'whose nature?'.

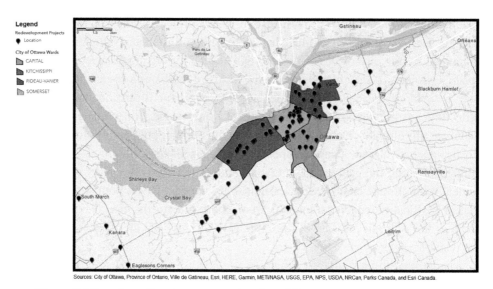

Sources: City of Ottawa, Province of Ontario, Ville de Gatineau, Esri, HERE, Garmin, METI/NASA, USGS, EPA, NPS, USDA, NRCan, Parks Canada, and Esri Canada

Figure 6.1 Location of projects across the city of Ottawa

cities (see also Leffers 2015a, 2015b). These used to be widely characterized as being driven by a 'growth coalition' consisting of property developers, city politicians, and bureaucrats, combined with a planning system which is restricted to zoning land according to use – agricultural, commercial, residential, and so on (e.g. Molotch 1993; Dowding 2001; this approach is relatively out of fashion in urban studies). The dynamic works such that residential construction occurs in outer urban areas because developers buy up cheap agricultural land on the urban fringe, and lobby to get it rezoned as residential or commercial, thus directly realizing speculative gains in the land value, but then build on it to maximize the value from that land. Since the land they buy is cheap, there is no particular reason to build at high densities. The other side of the equation is that developers provide the principal source of campaign funding for city politicians, who are not typically (with a few exceptions) in political parties that might provide alternative sources for such finance, and usually have few rules limiting such corporate campaign finance. Politicians are thus frequently beholden to developers' interests and see the interests of developers as coterminous with those of the city as a whole (Flyvbjerg 1998; MacLeod et al. 2011).

As various jurisdictions started to realize the contradictions of sprawl highlighted in Section 6.2, and developed the notion of intensification as a bureaucratic means of attempting to shift investment towards infill development and the redevelopment of urban areas at higher densities, this shift was not accompanied by shifts in the broader planning system to enable more strategic direction of investment or about where new building should occur. That part of the

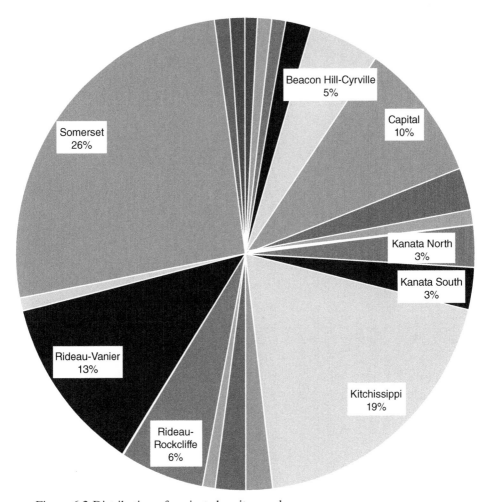

Figure 6.2 Distribution of projects by city ward

system has remained organized around the purchase of land by developers, applications to build or redevelop it – according to developers' existing business models – and pressuring councils to accept proposals for new buildings. Developers (some of them at least) responded to the intensification by identifying and purchasing land and then developing strategies for its redevelopment. Intensification thus operates in the manner of a 'spatial fix', where land zoning operates to construct market value for developers and create incentives for investment and a cycle of accumulation (cf. While et al. 2004).

In Ottawa, as in many cities, this has meant a preponderance of high-rise apartment buildings, where existing areas of un-built, brownfield, or low-rise buildings were converted into high-rise buildings. In some instances, these have been shaped by Community Design Plans (see Chapter 5), drawn up by the

Table 6.1. *Case studies of redevelopment projects and conflicts in Ottawa*

Case Study Project	City Ward	Project Description	Description of the Conflict
Lansdowne	Capital (Ward 17)	Lansdowne Park was a plot of 40 acres of undeveloped land with remnants of a stadium and heritage buildings by the Rideau Canal (a UNESCO world heritage site) in downtown Ottawa. The City entered a public–private partnership with the OSEG to redevelop the land into a mixed-use development featuring residential, commercial, and recreational uses.	Local community groups lobbied at City Hall, organized volunteers for door-to-door campaigning, and fundraised money to appeal at the OMB and to the Ontario Superior Court of Justice. They were supported strongly by their municipal councillors.
Laurier and Friel	Rideau-Vanier (Ward 12)	An acre of land was proposed for redevelopment into a mid-rise, mixed-use building to accommodate the rapidly growing student population of the nearby university. The building would be 9 stories, 190 units, and house more than 600 students in the downtown core.	The local community association, the councillor of the ward, the mayor, and most of the council opposed the project. Reasons against the project: Negative consequences to the heritage quality of the neighbourhood, the height of the building and effects on the streetscape, the consequences in terms of neighbourhood diversity and character (i.e. increased student population), and effects on the liveability of the neighbourhood.
114 Richmond	Kitchissippi (Ward 15)	A 5.5-acre convent, established in 1910, was purchased and a development plan was proposed along Wellington St West (an area where intensification was being promoted by the City). Of the three buildings proposed, two were to be built along the main street with heights of eleven and eight stories tall where zoning deemed six stories to be the maximum height allowance.	The convent site had not received official heritage designation, which resulted in the mobilization of the community to try to secure designation and public access to the site. Community associations appealed the approval of the project plan and entered into negotiations with the project proponent to alter the design plan.

Council in consultation with local community organizations, that make specific recommendations regarding energy efficiency, green roofs, solar energy, and similar specifically low carbon technologies, but these are never more than guidelines and are tangential to the main drivers of intensification. Frequently, developers applied to build buildings considerably higher than those specified in existing zoning requirements, in order to maximize returns on their investment in the land and construction. According to Bill Mahotra, founder of Claridge Homes (whose projects feature heavily in our data), intensification produced a sort of land speculation centred on the premium to be gained from projects meeting intensification guidelines. Projects that get constructed are determined by developers' judgement of profit potential, and for them this means the taller the better (Tencer 2004; see also Langston 2011). This has been intensified by the Council's strategy to focus intensification near key transit nodes, around stations in Ottawa's transitway and O-train (and especially near the light rail line, under construction as of 2017).[4] This is in line with planning notions of building along dense corridors, but has created intense spatial fix dynamics in particular parts of the cities near key transit nodes in gentrifying areas. Projects in Kitchissippi ward, along Wellington Street West (near Westboro station on the transitway), as well as at 500 Preston (by an O-train station) and near the Bayview transitway station, have all emerged rapidly, many of which have been highly contested.

Related, the form of the appeal system concerning development decisions similarly favours the strategies of developers. In the Ontario context, this is the Ontario Municipal Board (OMB) and, for the dynamics of sprawl, developers could normally rely on the OMB to overturn Council decisions should the Council turn down a specific development (Moore 2013, as cited in Leffers 2015b, 342). While the OMB would formally be required to take the intensification goals into account, the general consensus is that the OMB largely favours developers in their appeals. The same became true once intensification became a policy tool, although this time the appeals are not over being allowed to build on land zoned as agricultural or against the amount of land on the urban fringe zoned for residential development, but over questions of the height of buildings, set-back from the road, closeness to a property line, and the like. This ability to go to the OMB then structures debates within Council, since the Council would have to incur legal costs to go to the OMB (which, even if it would sometimes win, it may judge not worth the cost).

---

[4] Ottawa has had, since 1983, a dedicated bus only roadway, known as the transitway. It has one principal line running East–West across the city, and two lines running South from this line to other suburbs. There has also been one line of light rail operating, known as the O-train, on a North–South route West of the downtown core. A second line has now been built, running East–West along the current transitway line, but running under the city centre in a tunnel. After many delays, this opened in the end in September 2019, but has suffered various technical problems since opening.

Amongst opponents of intensification projects, this dynamic is reflected in what can be characterized as a 'developers vs. community' discourse. This is particularly prominent in the discourse of Clive Doucet, city councillor for Capital ward 2001–2010 (and, prior to amalgamation in 2001, councillor for the ward in the previous Regional Municipality of Ottawa–Carleton (RMOC) Council),[5] but is also frequently invoked by other councillors in the urban core, notably Diane Holmes and later Catherine McKenney (Somerset ward), Tobi Nussbaum (Rideau-Rockliffe, to the north-east of Rideau-Vanier), and David Chernushenko (Capital ward from 2010 onwards). This argument is that, in Chernushenko's words, 'private interests are determining the speed and character of urban intensification' (as quoted in Pilieci 2014, A6). In effect this is a left-populist opposition to intensification. At times it is connected to arguments that councillors are influenced by the money they get from developers, with one councillor, Tobi Nussbaum, proposing to ban corporate funding of municipal candidates in order to prevent this sort of influence.[6]

The project at Lansdowne Park exemplifies this sort of dynamic most effectively. Located next to the Rideau Canal in the downtown Glebe neighbourhood of Ottawa lies Lansdowne Park. The park, until construction began in 2012, was a plot of 40 acres of undeveloped land with a large but underused sports stadium and a few heritage buildings. The City of Ottawa was unable to invest in the land given budget constraints and that any funding secured through provincial or federal channels would be allocated to higher-priority areas (such as transit and affordable housing). The City entered into a public–private partnership with the Ontario Sports and Entertainment Group (OSEG) in order to redevelop the piece of land into a mixed-use development featuring residential, commercial, and recreational uses. The contestation between the community and the City/developers highlights this narrative as the planning process was largely ignored in favour of the developers' and City's goals.

There was an outburst of opposition from the community which led to what was described by one journalist as 'the opening shot of a war in which residents will fight to preserve the quality of their neighbourhoods' (Gray 2011, A6). The conflicts that arose as a result of the Lansdowne redevelopment project can be attributed partially to the demographic of the surrounding neighbourhoods. These neighbourhoods are affluent and contain a large number of public sector professionals (government, universities, hospitals); data from 2010 revealed the neighbourhoods as the most politically engaged in the country with reference to

---

[5] Doucet had left city politics in 2010. However, he later returned to stand, unsuccessfully, for mayor of the city in the elections that took place in late 2018.

[6] His campaign was unsuccessful, but the province did then ban corporate donations for municipal elections as of 2018. See Chianello (2016).

their political donations (*Ottawa Citizen* 2010). The mobilizing power of the neighbourhoods was extensive; Friends of Lansdowne was able to undertake exhaustive lobbying at City Hall, organize volunteers for door-to-door campaigning, and fundraise enough money to not only appeal at the OMB but also to the Ontario Superior Court of Justice. They were supported strongly by their successive councillors, Doucet and then Chernushenko.

It is difficult to say whether the Friends of Lansdowne would have just as fiercely opposed the development plan had it been accepted and implemented through normal planning and consultation processes. There were multiple design aspects of the original site plan that were changed throughout the appeal process, and many residents attribute the end result as a partial win for the community group. However, it is clear that the City's decisions to pursue a public–private partnership and their failure to host a sufficient consultation process with the community was a rallying point for those opposed to intensification, and provided support for the 'developers vs. community' narrative.

The City of Ottawa had started off with a design competition accompanied by a public consultation website which had been created in order to gather the necessary information to issue a Request for Proposal. This process was quickly suspended after the City received the proposal for the redevelopment of Lansdowne from the OSEG and a recommendation report from Council that favoured the pursuit of the OSEG partnership (Friends of Lansdowne Inc. v. Ottawa (City) 2011). The avoidance of a competitive bidding process and apparent disregard of public consultation led to the distrust of the developers and the City, with one newspaper article noting that 'residents, many of whom are property owners, wonder if the development community runs this municipality and if the city, overruled by the OMB, can do anything about it' (Gray 2011, A6).

Given the importance of intensification in creating the structural conditions for low carbon transitions, it is important to understand the underlying political–economic drivers and the conflicts that surround this process. The explicit mobilization of low carbon transitions or, more simply, the mention of climate change and GHG emissions is notably absent from the public discourse promoting intensification in Ottawa. Rather, the process of intensification is driven by the changes to the provincial planning rules that reshape incentives for developers.

6.5 Competing Narratives of Intensification

The 'developers vs. community' narrative underscores that the politics of intensification is less about whether or not to intensify, but rather about how to do it: Intensification is not one but could contribute to various paths to low carbon transitions (see Bernstein and Hoffmann 2018; Luque-Ayala et al. 2018). The second theme in the news stories is that the conflicts over specific intensification projects are not usefully understood as conflicts between proponents and opponents of intensification *per se*. Rather, they are conflicts between competing narratives of intensification, a tension that students of urbanism might recognize readily as 'Le Corbusier vs. Jacobs'. The former is the paradigmatic vision of a densely built hyper-modernist form of development centred on high rise buildings and car-oriented development; Jacobs is famous for a vision of dense, mixed use, 'organically' developing neighbourhoods centred on walking, cycling, and transit (e.g. Jacobs 1961; for a classic discussion of both, see Berman 1982).

These competing narratives reflect the political economy sketched in Section 6.4. The opponents of specific projects at times couch their opposition to high-rise intensification explicitly in terms of the approach to cities of Jane Jacobs,[7] notably Clive Doucet and David Chernushenko. Doucet routinely framed his opposition to high-rise buildings in these terms. There is recurrent mention about Paris not having buildings above eight stories yet being highly dense, on the importance of walkable neighbourhoods, of the roads they are on becoming 'traffic sewers', of the argument that skyscrapers in fact feed sprawl. On the last of these themes, this is stated to be because no-one in practice walks from them; instead they simply take the lift to the underground car park from where they drive. Moreover, they are family unfriendly and so feed the process of families moving to the suburbs, leading to a crisis of urban schools, which then becomes a self-feeding process. In Doucet's words, 'each decision will take us in one direction or the other: Toward creating a city based on vibrant, mid-rise urban villages connected primarily by rapid rail and rapid bus, or toward more of the same – more highrises downtown, more low-density, distant suburbs, and more traffic sewers to connect them to the malls and downtown highrises' (Doucet 2004, B4).

The narrative of proponents is never explicitly expressed in terms of Le Corbusier or his various disciples, but nevertheless the aesthetics associated with high-rise development, combined with the technocentric vision of urbanism associated with this, is clearly present (see Section 6.6, on height). Doucet in particular is framed by opponents as suffering from simple nostalgia (Denley 2010), reinforcing this association of high-rise intensification as modernist.

The conflict that arose when Viner Assets proposed a redevelopment project at Laurier and Friel in the downtown neighbourhood of Sandy Hill clearly

---

[7] Jane Jacobs has a particular resonance among Canadian urban political actors, especially on the political left (such as Doucet and Holmes in the Ottawa case), in part because she lived much of her life in Toronto and in particular was highly involved in the successful campaigns over the 'Spadina expressway' during the late 1960s through to its cancellation in 1971. See for example, Zielinski and Laird (1995). In Ottawa, as in many Canadian cities, community groups regularly organize 'Jane's walks' in her name to explore their cities – these are organized in many countries, but they are exceptionally widespread in Canada. See https://janeswalk.org/cities/, accessed 17 September 2018.

demonstrates the disconnect between how community members / council representatives and how planners/developers feel intensification should be performed. The site itself, consisting of almost an acre of land and four existing buildings, was slated for redevelopment into a mid-rise, mixed-use building to accommodate the rapidly growing student population of the nearby University of Ottawa. The building would be nine stories tall and consist of 190 units, providing housing for more than 600 students in the downtown core within walking distance to campus, amenities, and nearby transit stations. In a neighbourhood that was experiencing a housing crunch due to property owners rapidly converting their dwellings into student rental apartments, those proposing it expected residents to be pleased with the proposal. The introduction of more student-focused housing contained to one building managed by a group that had listed twenty-four-hour security and maintenance staff should reduce both the conversion of properties and the noise complaints in the area.

Conversely, the local community association, the councillor of the ward, the mayor, and the majority of council opposed the project. They felt that the building plan was 'too intense' for the area, and voted against the proposal when it reached council in spite of the planning committee recommending the project for approval. This was a unique situation, as it is rare that council goes against the planning committee's recommendations for redevelopment projects. The decision, and the subsequent overturn of that decision by the OMB, highlighted that there is a distinct difference in how each group views intensification in practice, with the community leaning towards an idealized version of Jacobs' liveable streets.

The analysis of the articles on the project revealed that residents were concerned about the heritage quality of the neighbourhood, the height of the building and effects on the streetscape, the consequences in terms of neighbourhood diversity and character (i.e. increased student population), and the liveability of the neighbourhood (e.g. Chianello 2014b). The community association and the council were clearly against the development because it was for students, suggesting that students should be redistributed across the city using transit-oriented development. When this argument was met by criticism from members on the planning council as 'blatant ageism', the community transitioned to an argument based on heritage and the liveability of the neighbourhood (Woods 2014).

Most of the area surrounding the site was low-rise buildings, and the area was zoned as a low-rise neighbourhood under the City of Ottawa's secondary plan for Sandy Hill. This zoning document, which was twenty years old at the time, did not reflect the intensification strategies that the city had since adopted. The city manager of development review testified at the OMB hearing in favour of the development, stating that the neighbourhood plan was outdated (Viner Assets Inc. v. City of Ottawa 2015). And while some buildings nearby are heritage designated and the site itself was on the heritage reference list (but not officially designated or protected), it was determined that the project would not adversely affect heritage buildings. The OMB, ruling in favour of the developer, signalled that this redevelopment project is in line with both the municipal and provincial statements on intensification and density targets.

To address the disconnect between what planners/developers and the community / their council members see as 'good practice' for intensification, the City of Ottawa has begun to manage expectations using city planning documents such as the neighbourhood secondary plans and zoning documents. As we saw in Chapter 5, Community Design Plans (CDPs) have emerged as documents that act as guidelines for increasing intensification while maintaining compatibility with existing neighbourhoods (City of Ottawa n.d.). These consultation processes allow residents the opportunity to give input on the physical attributes of future developments such as set-back from street, construction materials, green roofs, solar panels, drip irrigation, permeable site surfaces, and stipulations for green space.

6.6 Heritage and Height: The 'Character of the Neighbourhood'

These conflicts over competing narratives of intensification frequently played out in the language of the 'character of the neighbourhood'. This operates as a cipher for opposition to intensification projects (while not appearing to oppose intensification *per se*). Projects are often opposed on the grounds of their 'appropriateness' for the existing neighbourhood. In the Laurier/Friel project discussed in Section 6.5, this was usually couched, explicitly or implicitly, in terms of hostility to the neighbourhood becoming more dominated by students. The Mayor voted against the proposal, saying it 'would be wise to send a message that this is an important heritage community that's under stress' (Mueller 2014a). Another opponent stated that 'We will witness a moral decay of society and community living', a thinly-veiled reference to worries about student housing (Woods 2014). In other projects, anxieties about social class are associated directly with questions of 'appropriateness' (e.g. Stern 2010).

Beyond this reference to the specific social character of the neighbourhood, the two most significant bywords through which this unease is expressed are in terms of height and heritage. Conflicts over the number of stories of a building too often form the basis for much of the conflicts. Developers either apply for building permits to build higher than existing zoning allowances, provoking conflicts at that stage of the process, or then seek to build higher than the originally proposed height after a building has been approved. Either way they are seeking to increase the profitability of the project. Opponents emphasize the problems of the extra height in terms of the neighbourhood being disturbed aesthetically by the presence of high buildings, or also in terms of material effects – shadowing of other buildings, extra parking problems because of the increased number of apartments, and so on (e.g. Brady 2014b). In an interview, Chernushenko talked about projects where a small single family home was replaced by two much larger houses on the same lot (a common small-scale form of intensification), in terms of the creation of a 'monstrous mostly glass, you know, rectangular block that's almost all windows', highlighting this aesthetic dimension to objections. Conversely, developers at times explicitly promoted their buildings in terms of height: in Shawn Mahotra of Claridge Homes' words: 'point towers traditionally are beautiful buildings. When you have short stumpy buildings there's only so much you can do' (quoted in Langston 2013).

The heritage question is alluded to in Section 6.5 regarding the Laurier/Friel project. But it is perhaps most readily explored in relation to the project at 114 Richmond Rd (in Kitchissippi ward). This concerned a particular heritage building – an old convent, *Les Sœurs de la Visitation*. This convent, established in 1910, was put up for sale in 2009. The convent was on a 5.5-acre plot of land, most of which was undeveloped, along Wellington St West in an area where intensification was being promoted. The site was also two blocks west of a very significant conflict between a community association and developers over the construction of a large supermarket in the early 2000s (Fyfe 2014).

The convent site had been listed on the heritage reference list but had not yet received official designation or protection. After the piece of land had been put on the market, the City of Ottawa quickly lobbied for the building to be declared a heritage building, which would limit the type of development that could occur around it. Before the heritage designation process was complete, Ashcroft purchased the land.

Ashcroft released a design plan that kept pieces of the convent intact but doubled the height allowed in the neighbourhood's secondary plan. Unlike Laurier and Friel, city-wide consultations two years earlier had resulted in an updated plan for Wellington West that deemed six stories to be the maximum allowance on the main street. The first proposal set out by Ashcroft suggested a three-building redevelopment project with two buildings fronting onto the main street with eleven and eight stories. The design also outlined plans to preserve the convent and create walkways between the buildings on the main street that will enter into the convent grounds, allowing the space is be accessed by the public.

The result of the unveiling of Ashcroft's plan was the mobilization of the community in opposition. A heritage designation for the site had still not been secured and the local community groups had responded by creating petitions and lawn sign campaigns, writing to local newspapers, and calling for public meetings with their councillor. The city explored the idea of imposing a levy-tax to acquire a piece of the land and continued to delay the project using various legal techniques until a partial heritage designation was secured. The plan was eventually approved by the City and appealed by three local community groups at the OMB: Four months of negotiations resulted in the appeal being dropped. The project has since been constructed, with access to the convent maintained and a final height of nine stories on the frontage of the main street.

6.7 Ambivalence, Intensification, and Low Carbon Transitions

The observations in Sections 6.4–6.6 suggest and support claims that the political conflicts associated with low carbon transitions are expressed via a fundamental ambivalence. If we take the competing narratives around intensification, there is a paradox in that that those political actors who are most in favour of intensification *in general* (on the grounds of promoting both 'liveable cities' and addressing climate change – see Doucet 2007, for example) are simultaneously the most likely to be the most opposed to *specific* intensification projects (and never mention climate change in those circumstances, at least as represented in news reports). This is the case for most of the city centre councillors, such as Clive Doucet, David Chernushenko, and Diane Holmes. Opposition to intensification *per se* was relatively rarely expressed, and only by a handful of easily-identified Conservative journalists and politicians (but who were by no means a majority of Conservatives in the city). This is also underscored by considering the location of these conflicts within the city. The neighbourhoods where there has been most conflict are relatively mixed neighbourhoods but with a high percentage of public sector professionals. The electoral district that represents these neighbourhoods at the highest (federal) level (Ottawa Centre) has for most of this period returned a Member of Parliament from the New Democratic Party (NDP, the centre-left social democratic party in Canada), Ed Broadbent and then Paul Dewar, the latter in particular having made climate change action a significant part of his political profile. More recently, in the 2015 federal election, Ottawa Centre returned a Liberal MP, Catherine McKenna, who immediately on election became Minister for Environment and Climate Change in the Liberal government. By contrast, much of the rest of the city returns Liberal or Conservative MPs, none of whom have made climate change as prominent a part of their public profile as either Paul Dewar or Catherine McKenna. This is therefore the part of the city where action on climate change is given most attention. For example, CDPs in Ottawa Centre are more likely to cite energy efficiency technologies and sustainable architectural innovations.[8]

---

[8] This claim is based on reading the Community Design Plans across the city. These are available at: http://ottawa .ca/en/city-hall/planning-and-development/community-plans-and-design-guidelines/community-plans-and-studies/community-design-plans#alphabetical-list-community-design-plans, accessed 28 July 2017.

This paradoxical observation is reflected widely in the narratives around intensification projects, exemplified in the discourse of councillor Rick Chiarelli regarding various projects. Chiarelli states that he is in favour of intensification, but 'said he doesn't want to see the city go overboard' (as paraphrased in Johnson 2011). 'Extremism will be the death of intensification. And council needs to support moderate intensification and reject the temptation to accept overkill' (Chiarelli, quoted in Johnson 2011, C5). But even strong proponents of intensification effectively share this ambivalence and clearly circumscribe specific types of project they regard as 'good' intensification (interview with Chernushenko, January 2017, highlighting the housing project on oblate land off Main Street as such a 'good' project – see also Chapter 5). This is perhaps best expressed in the commentary by Joanne Chianello, prominent local journalist:

No one has to shed a tear for the plight of developers trying to sell homes, but it does make you wonder about the double-standard so many of us seem to have when it comes to infill.

Some residents are already complaining about backyard parking because they don't want to look at cars when they sit on their decks. They also don't want cars parking on the street because that inhibits snow removal (and where would their guests park?). They absolutely don't want to see front yards taken over by parking. Yet they claim to support intensification.

(Chianello 2014a, C1)

It is easy to see this as a question of hypocrisy (see Gunster et al. 2018), or of a simple 'Not In My Backyard' politics, but it is better understood as a deeper process of desiring mutually incompatible goals, and thus a complicated messy politics of the reconstruction of subjectivity entailed in low carbon transitions. People like the idea of walkable neighbourhoods, great transit provision, services close to home, as well as the idea of being a low carbon city, but at the same time have deep attachments to large single family homes, presuming to have more than one car (and thus the space to store it), and the like, as well as to the specific sort of urban environment, the history it embodies, and the meaning that history gives to daily lives.

Much political action aims at closing down this ambivalence, of purifying it in the sense outlined in Chapter 2. Developers and the political right seek to limit the destabilizing effects of ambivalence, either by articulating intensification as a continuation of existing 'normal' patterns of development (as done mostly by the developers in our research) and in some cases seeking to imbue it with more powerful affectively positive associations, or by resolutely resisting the normative value of intensification itself (as in the case of some 'backlash' political statements by those on the right). Opponents tend to elide the ambivalence by creating the simpler 'developers vs. community' narrative.

A better starting point is to recognize this ambivalence and use it to open up space for asking what sorts of subjects we want to become in low carbon urban transitions, and what sorts of urban political economies might better enable these subjectivities to emerge? In our case, the relevant contexts are the pre-existing planning process centred on passive zoning and active private developers, the other drivers for intensification as a project of increasing urban density, and the set of attachments and desires that generate resistance to specific intensification projects. I come back to the question of ambivalence in the Chapter 10.

6.8 Conclusions

Intensification politics shows the intrinsically agonistic qualities of climate politics. If cities need to become denser, especially in those parts of the world where they are currently low-density, then the conflicts over increasing density express very clearly that pursuing this goal is unlikely to be a smooth consensual affair. But this agonistic quality is both between different groups with their competing interests, power resources, and visions for the city, and within individuals and communities, shaped by conflicts over their mutually contradictory values. The tendency in these dynamics is clearly towards politicization, and actors seeking to depoliticize urban density struggle to do so. At the same time, however, the particular character of these conflicts, both between groups and within individuals, can be understood in cultural political economy terms. With developers this is clear – they pursue specific forms of intensification as part of a specific business model, and city planners enable this because of prevailing patterns of state–corporate relations in the city. Opponents also articulate their opposition as resistance to corporate power. But both proponents and opponents also articulate their orientation to specific intensification projects in terms of visions of the good life, and the daily practices, whether car driving on freeways or walking to the local farmers' market.

7

Mapping Climate Experimentation in Ottawa

MATTHEW PATERSON AND XAVIER P-LABERGE

The previous chapters started with the simple idea of politics as a specific site, focused on the public authority of the City Council. However, we quickly showed the limits of this one-dimensional account of politics as a site, exploring its various other dimensions within the processes of the City. Nevertheless, we remained within the City Council as the central site of politics, despite the odd foray into other arenas such as Carbon 613, which we discussed to show how the City as a site of climate politics was in part being constituted.

We return to the question of politics as a site in this chapter, but by explicitly showing its multiple sites. While the City Council went from leadership to faltering in its efforts to set targets for greenhouse gases (GHG) emissions and implement plans to achieve those targets, as we saw in Chapter 2, across the city all sorts of other initiatives to govern climate change emerged. In this, climate politics within the city mirrored broader patterns, where the attempt (more successful in some places to others) to govern climate change via through targets and their implementation has been accompanied by, or perhaps surpassed by, a mode of governing via experiments (see especially Hoffmann 2011; Bulkeley and Castán Broto 2013; Bulkeley et al. 2015). Some experiments are stimulated by the more traditional forms of governance via targets, operating in niches that are created by those policies (the classic example of this is in carbon offset certification, see notably Green 2013), while others emerge precisely because of the perceived inadequacy of such traditional forms of governance.

This chapter explores the broad patterns in these initiatives within Ottawa. Chapters 8 and 9 then explore two specific sets of initiatives in more detail. Here we are concerned with underscoring that climate politics exists in diverse sites, and enrols various types of actors, seeking to govern in many ways. That is, it has great complexity that stands in tension with the desire of many actors to 'purify' it through a single narrative.

97

It does so on the basis of a survey of initiatives in Ottawa on climate change. The net was drawn wide, to catch those initiatives that used climate change as one of their rationales, even if it was not the principal focus. Nevertheless, this produced some important exclusions: Notably the construction of the new light rail line that was started during this period, which, at least at the point when we constructed this database, was not integrated into the city's rationales for action on climate change.[1] The notion of governance underpinning it was also broad, following the practice of similar research in other contexts (see Castán Broto and Bulkeley 2013; Bulkeley et al. 2014; McGuirk et al. 2014). Governance is taken here to refer to processes concerned with 'realizing public goals', involving 'steering a particular constituency of actors', and 'regarded as authoritative' (Andonova et al. 2009; Bulkeley et al. 2014, 14). The survey was carried out during 2014–15 and covered any initiatives we found that were active during this period; others that have emerged since then may not be covered even if they are mentioned elsewhere in the book, and the aim here is not to capture the change, but the patterns in the types of initiative we see across the city. We also disaggregated significantly so that, for example, each individual project of the Ottawa Energy Renewable Coop (see Chapter 8), each of which is a solar pV initiative, was coded separately: This has the effect perhaps of exaggerating the effect of individual organizations but enables the specificity of each to be analysed (for example to distinguish between Ottawa Renewable Energy Cooperative (OREC) projects that involve collaborations with community organizations from those involving school boards). This produced a total of 136 initiatives. We then collected documentary materials from each initiative and coded them according to the types of actors involved in producing the initiative (both at a broad level, as public/private/non-governmental organization (NGO)/ hybrid, and for specific types of actor – church, education, for example), the issue areas related to climate change that they focus on, and the ways that they seek to govern, or 'steer' the city in relation to climate change. The specific codes are presented in Table 7.1.

7.1 The Patterns of Climate Governance in Ottawa

This section provides a basic mapping of these initiatives. It briefly describes the actors that generate the initiatives, the issues they focus on, and the ways they seek to govern. This is intended to set the scene for a fuller analysis of the principal ways that actors are experimenting on climate change in Ottawa.

---

[1] Since then, and in particular once construction started on the light rail system, the City started promoting the GHG reductions they thought would come from it more aggressively.

Table 7.1. *Actors, issue areas, and forms of governance*

Actor Type I	Public, Private, NGO, Hybrid
Actor Type II	City, Environmental NGO, Faith-based, University, College, School Board, Hybrid, Company, Business Association, Community-based Group, Event, Foundation
Issue Area	Water, Transport, Energy Demand (efficiency, consumption), Energy Supply (production), Air, Waste, Infrastructure/Building, AFOLU (Agriculture, Forestry and Other Land Use), General Climate Change, General Environment
Form of Governance	Information Sharing, Capacity Building, Direct Action, Monitoring and Certification, Target Setting, Funding, Rule Setting

First, who is involved in climate governance experimentation in Ottawa? Figures 7.1 and 7.2 show that, at the broad level, it is dominated by initiatives carried out by public sector actors, followed by NGOs, and with relatively little participation by the private sector.[2] In particular, there are relatively few 'hybrid' initiatives compared to existing studies (e.g. Bulkeley et al. 2014, chapter 2; McGuirk et al. 2014, 140).

Figure 7.2 breaks this down further. It shows that the nature of public sector action on climate change is quite diverse: The city council itself only accounts for 15 per cent of all initiatives (so 25 per cent of 'public' ones), while the city's two universities (18 per cent) and school boards (8 per cent) both play significant roles in public initiatives.[3] Again, these patterns seem quite different to that reported in other surveys of city initiatives: McGuirk et al. (2014, 140) do not report initiatives by universities, for example.

Second, if we look at what these initiatives focus on, we can see that around 60 per cent focus on either energy supply (fifty-seven initiatives) and/or energy demand (forty initiatives), and 31 per cent (forty-two initiatives) are broadly focused on a range of environmental issues (see Figure 7.3). The rest focus on a range of different issues or sectors in relation to climate change.

Third, these initiatives seek to govern climate change in Ottawa in a variety of ways. The most common is in direct action, that is, projects that seek directly to reduce emissions or otherwise address climate change. But information sharing,

---

[2] Some other work developing similar datasets of climate initiatives has a simpler distinction public/private/hybrid (e.g. Bulkeley et al. 2014), where 'private' includes both corporate/commercial actors and civil society/NGO actors. The significant differences in forms and issue areas between these seem to confirm the value in keeping these separate. Here, the distinction is that private refers to for-profit organizations, while NGO refers to non-profit organizations, so there are some organizations (e.g. the Ottawa Centre Ecodistrict) that are treated as NGOs even thought they are collectives of companies.
[3] School boards in Canada, as in the US (but differently to most European countries), are instituted as separate to municipal governments, with their own elected officials.

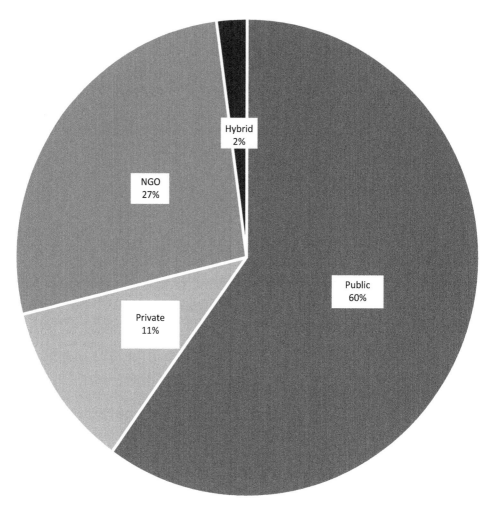

Figure 7.1 Types of actor involved in climate governance in Ottawa

capacity building, and target setting are all important means of pursuing climate governance in these initiatives (see Figure 7.4).

Another way of illustrating patterns across the initiatives is presented in Figure 7.5. It shows, as a network, the principal connections across these various aspects of the initiatives (for actors, these remain at the broad level of abstraction rather than the more specific one). In Figure 7.5, ties connecting each node indicate that specific initiatives connect the nodes; for example, a tie between 'public' and 'direct action' means that at least one initiative is a public actor doing direct action. In order to simplify the figure and identify the principal patterns, this is a 'four degree network': That is, each tie indicates at least four initiatives connect each node, giving a stronger sense of the patterns than if each tie indicated only at least one initiative connecting them.

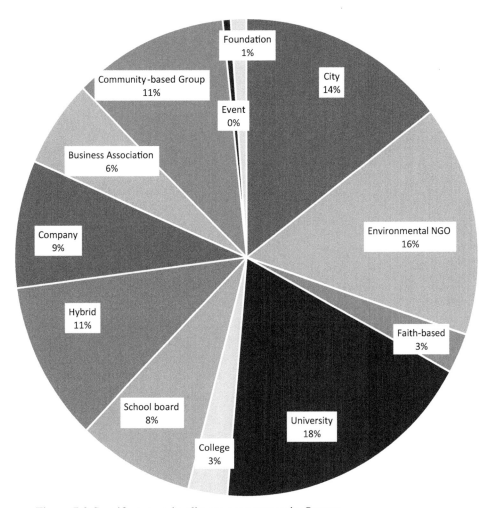

Figure 7.2 Specific actors in climate governance in Ottawa

A rough pattern involving three clusters of initiatives can be discerned in Figure 7.5, which we use to organize the rest of the chapter, and informs the selection of cases for fuller analysis in Chapters 8 and 9, as well as being the focus on carbon accounting in Chapter 3. First, at the core are initiatives centred on direct action and target setting, focused on infrastructure building, energy demand, and more general environmental issues. These initiatives are organized most commonly by universities, and to a lesser extent the City Council, so are public initiatives. Second, there is an important second cluster centred on information sharing and capacity building, where the principal actors are environmental NGOs and to an extent community groups. Finally, the issue of energy supply, that is numerically dominant, are nevertheless relatively marginal to the network, and are

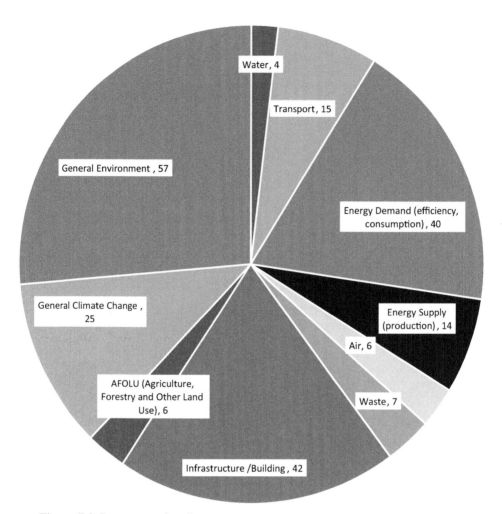

Figure 7.3 Issue areas in climate governance in Ottawa. Note that individual initiatives can be involved in more than one issue, so percentages are not given here

not associated with the dominant actors but rather with private companies, community groups, and hybrids. These three clusters of initiatives will be used to structure the rest of the chapter.

7.2 Public Initiatives on Energy Demand and Infrastructure

In Ottawa, public initiatives addressing climate change come from universities, schools, school boards, and the City Council itself. As illustrated in Section 7.1, these initiatives are disproportionately focused on either managing energy demand or on building infrastructure.

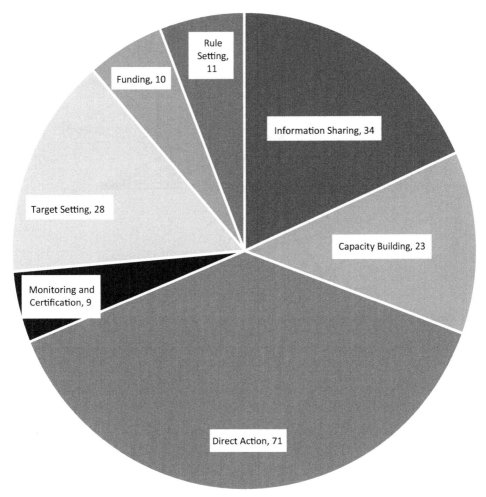

Figure 7.4 Ways of governing climate in Ottawa. Note that individual initiatives can seek to govern in more than one way, so percentages are not given here

Universities are particularly active and have a large number of projects. With many buildings, several initiatives aim to reduce the demand for energy. In addition, the vast majority of these initiatives use direct action or target setting. The reason for public institutions to develop so-called green initiatives to reduce energy consumption comes, among other things, from the pressure of citizens, who can more easily put pressure on these groups than on private institutions. There have been a number of citizens' movements advocating for environmental measures at their universities. We focus here on action at Carleton University: We detail the initiatives and their politics at the University of Ottawa in Chapter 8.

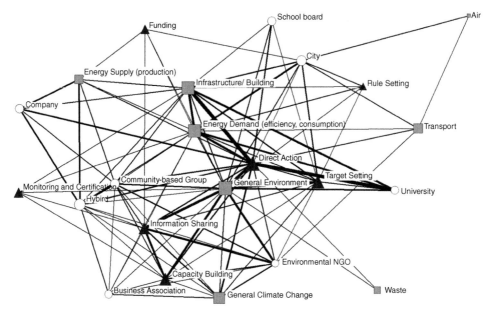

Figure 7.5 Actors, issue areas, and forms of governance in Ottawa climate initiatives. Figure drawn using Ucinet/Netdraw (Borgatti et al. 2002). The thickness of the line indicates the number of initiatives connecting each node. The shade and shape of notes indicate the type of attribute: White circles indicate the type of actor, grey squares the issue area, and black triangles the form of governance. The size of the nodes indicates 'node degree', i.e. the number of other nodes to which the node is connected. Four-degree network: Note that the node degree is calculated (giving the size of the node) when the network degree was one (i.e. when only one connection between two nodes was necessary for a tie to be recognized)

Carleton University has developed a number of programmes and projects aimed at reducing energy consumption. One is the development of a co-generation energy plant on campus, due to start in 2019, similar to that which long existed in the University of Ottawa campus (see Chapter 8). This is aimed to provide 40 per cent of the campus' electricity, while distributing the waste heat to buildings across campus. They envisage this will cut CO_2 emissions by 5,000 tonnes annually (Carleton University 2018, 11). It has also established a Green Team Programme consisting of twenty eco-representatives that focus on workplace sustainability initiatives. Carleton also has a number of transport initiatives (more than the University of Ottawa, perhaps reflecting that it is not a downtown campus and more students and staff are car-reliant), including the expansion of car-share programmes on campus, such as VirtuCar, StudentCarShare, and Zip Car, installing electric vehicle charging stations on campus, and having a bike-share programme to offer bikes for hire.

Linked to the overarching process of target setting and emissions monitoring detailed in Chapter 2, the City of Ottawa has several energy demand reduction projects. These include a green building municipal policy focused on making buildings more efficient and Leadership in Energy and Environmental Design (LEED) silver certification for any building over 500 square metres, and a greener fuel use plan and the purchase of electric vehicles. This plan has been updated many times and contains plans, among others, to increase the size of parks, cycling, and hiking areas, improve public transit, and reduce the city's overall energy consumption.

School boards have also developed a number of energy initiatives. More than fifty schools in the Ottawa Catholic School Board are EcoSchools certified, which means they have demonstrated goal achievement in the following four areas: Energy conservation, waste minimization, ecological literacy, and school ground greening. Schools are rewarded for having EcoInitiatives, such as projects with students learning the importance of saving energy, and how this reduces greenhouse gas emissions and pollution.

The schools in the area do not have the same sort of social movement pressure that generates some of the activity in universities or at the City of Ottawa. However, they often justify their projects for educational purposes for their students. Thus, the initiatives presented have generally been designed and installed by teachers and their students. The projects are certainly smaller than those of the other two types of institutions but are also completed more quickly. As a result, schools will usually move from project to project and continue to learn from the young people involved.

For example, the Central East Catholic School Board has an energy conservation goal for its schools consisting of energy efficiency measures, including efficient lighting, motion detection for lighting, heating control, ventilation, and air conditioning, better windows, roof insulation, and awareness of the occupants and their habits. In addition, in all of its schools, the Board proceeded with the installation of hand dryers to reduce the consumption of brown paper and the installation of solar panels on schools with a roof structure capable of accommodating them. Another project has been developed by Samuel Genest High School, in a partnership with the Ottawa Renewable Energy Cooperative (see Chapter 9), which leases the school's roof space for their solar panels.

7.3 NGO Initiatives Using Information Sharing and Capacity Building

As Canada's capital, Ottawa is at the heart of the work of many non-governmental organizations (NGOs). Many of these organizations have developed initiatives using capacity building and information sharing to achieve goals. Through capacity building, NGOs aim both to develop their ability to get the attention of policymakers and politicians but also more directly to enable themselves and other organizations to effect change in GHG emissions directly. It should be noted that there are different types of initiatives, those coming from more critical environmental groups, those coming from less critical environmental groups and closer to government and receiving mainly subsidies from it, and finally groups including companies, and thus, being more focused on the relevance of energy-saving measures for corporate performance.

The Community Energy Network of Eastern Ontario is a community network focusing on renewable energy and energy efficiency issues. The network is active in Eastern Ontario and the National Capital Region. It includes, among others, Ecology Ottawa, Sustainable Ottawa, and Sustainable Enterprise Alliance. The intention of the group was, when it was founded in 2010, to build a broader network that went beyond just the non-profit sector to engage businesses, municipalities, and community groups.

Also focused on sustainable energy, EnviroCentre was established in 1999 in Ottawa, and provides services and programmes to residents, businesses, and other organizations focused on conserving energy and reducing the associated environmental impacts. EnviroCentre features information on energy efficiency, workshops on sustainable transportation, and the benefits of alternative transportation for businesses. The organization even offers practical and environmentally friendly products that reduce energy consumption and waste generation at their *EnviroBoutique*.

The EnviroCentre has three main initiatives. The first is Carbon 613, which we discussed in Chapter 3. The second initiative is called Sustain Your Community. This project lasted from 2014 to 2017 and was intended to promote citizen engagement for the protection of the environment by encouraging their participation in their community to reduce GHG emissions. Among other things, the project teamed up with Sustain Kanata North to organize Pedal Play, an educational activity focused on cycling. The project also supported Sustain Lowertown in the creation of five community gardens, and subsidized West Carleton to build a community vegetable cellar. The latest initiative of the EnviroCentre is the Ottawa Sustainability Fund. This is a funding programme run by volunteers affiliated with the Ottawa Community Foundation and the EnviroCentre. Since its foundation, in 2006, the fund has contributed more than $100,000 to community projects and Ottawa organizations such as RightBike, the Natural Step of Canada, the Matthew House of Ottawa, and the creation of the National Capital Environmental Nonprofit Network for projects that contribute to greenhouse gas emissions reduction.

The focus on capacity building means that some organizations' focus is precisely on orchestrating a range of other organizations. Sustainable Eastern

Ontario has as one of its activities coordinating the National Capital Environmental Nonprofit Network and the Community Energy Network of Eastern Ontario in partnership with EnviroCentre. Sustainable Eastern Ontario is a network of organizations that promotes partnership and collaboration on sustainability issues. It develops strategic collaborations across the sector, to build their administrative and operational capacity. This organization provides shared office space called the Sustainable Capacity Centre. It has also created a National Capital Green Pages Directory that contains the list of local eco-friendly and sustainable products, services, businesses, and organizations of Eastern Ontario and Western Quebec.

The National Capital Environmental Nonprofit Network (NCENN) is an important programme of Sustainable Eastern Ontario. It is a network that provides capacity-building opportunities to all environmental non-profit organizations within the National Capital region. The NCENN currently connects 154 environmental NGOs across Eastern Ontario. It offers a range of services to support boards in taking a leadership role in their organization.

The Canada Green Building Council (CaGBC) is a non-profit organization that has been working since 2002 to advance green buildings and sustainable community development practices in Canada. The organization is the license holder for the LEED green building rating system in Canada. The CaGBC has a chapter in Ottawa representing fifty firms and over 300 green buildings. Its main objectives are to connect people, to facilitate learning, to drive changes, and to build a community. Most of the work of the organization is promoting LEED certified buildings and zero-carbon building initiatives. It aims to reduce GHG of buildings, landfill waste from construction and demolition activities, and municipal water consumption.

Religious organizations are also focused on capacity building. The Anglican Church of Canada has an Environment Subcommittee, known as Creation Matters, that focuses on 'greening' churches. The Anglican Diocese of Ottawa plays an active role in Creation Matters for parishes of Eastern Ontario and Western Quebec. It often deploys the more combative language of climate justice and has participated in the Conference of Parties of the United Nations Framework Convention on Climate Change (UNFCCC). The Ottawa Diocese works on giving information and material to churches, while the Archdiocese of Ottawa has a programme of environmental stewardship that assists parishes in the implementation of ecological initiatives and promotes ecological responsibilities.

The religious orientation of some NGOs has also produced novel initiatives such as ClimateFast, a religious version of carbon dieting (Paterson and Stripple 2014). This is part of the Fast for the Climate international organization. It strives to build political will and to persuade parliamentarians to work towards urgent and substantial action on climate change, through the medium of going on public fasts, deploying the slogan 'Hungry for Climate Leadership'. ClimateFast publishes a newsletter and engages in protest action such as vigils on Parliament Hill.

Another NGO working in Ottawa is 350 Ottawa, which is a local chapter of 350. org. 350.org was created in 2008 by a group of university friends in the US along with author Bill McKibben. 350.org was named after 350 parts per million – the concentration of carbon dioxide in the atmosphere that is said to be not too harmful for the climate. The group has three principles: Climate Justice, groups are stronger when they collaborate, and mass mobilization can make change. 350 Ottawa is campaigning for divestment by universities, community associations, religious institutions, and municipal governments in the National Capital Region, as well as individuals. The organization works with its allies: Citizens Climate Lobby, Climate Action Network, Climate Fast, Climate Reality Project Canada, Council of Canadians, Ecology Ottawa, Greenpeace Ottawa-Gatineau, and Price Carbon Now, ON! Other than engaging in protest, the group also gives a lot of information and resources to counter fossil fuel industries. It gives support to other organizations, such as the divestment campaign at the University of Ottawa (see Chapter 8).

In Ottawa, there's a group called Green Ottawa working on environment, sustainability, conservation, renewable energy and healthy, human-powered lifestyles for organizations, and green businesses by doing conferences, events, volunteering, and more. The group mostly serves, with its website, as a link for networking on any issue on environment in Ottawa. Other groups focus on sharing learning and skills, such as The Natural Step Academy that has a Youth Sustainability Leadership programme and online Sustainability eLearning courses. The aim is to form sustainability practitioners and change agents. The Natural Step also has an initiative called the Sustainability Transition Lab in order to address complex sustainability challenges by using collaboration and new ways of working across sectors and across scales. The project has since initiated different laboratories, such as the Natural Capital Lab, that measures and manages the value of Ontario's nature, the Circular Economy Lab, that brings together private and public-sector leaders and innovators from across Canada to co-design, pilot, and test circular economy solutions, and the Future-Fit Business Benchmark, which is trying to equip business leaders and investors with the means to quantify how their actions are contributing to a better future.

Some groups work more on trying to get many actors together to get concrete projects done. For example, Depave Paradise, a project of Green Communities Canada that works with local partners in communities across Canada, works on transforming asphalt into green space. The reference is to a song by iconic Canadian singer Joni Mitchell, with the line 'they paved paradise and put up a parking lot' (Mitchell 1970), although there is also perhaps an allusion to the

1968 Parisian protest slogan 'under the paving stones, the beach'. In Ottawa, the group – in collaboration with Ecology Ottawa – depaved 92 square metres at St Anthony's Catholic School in 2015 and 102 square metres at Kitchissippi United Church. Other more 'direct action' oriented NGOs include Tree Ottawa, which is focused on protecting, planting, and promoting trees in the City of Ottawa, and Right Bike, which focuses on helping Ottawa residents get around and stay healthy through community bike repair events and bike mechanics training programmes.

A number of groups and networks active in Ottawa focus on agriculture and the food system in relation to climate change. Just Food focuses on pursuing a just and sustainable food system. The Ottawa Community Urban Food Forest is a project of Permaculture Ottawa, in conjunction with Just Food Ottawa, creating a Food Forest to act as a demonstration project. Permaculture Ottawa is focused on delivering popular education, supporting community projects, and advocating for sustainable and socially just living spaces in Ottawa through permaculture.

7.4 Private/Community Initiatives on Energy Supply

The last cluster of initiatives come from private and community-based projects on energy supply. Several alternative energy projects have been developed in recent years. Some are local initiatives, while others are more provincial or even national initiatives. Most of these initiatives presented are generated by private businesses. As a result, these projects generally aim at producing economic benefits for investors or companies implementing energy supply initiatives. Several projects come from cooperatives that seem to desire to be pioneers in the development of clean energy, mainly solar.[4] These initiatives mostly aim for long-term savings or profits. It can take a long time to amortize the costs of installing and purchasing solar panels or technologies decreasing GHG emissions. The OREC is one of the main examples of this type: We ignore it here and discuss it in Chapter 9.

Founded in 2005, Bullfrog Power provides renewable electricity to individual and corporate customers across Canada. Generally, Bullfrog plays the role of intermediary between renewable energy providers and customers that want to fund more renewable energy (RE) in the grid.[5] In Ottawa, Bullfrog provides 100 per cent RE energy to various companies, including Hub Ottawa, an organization focused on sustainability-focused approaches to improving Ottawa's downtown core; Thyme and Again, a local catering and food shop; Egg Farmers of Canada, that has its head office in Ottawa; Your Credit Union, a financial services

---

[4] This is largely because the Ottawa valley has very good solar availability. By contrast it has relatively low wind speed values. See the Government of Canada's data at: www.nrcan.gc.ca/18366, accessed 30 July 2018.

[5] From 2009 onwards, this was stimulated significantly by the feed-in-tariff included in the Green Energy and Green Economy Act, enacted by the Ontario Provincial Government. See Chapter 5 for details.

cooperative with a branch in Ottawa; Westin Ottawa, a 4-star hotel in Ottawa; Simons, a clothing store in Ottawa's Rideau Centre; a screening of motion picture Deepwater Horizon; Forest Products Association of Canada; the Canadian Wood Council head offices in Ottawa; and the Ottawa River Runners White Water Club Inc. clubhouse. Bullfrog also collaborates with other organizations (including OREC, see Chapter 9). In a partnership with Beau's Brewing Co. and Just Food, Bullfrog launched a new solar project in Ottawa. Also, on Earth Day of 2017, the Bayshore Shopping Centre purchased 470 MWh of green electricity from Bullfrog Power. The equivalent to what 498,640 homes in Ottawa would use in one hour.

Not all energy supply initiatives are from private and/or community actors. Energy Ottawa is an affiliate of Hydro Ottawa, the electricity generation and distribution company owned by the City of Ottawa. Energy Ottawa owns and operates sixteen run-of-the-river hydroelectric facilities, including six in Ottawa and ten in Eastern Ontario and New York State, making it Ontario's largest municipally owned producer of hydropower. The six hydroelectric stations in Ottawa are at the Chaudière Falls on the Ottawa River and have a total capacity of 38 MW. Energy Ottawa also has a landfill gas-to-energy generating plant that turns methane gas into renewable energy. It generates over six MW of electricity each year, representing electricity for 6,000 homes. It has also installed solar systems on municipal buildings, with a combined capacity of roughly 2.3 MW.

One of the more distinctive or unusual initiatives is LiVE88.5. This is Ottawa's 'alternative rock' radio station. It decided in 2011 to become carbon neutral, and is the first and still the only carbon neutral radio station in Canada. Each year, the radio makes a $10,000 donation to the Rideau Valley Conservation Foundation (RVCF) to offset the 424 tons of carbon it produces annually. Over the years, the RVCF has planted 34,000 trees with these donations.

7.5 Conclusions

Many cities round the world have similar sets of initiatives. Each will have their own quirks, reflecting local circumstances: Dominant economic actors, jurisdictional arrangements, availability of particular energy sources, and so on. Each initiative often looks rather weak or insubstantial when viewed in isolation. For the most part, these reflect the 'complexity' point sketched in Chapter 2: The patient working on initiatives by myriad different actors, interacting in novel and interesting ways. The complexity is the central point to draw out: While the general arguments are about politics, and cultural political economy can be brought to bear on these initiatives, to expect a single logic across all of these sites of climate politics is to miss the point. So while it is arguable that many of these initiatives display the qualities of depoliticization we have seen in various contexts already in the book – eschewing questions of power and overt conflict in favour of partnerships, collaboration, and (socio-)technical 'solutions' – there are never-theless a number of initiatives, such as Depave Paradise or Climate Fast, that reflect the point about politics as intrinsically agonistic. We see thus glimmers of contestation and repoliticization. We see this dynamic in more detail in Chapters 8 and 9 that focus on two specific arenas in this landscape of climate initiatives – the University of Ottawa and the OREC – where technocratic initiatives combine with attempts to reclaim political space for more transformative action.

8

The University of Ottawa

Strategic Energy Management, Experimentation, and Repoliticization

As we saw in Chapter 7, educational institutions – the city's two universities, two colleges, and two school boards – play a large role in generating governance initiatives on climate change in Ottawa. They are central to the cluster of public initiatives focused on building new sorts of infrastructure and managing energy consumption. Of these, the University of Ottawa (I will use either UofO or simply 'the University' as shorthand) is significantly the most active. This chapter explores in more detail climate politics within that university.

As institutions, universities are relatively little studied in analyses of responses to climate change.[1] But their potential to play important roles in shaping climate governance is clear. First, in many of the cities and towns where they are to be found, they constitute often one of the largest employers, and the largest single concentrations of commercial buildings and thus energy use. UofO, for example, has a total campus population of almost 50,000 students and staff, i.e. around 5 per cent of all Ottawa residents, and manages the buildings associated with that number of people.

Second, they are focused on the production of knowledge, and thus central to those processes of low carbon development that entail producing new knowledge, both in terms of specific technologies but also knowledge regarding the socio-technical dimensions of low carbon transitions. In some instances, universities have explicitly deployed this quality, turning university campuses into 'living labs' focused on using the expertise and research skills of both staff and students towards the pursuit of low carbon shifts (Evans et al. 2015), although, as this chapter will show, there is relatively little that fits this pattern on the UofO's campus.

---

[1] For a few examples, see Trencher et al. (2014) or Evans et al. (2015), and on fossil fuel divestment campaigns on campus, see Grady-Benson and Sarathy (2016) or Bratman et al. (2016).

Third, as non-profit institutions (for the most part) and in many cases, including in Canada, public sector institutions, they are at least in principle not driven by profit motivations and usually have an explicit broad social mission of some kind enshrined in their founding documents. These can and in many cases have been adapted to extend to regarding the promotion of 'sustainable development' (slippery though that term is). UofO's strategic plan for example gives this as one of its five core values:

We value and teach an ethic of service and civic responsibility. We help forge a stronger society by combining scholarship and social purpose. We value service to others and foster community partnerships in learning and discovery. We are committed to academic freedom, equality, cultural diversity, integrity, respect for others and sustainable development.

(University of Ottawa n.d., 2)

After a short section contextualizing the University, this chapter discusses four overall dynamics within climate governance and politics within the University. First, the University has focused for a long time on systematic energy management of campus facilities, and its climate approach is driven by this pre-existing disposition. This has enabled it to develop a targets-and-monitoring approach to climate change and to produce significant greenhouse gas (GHG) reductions and feel fairly comfortable with the possibility of more radical reductions, such as those that have been envisaged by the province of Ontario (80 per cent cuts by 2050), at least prior to the election of Doug Ford as premier. Second, it has developed a number of experimental initiatives, driven in particular by engineers within the university and by an activist Office of Campus Sustainability. Third, it has engaged in a series of initiatives to generate participation by campus members in low carbon activities. And fourth, it has been the site of conflict, as have many university campuses, over the question of fossil fuel investments in the university financial portfolio.

The story at the University at one level is therefore one where patient, sustained attention to managing and shifting the energy performance of the University's infrastructure can, at least in this sort of institutional context, deliver significant payoffs in terms of GHG emissions. That is, it is in many ways a story of complexity and depoliticization, but one where this can be made to produce significant results. The combination of target setting and experimentation reflect well the conditions of complexity that characterize climate change and its responses. It is notable that the active politicization of climate change on campus occurred over divestment, spread from other sites of divestment campaigns, and not over the on-campus initiatives by the University. Nevertheless, climate change was politicized in the divestment campaign.

8.1 Context

The University of Ottawa is a large institution. In 2016–17 it had 41,880 students, 3,187 permanent academic staff, and 3,043 other staff.[2] Its two campuses (the city centre general campus and the Smyth Road hospital campus) together cover 42.5 hectares of land, and it has 37 large buildings (excluding student residences) and numerous smaller ones. In 2016, the replacement value of its assets was estimated at $2.03 billion and its income in 2016 was $1.175 billion (University of Ottawa IRP 2017).

As with most universities in Western countries, it has grown very substantially over the last 30–40 years. Its population (students and staff) tripled between 1974 and 2013 and the amount of built space increased two-and-a-half fold (University of Ottawa 2015, 7). But the UofO instituted an energy management plan in 1974 (hence why the reporting starts from that date in its reports) and, long prior to starting to work explicitly on climate change, had worked to maximize energy efficiency, conservation, and also to generate its own electricity and heat. The overall effect of this is that, despite the rapid rate of campus growth, total energy consumption by the University only increased by 3 per cent during the same period. Furthermore, because of a number of initiatives discussed in Sections 8.2 and 8.3, direct GHG emissions (i.e. only immediate emissions on campus, 'Scope 1 emissions' in carbon accounting terms) declined 41 per cent between 1974 and 2015 (University of Ottawa 2015, 10).[3]

This engineering-centred background drives much of the response to climate change within the university. In 1974, the university hired an engineer to manage energy consumption on campus (University of Ottawa 2015, 3). This figure is now housed within the University's Facilities Management office, which is the principal site of new initiatives on sustainability: The Office of Campus Sustainability is housed within Facilities Management, tellingly. This means that there is both a long-established experience of managing energy on campus, focused on maximizing efficiency to reduce operating costs, and thus a well-established set of decision-making norms and processes that favour actively managing energy use, especially within the campus' buildings.

---

[2] This figure almost certainly excludes the very large number of casual teaching staff on sessional (course-by-course) contracts. This data includes 212 'adjunct professors' but these must be staff on more secure, if non-permanent, contracts, given the proportion of courses given by sessional staff.

[3] This is of course limited as an effect, excluding indirect emissions (from electricity production generated elsewhere). The University already had, since the 1950s or 1960s according to Jonathan Rausseo (interview, January 2018), its own power plant working as a combined heat and power plant, which would move emissions from indirect to direct (although as we see later, it has recently abandoned the electricity generation aspect of the power plant). Nevertheless, the other emissions (produced by people commuting to campus, from the waste generated, and by travel on university work business) now dwarf both direct and indirect emissions (see Rausseo 2016).

8.2 Setting Targets and Managing Progress

This context helps us understand the first way that the University has approached the question of climate change. The University has managed GHGs since 2006 by introducing a target of cutting energy use by 2 per cent per year (Rausseo, personal communication), as an extension of its energy management traditions. It set a target to reduce its direct GHG emissions by 34 per cent over 2005 levels by 2020 (University of Ottawa 2015, 10). These emissions were already down by 23 per cent in 2015 according to the Sustainable Development Report (University of Ottawa 2015, 10).[4] This overall approach then is very like that of the City of Ottawa, with a technocratic, depoliticized focus on carbon accounting, and target setting, with the difference that, at the University, emissions have in fact gone down significantly.

This managerial approach has been intensified by the development of the Ontario long-term GHG targets and the cap and trade system, established in legislation in 2016 (see Government of Ontario 2016), but abandoned after Doug Ford's election in 2018. This set out an overarching goal to reach 80 per cent GHG cuts by 2050, and requires large emitters (including UofO) to establish measurement and monitoring of their emissions to participate in the cap and trade system. This shifted the logic of the University's focus on its emissions from cost towards compliance with legislation. The university had been making CO_2 cuts of around 1 per cent per year (better than most similar institutions, and currently has about half the emissions of similar-sized institutions) but now needed to be aiming to improve this towards a 4.5 per cent cut annually (interview with Jonathan Rausseo, 2016).

However, universities across the province lobbied to be exempted from the cap and trade system, and gained an exemption through to 2021. Actors from the UofO were disappointed with this result as they felt it was ready not only to comply but to be able to generate enough emissions reductions to be a seller of allowances. Other universities also lobbied to have co-generation facilities exempted. They brought in a Danish delegation in support of this campaign. However, the UofO successfully showed that the Danish experience was not transferable to the Ontario situation since coal had already been eliminated in Ontario but was still significant in Denmark, so what appears as a benefit in Denmark (natural gas electricity with waste heat distribution) becomes not so in Ontario (as the natural gas electricity is higher carbon than the provincial average). The UofO also acted to persuade other universities that increasing emissions prior to being in compliance (to get higher

---

[4] The University's Office of Campus Sustainability gives a figure of a 17 per cent cut by 2005 on its website (http://sustainable.uottawa.ca/emissions-and-climate-change, viewed 20 November 2017), presumably reflecting updated or recalculated figures.

numbers of allowances) was a daft approach, since it entailed increased consumption of natural gas, at around $144 for the amount of natural gas that would generate a tonne of carbon, with allowances trading currently at around $17 a tonne. But the exemption of universities from the cap and trade has also meant that the UofO is unable to sell its early action credits into the system. The UofO is the only university to generate such credits (and perhaps the only organization overall), and while the province has acknowledged their validity, it has not 'authenticated' them, which would enable them to be sold.

The University's overall plan to reach these targets is articulated in terms of 'wedges', focused on conservation, innovation, and generation, with any remainder (anticipated to be very small) being taken up by substitution (for example shifts to electric vehicles in the University's fleet) and offsets (Rausseo 2016). I deal with conservation and generation here, and innovation in Section 8.3.

Energy conservation and efficiency in buildings is integral to the GHG strategy, anticipated to account for perhaps half of the overall emissions cuts (Rausseo 2016). The university aims to reduce energy use by 2 per cent annually. Conservation is principally to be pursued through carrying out 'deep energy retrofits' in existing buildings. The university had already started a programme of these in 2010, called the 'EcoProsperity' programme (University of Ottawa 2015, 6–7). These entail extensive retrofit work across the energy-consuming systems in the University's buildings that have been able to reduce energy use in a building by 30–40 per cent. It also entails reusing waste energy in other secondary uses. The Office of Campus Sustainability manager, Pierre de Gagné, explained: 'in a deep energy retrofit, we go in and try to reuse the energy we have, cascading it down to a different use and substituting it for expensive purchased energy' (as quoted in Gillet 2017). Integral to this strategy is the existence of a Combined Heat and Power system on campus which entails a system across buildings for redistributing waste heat where needed. University documents show the centrality of a cost-orientation, emphasizing that the EcoProsperity programme has saved the University $18.5 million from 2010 to 2015 (University of Ottawa 2015, 7). The University had a well-established rule that if an investment in energy savings had at least a five-year payback period, then the investment could go ahead (interview with Jonathan Rausseo, 2016).

Generating electricity provides another 'wedge' of emissions cuts. The University's plan aims to develop a series of other sources of energy on campus, including solar thermal and pV, geothermal, and off-site generation. Some solar pV has already been installed on campus. However, the historically principal source of electricity generation on campus has been abandoned, also in part for GHG reasons. Historically the university had a co-generation power plant that provided electricity to the campus but also significant amounts of direct heat to campus buildings. However, in around 2013 the electricity part of this was abandoned and it is now solely a heating/cooling system, for a number of reasons. In carbon terms, the province's electricity system was already lower carbon on average than the natural gas used in the power plant. But also, the efficiency in the boilers is lower if generating both heat and electricity, and there is a strong and inverse seasonal variability – electricity needs are high in summer while heating needs are minimal, and the opposite is the case in winter. As a result, combining the two made less sense over time (interview with Jonathan Rausseo, 2018).

8.3 Experimental Initiatives

Alongside technocratic planning focused on targets, monitoring, and systematic overhaul of the campus buildings, and integrated with it to an extent (in that these initiatives are expected to produced measurable GHG reductions) are what the University calls 'innovative' initiatives but which might, following Hoffmann (2011) or Bulkeley et al. (2015), be called experimental ones.

Some of these are fairly well-established practices that the University took on systematically. Notably, with new buildings, the University decided to require all new large buildings (over 100,000 square feet) to be built to be at least LEED-Silver standard.[5] Four such buildings were constructed by 2017, including the Social Sciences building and the Advanced Research Complex, which both gained LEED Gold certification (University of Ottawa 2017, 11). The University participates in a number of the Ontario government's programmes, of which the most important is the Global Adjustment programme. This involves the university implementing energy reduction measures such as turning off non-essential lighting and rotating ventilation during the hottest days of the year, and produces significant income from the provincial government in electricity rebates.

But others are more properly experimental, where the intention is not to squeeze extra efficiency out of existing building designs, but to more radically work on the fabric and processes of buildings. A good deal of this is through the way the CHP system works. Rather than a relatively simple system for distributing the waste heat from the power plant to the buildings, this is a much more complex system for managing both heating and cooling across the campus: 'all the buildings are connected by tunnels under ground that allows energy to be shared between the power plant and buildings' (University of Ottawa Office of Campus Sustainability n.d. a). It is also

---

[5] LEED, or Leadership in Energy and Environmental Design, is the principal North American certification system for the environmental performance of buildings. Rausseo notes (interview, 2016) that the internal politics of this are complicated in that Faculties pay for the capital costs of new buildings but not for the running costs, generating resistance to paying upfront for more efficient buildings if they cost more, and thus the LEED requirement has relied also on pro-active Deans.

integrated with other sources of waste heat: For example, the main data centre with the University's servers also provides significant amounts of waste heat that is then circulated across the campus. Waste heat is now being captured on campus in large teaching rooms (from body heat), kitchens, and showers (through heat exchangers on the outflow pipes), among other sources (interview with Jonathan Rausseo, 2018). The air-conditioning systems in the buildings[6] is mostly done via the circulation of chilled water, which also enables the heat gained as the water circulates to be retained and recirculated for use (University of Ottawa Facilities n.d.).

Most recently, the University has introduced what it calls 'Smart Intelligent Building Automation' in the Desmarais building. This entailed introducing around 1,000 sensors into the building to monitor usage (most commonly these are motion, sound, and CO_2 sensors, the latter as measures of the number of people in a space given how fast the CO_2 levels are going up or down), and connected to mobile phone apps to connect this to individual building users' patterns. These have enabled a much more varied application of heating and cooling across the building: Instead of turning on the whole building shortly before the first person typically arrives in the morning, the system is able to learn about that person's habits and heat specific parts of the building (the toilets, the kitchen, their office) accordingly. Even after having carried out a deep energy retrofit on the building, this system still produced another 70 per cent reduction in energy use in the building (interview with Jonathan Rausseo, 2018).

The Social Sciences building, opened in 2012, is the site of a number of these experimental initiatives, which result it in it consuming approximately 50 per cent less energy than required by national building codes (University of Ottawa Faculty of Social Sciences n.d.). It is a fifteen-story building housing all the departments in the Faculty of Social Sciences (apart from the School of Psychology), within which around 10,000, or 25 per cent of the University's students, study. Heating and cooling in this building operates without direct thermostatic controls, but rather by in one sense a much simpler system but in other senses a much more subtle process of 'indoor climate change' (Shove 2012) than standard systems. It does so by simply circulating cooler or warmer air from elsewhere on campus when CO_2 levels within the building reach specified levels.[7] Eighty per cent of the heating needs come directly from circulating waste heat from the University's data centre housed in the building's basement (Lévesque et al. 2010, 10; University of Ottawa Faculty of Social Sciences n.d.).

---

[6] While Ottawa rightly has a reputation for its cold, summer temperatures are nevertheless hot and humid, with an average high in July of 27°C, requiring air conditioning, especially in large buildings with considerable thermal gain from the concrete.

[7] Teaching in that building was quite instructive. Seminar rooms have CO_2 monitors in them. In a seminar room, when you enter, CO_2 levels would typically be around 500 ppm (as opposed to the ≈400 ppm and rising outside, of course). By the end of a two-hour seminar, levels could be as high as 800 ppm.

Figure 8.1 The living wall in the FSS building.
Source: Dufresne (2013)

These systems have a living wall as an integral element (see Figure 8.1). At twenty-four metres (seventy-eight feet) high it is the highest in Canada and one of the largest in North America. The air circulation system directly circulates air through this wall, using the plants not only to absorb a good deal of the CO_2 generated by people breathing, and thus reducing the need for ventilation (with associated energy losses), but also a range of other air contaminants – Volatile organic compounds, airborne bacteria – and also reduces significantly the need for mechanical humidifiers (Dufresne 2013).

8.4 Participative Climate Governance

A good number of the experiments on campus have recognized that low carbon shifts, like other sustainability shifts, need to enrol campus members in changes to daily practices. The university has engaged in a number of activities that seek to either engender changes in daily practice by students and staff, and/or to generate participation in collective decision-making within the university. The Office of Campus Sustainability is central to these activities. At the more straightforward end, the university has negotiated with the city's public transport operator, OCTranspo, for a reduced rate pass for students, the U-Pass, since 2010, and obliges students to pay for the pass as part of registration. This, plus the city centre location of the University and the presence of the Transitway, a bus-only road that passes by the campus, means that the University estimates that only 17 per cent of campus members travel to the campus by car (University of Ottawa Office of Campus Sustainability n.d. c). The office also organizes extensive recycling facilities, including a bespoke recycling company to collect and manage its recyclables (rather than using the City's facilities), and claims to be able to recycle 98 per cent of waste on campus.[8] The University enrols some of its staff in low carbon initiatives via the bike fleet for facilities staff and (in a much more modest way) procurement of hybrid vehicles for the campus security staff.

At the more experimental end, the university operates a free store where students and staff can exchange unwanted items, has on campus bike maintenance stations equipped with pumps, Allen keys, etc., and operates a community garden programme with fifty plots. And it operates a green reps system within the on-campus student residences, to encourage participation in the initiatives on campus (University of Ottawa Office of Campus of Sustainability n.d. b).

8.5 Fossil Fuel Divestment and University Politics

But participation came 'from below' also in the University. Alongside these technocratic and experimental initiatives, the University became a site for contestation of climate politics. In 2013 UofO students, led by a 350 Ottawa group, organized a fossil fuel divestment campaign, Fossil Free uOttawa (see www .fossilfreeuo.org/). Divestment movements spread rapidly on campuses across North America in particular, mobilized by 350.org and triggered by Bill McKibben's two articles in *Rolling Stone* (2012, 2013) and the initial campaign at Swarthmore College in the US (on divestment generally, see Rowe et al. 2016;

[8] In the 2015 Sustainable Development Report, the University reports a 60 per cent waste diversion rate, with a target of achieving 75 per cent by 2017. This includes large items such as furniture. This placed the University first in recycling rates among Canadian universities, for the seventh year in a row (University of Ottawa 2015, 8).

Hopke and Hestres 2017; Mangat et al. 2018). The students got considerable support from professors and organized a petition supporting divestment. They asked the Board of Governors to answer the campaign by:

Immediately freezing any new investment into the 200 largest publicly traded fossil fuel companies, plus Enbridge Inc., Kinder Morgan Inc. and TransCanada Corporation;
   Fully divesting its endowment and pension funds from fossil-fuel public equities from these same companies over the next five years.

(Fossil Free uOttawa n.d.)

The Fossil Free uOttawa campaign used a broad range of arguments for divestment (see Mangat et al. 2018 for analysis of these arguments). They argued that divestment is a moral imperative in order to support the limit of 2°C of warming and that it could be a driver for social change (Fossil Free uOttawa 2014). Like many other divestment campaigners (Mangat et al. 2018), they used the analogy to the role that divestment played in campaigns against the apartheid regime in South Africa (Fossil Free uOttawa 2014). They also made an economic argument, arguing that there is a carbon bubble and that divesting can be profitable since the value of fossil fuel stocks will go down as their assets are 'stranded'. They argued that 'uOttawa could have saved $21.5 million by divesting from fossil fuels 3 years ago' (www.fossilfreeuo.org/). Finally, they argued that divesting in fossil free could support 'green jobs and a sustainable future' (Fossil Free uOttawa 2014).

As sketched in Chapter 1, the outcome of this campaign could be termed a 'reverse passive revolution'. The administration sat on the report and petition from the students for a while, and the sense was that they were trying to wait for the issue to go away. Then, at the beginning of 2016, the University sent an email around to the student group and various people on campus (academics with relevant expertise, the campus sustainability manager, etc.) and a couple of consultants they had used for an internal evaluation to organize a public meeting to air views and feed into a decision to be made by the Board of Governors in April 2016. The messages were decidedly mixed. As part of this process, the University held a conference entitled 'Easing Global Warming' on 21 March 2016. The conference involved a series of panels with academics, participants in the University's internal evaluation of the case for divestment, and student activists, and senior university officials attended, including the University President Allan Rock, to hear a range of views on the question.

The outcome was very interesting. In effect, the University's official decision was that it would not divest, but that instead it would produce a range of measures that continue the University's work of shifting the campus operations, including its investment portfolio, away from fossil fuels and GHG emissions (University of Ottawa Executive Committee of the Board of Governors 2016; University of

Ottawa Finance and Treasury Committee 2016). The University was already in fact very well placed to make leadership claims in this regard, with relatively low levels of GHG emissions already in place and a credible strategy for further reductions, as outlined in Section 8.2. In terms of its financial portfolio, the University was at that time already the only university in Canada and still only one of three universities in the world that has signed the Montréal Carbon Pledge (PRI n.d. a). The signatories of the Pledge will measure their portfolio's carbon footprint in order to add to pressure for 'companies and the investors that hold stakes in them to measure and reduce their carbon footprint' (PRI n.d. b).

But there in the detail was the statement that they would take their investments out of the fossil fuel interests they had remaining and shift that money into 'clean energy' investments. In other words, the University decided to divest its money while saying it had decided not to do so. Divestment activists and their supporters claimed success. The progressive online paper rabble.ca proclaimed that the University became 'the first Canadian university to divest from fossil fuels' (Kotyk 2016), and quoted Fossil Free uOttawa campaigner Megan Bowers as stating the University had committed itself to divestment, invoking the University's slogan 'defy the conventional' to underscore the historic nature of the decision. Local newspaper the *Ottawa Citizen* was more measured, reporting that the University 'rejected the idea of divestment as an insufficient response on its own to the climate challenges we face', although emphasizing that the University would instead aim to reduce the carbon intensity of its investment portfolio by 'at least 30 per cent by 2030' (Crawford 2016). The University's Finance and Treasury Committee Report was explicit in rejecting divestment, arguing it would be purely symbolic and ineffective compared to a strategy of actively managing the entire portfolio (University of Ottawa Finance and Treasury Committee 2016).

What to make of this story? It seems to me that it is evidence of the increasing recognition by mainstream institutions such as the UofO that the long-term goal is zero fossil fuels, and that it thus is sensible to take long-term investment out of fossil fuel investments. But at the same time the university baulked at the political logic of this – not wanting to be seen to take sides in the 'war on coal' (or oil and gas in the Canadian case, coal being almost already eliminated from the fuel mix). They deployed the more technocratic 'stranded assets' storyline, as well as a more feel-good 'playing a part in the energy sources of the future' sort of rationale, for their investment switching.

8.6 The Politics of Low Carbon Universities

According to Rausseo, the three internal logics driving forward climate action in the University are 'money, reputation, and compliance' (interview with Jonathan

Rausseo 2016). For the first of these, the five-year payback has operated as a stable decision-making framework that has enabled many initiatives such as the deep energy retrofits. In the second, the University's strategic plan Destination 2020 made a series of general claims about campus sustainability that it has thus been forced to deliver on. Rausseo suggested that these sustainability claims were particularly important for pre-students and thus for recruitment to the University's programmes. Internal pressure such as from divestment groups has also worked to make the University step up climate-related action. Increasingly however, compliance with provincial targets – the GHG one explicitly but also those concerning waste diversion – drive a more strategic orientation towards long-term decarbonization goals (interview with Jonathan Rausseo 2016).

Over time, we can discern a shift in the drivers of climate politics within the University. Initially, the driver was clearly the Facilities management office, with its engineering focus on maximizing efficiency in buildings and solving problems with innovative uses of energy through the combined heat and power plant and later on with more novel means such as heat harvesting, ice storage and cooling, the living wall in the FSS building, and so on. They were aided by the 5-year payback rule accepted by the University senior administration which enabled an easy route to arguing for the upfront capital costs. But from 2014 to 2017 these drivers have subtly shifted. In the first report of the 'addressing global warming' plan adopted by the senior administration in 2016, the question of a 'sustainable campus', focus on these building initiatives is somewhat relegated to part four of the document, after sections on teaching, research, finance, and external relations.

This shift seems to be the result of two dynamics that intervened from around 2015 onwards. The first is the development of the Ontario government's climate change act, containing a plan more or less for the decarbonization of Ontario by 2050. This had the effect of significantly increasing the profile of climate change within the University's administration, since it now had to focus on complying with provincial legislation rather than simply focusing on saving money and gaining some reputational benefit by being one of the most energy efficient campuses in Canada. The central administration thus got more directly involved in climate change strategy on campus and has decentred the question of buildings management somewhat.

Conversely, however, this has also produced new sources of finance. The cap and trade system generated approximately $2 billion of revenue to the province annually, which is not 'revenue neutral' but being disbursed directly on projects within the climate change strategy of the province through its 'Greenhouse Gas Reduction Account' (Government of Ontario 2017). The University has applied for and got significant amounts of this money. The province also has a 'global adjustment' system in the regulation of electricity markets, which entails real time electricity pricing based on demand but with paybacks to those engaged actively in 'peak shaving' of their demand. The University earns approximately $1 million annually from this programme because of its various programmes that enable it to shave peak demand effectively. This has meant also that the Office of Campus Sustainability has been able to find new ways of keeping in control of the University's climate strategy in relation to the increased interest by the central administration, often by simply using this external funding option to turn projects that had, say, a seven year payback, into ones with a five year payback. A recent development has been the development of a discourse of 'deferred maintenance' (interview with Jonathan Rausseo, 2018). The University estimates that its estate needs roughly $200 million of annual maintenance, and given it doesn't spend this, the potential costs of such maintenance or problems that arise because of lack of maintenance generate huge risks. The Office of Campus Sustainability is able to use this to argue for various energy initiatives since they can be partly justified in relation to the deferred maintenance logic, aligning the finance office's risk management with the University's climate strategy.

The second is the effect of the Fossil Fuel Divestment campaign. This also had the effect of increasing the interest of the central administration in climate change but focused on the financial dynamics of the University – its endowments and pension funds, and on strategic reputation management both within and outside the University. Finance is part two in the University's first annual report (University of Ottawa 2017) and there they detail a number of ways the University is using its money strategically in relation to climate change.

In contrast to those identified in some of the existing literature on climate change in universities (e.g. Trencher et al. 2013, 2014; Evans et al. 2015), the University of Ottawa plays relatively little role in the broader community's efforts on climate change. There are specific initiatives such as the U-Pass where the university engages the City in order to contribute to reducing its own footprint. And individual academics get involved in aspects of city climate politics. But there is no sustained engagement. There is no using the university as a 'living laboratory' to generate wider low carbon transitions. The University's experience with deep energy retrofits seems a particularly obvious plausible initiative where it could work with the owners and managers of the many other large buildings in the city to trigger a broader shift in energy use across the city. But there is little of this, as yet.

8.7 Conclusions

In the University of Ottawa, we see the dominance of a combination of managerial/ technocratic and experimental governance, classic examples of Bulkeley's (2016) 'accomplishing' logic of climate governance. However, in the case of the University (unlike the City Council, for example), this combination has delivered significant gains in climate change performance, and the University is continuing to work in this vein very productively. Perhaps this is in part because of the particular sort of jurisdictional authority university managers have within their bounds.

But this technocratic management has been accompanied by recurrent repoliticization of climate change, notably in the divestment campaigns. This repoliticization has had effects in disturbing the field by shifting relations among university managers, reframing climate change as a question of finance as much as of on-campus energy management, and contributing (along with the province's regulatory and funding arrangements for GHGs) to shifts in authority among different parts of the University. It is not obvious if this will be positive in terms of the future trajectories of the University's climate strategy: Enhancing the authority of financial managers compared to buildings engineers within the University may work to undermine the focus on energy management and improvement. More broadly, the story underscores the importance of taking the 'complexity' side of the 'purification vs. complexity' argument seriously. It could even be read to imply that 'purification' is a distraction: The University was already doing a good job of addressing climate change internally and the divestment campaign was a simplistic attempt to focus on one, perhaps relatively unimportant aspect of the University's climate-related operations. But this I think would be premature: The divestment campaigns have contributed to making senior managers focus on areas of their operations they had not previously considered, and added a politicized pressure to act to the more managerial, efficiency-oriented one.

9

Renewing Democratic Politics

The Ottawa Renewable Energy Cooperative

BORA PLUMPTRE AND MATTHEW PATERSON

9.1 Introduction

If the University of Ottawa exemplifies the ways that public institutions have focused on energy demand management and new forms of infrastructure (in their case, innovations within buildings), we also saw in Chapter 7 that there has been significant activity by community and private sector initiatives focused more on changing energy supply. Here we focus in more detail on one particularly prominent initiative, the Ottawa Renewable Energy Cooperative (OREC).

OREC is important in Ottawa climate politics in part because it is the largest organization, outside the City of Ottawa itself (through its ownership of Energy Ottawa, which runs the hydroelectric plant on the Ottawa River), involved in renewable energy (RE) development. But it is also important because it signals in interesting ways the tensions between the agonistic politics of identifying enemies to struggle against, exemplified by the divestment campaign discussed in Chapter 8, and the relatively patient, potentially co-optable, politics of working to generate transformations of energy away from fossil fuels. But even where it does so, OREC shows that an energy investment is never simply an energy investment: It entails specific forms of politics.

Much of the impetus and desire that animates organizations such as OREC is that not only are citizens enabled to promote renewables and help address climate change, they contribute to important transformations in democratic practice. 'Energy democracy' is a term used by many such groups, including OREC (Peters 2016, 5), which has also emphasized its adherence to the seven principles of cooperative governance, including democratic member control and cooperation among cooperatives (OREC 2018). We can see OREC, therefore, as a sort of repoliticization of climate change in terms of new and revitalized democratic institutional forms, although it lacks the focus on challenging existing power structures, or at least only implicitly does so. OREC frames its mandate as being 'to empower Eastern Ontario residents to support the growth of the local RE sector through responsible long-term investments [made] together as members of a democratic co-operative' (OREC 2017c). As such, this reflects much of the shifts to renewables in many countries – community control is an important feature that accelerates the shifts to renewables, meaning that renewable energy renews politics as well (e.g. Strachan et al. 2010; Mabee et al. 2012; Nishimura 2012; Winfield and Dolter 2014; Oji and Weber 2017). Between the practical need for a transition to low carbon energy systems and the opportunity to promote democratic renewal through infrastructural and technological change, a zone of experimentation has opened in which advocates of energy democracy have begun to propose, as well as to put into practice, different visions of a reconfigured energy system based on a socially and economically just transition to renewable sources (Sweeney 2014; Angel 2016; Burke and Stephens 2018).

These shifts however can be understood as a revitalization of older debates: Arguments in the 1970s about the contrast between 'soft' and 'hard' energy paths (Lovins 1977), or the authoritarian qualities of centralized (and especially nuclear) electricity systems vs. the democratic qualities of small-scale, renewable systems (Gorz 1980; Winner 1980). As such, they retain some of the tensions within those debates, resembling the 'purification vs. complexity' argument running through this book. For some, 'energy democracy' is decidedly counter-hegemonic: Sweeney (2014) explains energy democracy as a three-part agenda to 'resist [corporate fossil fuel interests], reclaim [privatized energy systems to the public sector], and restructure [the governance of energy toward democratic, just, and sustainable low-carbon configurations]' (p. 218). But for others (and as we shall see, this is OREC's way of deploying it), it works more consensually, building new community political structures as it builds new energy infrastructure.

9.2 Promoting Renewable Energy Cooperatives in Ontario and Ottawa

The background for the emergence of OREC, and many similar organizations across Ontario, is the development of a climate change strategy within the province designed to promote renewable energy (RE).[1] There was also an important legacy of energy politics in the province, with the restructuring and privatization of electricity, the blackout crisis of August 2003 across eastern North America – the result of under-investment and regulatory systems focused on low consumer prices (Martin 2007) – contestation over the air quality problems associated with coal

---

[1] It is worth underscoring that our analysis was completed prior to the election of Doug Ford as Premier of Ontario, and we don't get into the implications of his radical shift of policy direction on climate change and energy here, although it is worth noting that at least some OREC projects have been cancelled because of his rejection of the support for RE in the GEGEA.

which had produced a commitment to phase out coal, and active lobbying by renewable organizations such as the Ontario Sustainable Energy Association. All of these created impulses to seek to increase electricity supply (as well as manage demand) and in particular to diversify supply (in a province that by around 2010 got 59 per cent of its electricity from nuclear) to take up the slack from the coal phase-out (Rowlands 2007; Stokes 2013; Rosenbloom and Meadowcroft 2014).

Efforts to address these intertwined problems resulted on the one hand in an attempt (which failed by 2013) to privatize the electricity supply, following from the restructuring the previous Conservative government had carried out from the late 1990s onwards (some of which had contributed to the blackout), and on the other hand in the *Green Energy and Green Economy Act* of 2009 (GEGEA). This legislation contained a number of measures, of which the most important for the emergence of organizations such as OREC was the Feed-in-Tariff programme which provided significant incentives for solar and wind installation (Yatchew and Baziliauskas 2011). This approach was directly borrowed from similar policies in Germany, where a FIT policy was shown to have accelerated the uptake of RE more than other possible policies, such as the Renewable Portfolio Standards adopted in many US states (e.g. Dong 2012). But at the same time, the province enacted an amendment to their regulation of cooperatives under the *Co-operative Corporations Act*. This amendment was designed specifically to enable and promote the emergence of RE cooperatives. Prior to the amendment, Ontario's regulation of cooperatives had a '50% Rule'. Under this requirement, at least half of a registered cooperative's 'business' (variously defined) must be conducted with its members, a stipulation that would clearly have been impossible to satisfy when the business in question consists of the generation and sale of electricity (Shewan and Sadler 2012). The amendment exempted RE cooperatives from the rule.

While this regulatory change at the provincial level is the important context for understanding the emergence of OREC, the City has also started to actively promote community development of RE. On 8 July 2015, the City Council approved the development of a Renewable Energy Strategy as part of the *2015–2018 City Strategic Plan*. (We saw in Chapter 3 that this had started life as a more ambitious project by David Chernushenko for a '100% renewable Ottawa' strategy). According to municipal documents provided to the Environment Committee,

The purpose of the strategy is to increase energy conservation, energy efficiency, and renewable energy generation in Ottawa in collaboration with community partners. The strategy will build on the City's 2014 Air Quality and Climate Change Management Plan (AQCCMP), including the goals and objectives set out by that plan to reduce energy demand, reduce dependence on fossil fuels, and transition towards increased use of renewable energy sources.

(City of Ottawa Environment Committee 2016, 1)

This policy shift provided the basis for partnerships between OREC and the City, helping OREC grow.

9.3 OREC: Origins and Current Projects

OREC was incorporated in September 2010 under the *Ontario Co-operative Corporations Act* (OREC 2015a). It was formed from the remnants of a cooperative named Sustainable Ottawa, a similarly non-profit proponent of community energy systems whose main initiative, *H2Ottawa*, focused on domestic solar water heating. While this programme was largely informational and focused on raising public awareness, it also provided limited funding for solar water heater retrofits, and provided beneficiaries with access to negotiated discounts from certain installers and contractors. This precursor organization ultimately suspended operations 'due to a lack of interest from members' (Sustainable Ottawa 2010).

However, as the organizational fortunes of Sustainable Ottawa flagged, the Liberal energy minister at the time, George Smitherman, announced the Government of Ontario's intention to develop a feed-in-tariff (FIT) programme open to community-led RE projects. Having heard the news, five members of Sustainable Ottawa were eager to continue advancing their vision of an enhanced role for small-scale solar technology in local energy systems. Driven by several continuing, intersecting beliefs about the future of energy at the local level, these volunteers capitalized on the new policy reality by founding OREC – an organization which, structured as a cooperative, would be better positioned to push a local sustainable energy agenda forward, since it would be eligible to apply for contracts with the provincial electricity system. While OREC was one of the earliest to form, it is now one of seventy-seven such cooperatives across the province (of which forty-seven are estimated to be active, see Lipp et al. 2016, 9–11), stimulated by the FIT and the changes to the regulation of cooperatives (FSCO 2017, our calculations). While some of these have broader operations (wind, biomass), to date, OREC has focused exclusively on selling electricity generated by solar photovoltaic installations; however, its Board of Directors remains open in principle to developing alternative kinds of energy (personal observations, OREC Board Meeting, 23 June 2016).

In addition to a desire to strengthen community ties, OREC's early leaders were also motivated by beliefs about the need to develop greater energy literacy amongst the general public, and about the need to demonstrate and prove the technical and financial viability of collectively owned RE systems. With the legislative framework to support its vision now in place, OREC held its first public meeting in April 2011. The young organization hosted a screening of *Powerful: Energy for Everyone* – an independent documentary film about grassroots efforts to bring about change in the energy sector, directed by a local city councillor

(David Chernushenko) – and followed this with a discussion panel that included a local solar developer and the local Member of Provincial Parliament (Yasir Naqvi).

OREC provides interested citizens across Eastern Ontario with the chance to jointly own and invest in local RE generation projects. Operating as a for-profit corporation within a cooperative organizational structure, OREC finances RE projects through share offerings that are made available to its paid members. It develops projects by entering into long-term lease agreements with property owners who own roof space or land that OREC's staff and management identify as being viable for solar generation.

As with OREC's investors, these partners are remunerated through revenue made from the sale of power produced over the lifetime of the project. To date, revenue has been guaranteed by the provincial FIT programme, through which OREC is able to hold contracts for the purchase of power by the Independent Electricity System Operator (IESO; formerly, the contracts were held with the Ontario Power Authority). Since its establishment, the cooperative had grown to a membership of over 700 Ottawa residents by 2017, who had collectively invested over $7 million in its various projects. OREC currently manages a portfolio of seventeen solar power installations totalling 1.7 megawatts (MW) of installed capacity, with more currently under development. Existing individual projects range in scale from 10 to 500 kW and are generally situated on the rooftops of schools, non-profit housing, and private barns and warehouses in Ottawa; there is also one ground-mounted project (OREC 2017a).

9.4 OREC's Business Model

OREC's model of operation consists essentially of four elements. First, to develop its project portfolio, it explores and solicits partnerships with Ottawa-area property owners with a view to siting OREC-owned RE systems. When a viable project site has been identified, a lease agreement (usually for a twenty-year period) is negotiated. Because of the necessarily long-term nature of the contracts OREC can sign, its ideal project partners are those with stable institutional, private, or non-profit backing, who have the space to accommodate an economically sized solar array atop a suitably large building or section of land.

Second, to finance and develop new projects, OREC has regular investment rounds in which members are offered the opportunity to buy securities (either shares or 'member investment notes', see below) within a time-limited window.[2]

---

[2] Members are allowed under the energy cooperative regulations to use these investments as part of their Registered Retirement Savings Plans or Tax-Free Savings Accounts, both of which are Canadian pension/savings tax incentive systems. Investments in OREC are thus in effect tax-free, a significant incentive (and especially for higher earners, of course, giving rise to some criticisms of OREC's model).

Projects are typically solely owned by OREC, but in some cases larger installations are co-financed, with ownership and revenue from FIT income shared through a joint venture arrangement (for example, with a local school board such as the Conseil des écoles catholiques du Centre-Est). From 2012 to 2017, OREC led five share offerings, with the 2017 one having raised $1.98 million from 160 members over the course of January to April 2017 (OREC 2017a). This last round financed the construction of four new solar projects, and saw OREC establish partnerships across the Ottawa region – including a joint venture between the municipality of Alfred and the Keewaywin First Nation, as well as projects at a rugby stadium run by the Eastern Ontario Rugby Association, a winery, and a commercial building (OREC 2017a).

The third element in the business model is selling electricity to the grid. Each of OREC's solar systems is connected to the Hydro One or Hydro Ottawa grid, earning revenue from the power it feeds into the grid. To secure its projected revenue for a project, OREC applies to the grid operator (the IESO) during its latest round of contract offers under the FIT programme. Once a project receives approval, OREC signs a (typically) twenty-year FIT contract with the IESO, which agrees to buy every kilowatt-hour (kWh) the project generates for the grid at a set rate. At the end of 2017, the IESO completed its fifth and final round of FIT contract bids, during which OREC successfully secured power purchase agreements for an additional four projects.

The final element in OREC's business plan is the distribution of revenue. For those who buy shares, in return for members' long-term investment commitment (since shares usually cannot be sold early), OREC offers an annual dividend on the value of an individual member's share capital; the dividend for shares was originally targeted at 5 per cent (Foon and Dale 2014), but is now targeted one point lower. Historically, the performance of the cooperative and its energy systems has enabled it to return a 4 per cent annual dividend (OREC 2017b). Repayment of the principal amount typically commences in the sixth year of investment (at 1/15th annually), and comes in addition to continued dividends on the declining value of the remaining share capital. In its model investment scenario, OREC anticipates full repayment of the principal after twenty years (i.e. the standard duration of FIT contracts). By contrast, purchasers of the member investment notes can expect a 3 per cent annual interest payment and to see their capital reimbursed after five years. Though OREC is prevented legally from guaranteeing dividend payments, its promotional literature and informational materials stress that its expected revenue is backed by a firm contract with the IESO.

9.5 OREC and the Remaking of Democratic Politics

Some of the reasons for OREC's success in rapidly generating significant investments in renewables in the Ottawa area are beyond the realm of its own practices. The provincial legislation, specifically the FIT programme and the new regulations for energy cooperatives, provide the institutional context for the flourishing of organizations such as OREC. Also, Ottawa's physical location and seasonal environmental conditions are highly favourable to the production of solar power. Ottawa has higher-than-average (across Canada) annual levels of solar irradiation (Natural Resources Canada 2017). And since colder temperatures enhance solar panel efficiency, Ottawa's long winters also help somewhat to increase solar generation in the region.

But integral to OREC's success as a project, and community energy initiatives like it in many other contexts, is an attempt to connect the shift to renewables to a renewal and transformation of democratic politics. As hinted in Section 9.1, OREC frames its own practices in relation to an emerging discourse of 'energy democracy' – a variety of claims that the low carbon transition in energy goes hand in hand with a democratization of energy itself (see variously Sweeney 2014; Angel 2016; Burke and Stephens 2018). Of course, what this means in practice can vary considerably, and it is not our aim here to romanticize initiatives such as OREC. However, there are interesting aspects of OREC's practice that are useful in helping us understand the ways in which low carbon transitions are generative of political change.

Three aspects of democratic practice can be usefully used to unpack OREC's democratic claims: Participation and inclusion, control and accountability, and the deliberative qualities of its activities (this typology draws on Kronsell and Bäckstrand 2010). Overall, we suggest that the principal contribution to democratization is through the construction of novel public spheres.

9.5.1 Participation and Inclusion

A major part of the claim of 'energy democracy' is that the possibilities for direct participation in energy initiatives are greatly increased by the shift to small-scale renewables across many energy systems. OREC attempts to perform this partly by simply enabling citizens to be involved in energy generation and also in the specific ways it acts internally and externally.

Internally, as a mode of governance, OREC, like many initiatives in climate change governance (e.g. Bulkeley et al. 2014), defies simple categorization as either a wholly public or wholly private approach: Politics is being remade in the process of developing initiatives on climate change. On the one hand, it is a private venture in the sense that it is incorporated as a for-profit entity that is managed by, and answerable to, its members. On the other hand, its development (to date) has been dependent on the particular form of public policy in Ontario – the FIT programme and changes to the regulation of cooperatives. To adopt the language of Kronsell and Bäckstrand (2010, 36–37), Ontario's RE cooperative sector arguably works primarily through a networked organizational form – though it also exhibits the self-organizing properties of a market. Meanwhile, in terms of the 'rationalities' of governance, OREC and its peers appear to enact and enable a blend of administrative (since the market for community solar was essentially brought into existence by regulatory fiat), economic (since members pursue their perceived self-interest by making contracts), and deliberative logics (Kronsell and Bäckstrand 2010, 30–35).

OREC's hybrid nature as a mode of steering for RE transition nonetheless points to the structural influence of public policy on the participatory possibilities of the cooperative. As one board member remarked,

Policy plays a big role for community solar or solar of any kind, to be honest. Energy in general is very regulatory-based and policy-based, even for oil and gas . . . I think that if the work that CANSIA [the Canadian Solar Industries Association] was doing didn't materialize, I don't think OREC – definitely not in its current form – would be as successful [and] may not even exist at all.

(personal interview)

From a broad perspective of inclusiveness, then, OREC shows how public policy opened up the possibility for ordinary, motivated individuals and groups to shift from their conventional roles in the electricity system – as passive consumers and service users – into less familiar public roles, such as RE project proponent, project participant, local beneficiary, financial investor, and technology host (Walker and Cass 2007, 464–65). OREC and the community energy model are notable for the way they expand the scope of potential identities and relationships that 'the public' may hold with respect to RE technologies and the broader energy system. This is clear from the Cooperative's statement of its goals, which are to:

1. Generate decentralized renewable electricity in Eastern Ontario;
2. Create a democratic, self-reliant, environmentally, socially, and financially sustainable business model for community power in cooperation with other community-based co-operatives in Eastern Ontario;
3. Increase the accessibility and awareness of sustainable energy technologies by providing leadership and advocacy and building social capital;
4. Through social financing improve the market for renewable energy and other forms of sustainable technology in Eastern Ontario;
5. Provide a fair return for co-operative members who wish to invest in local renewable energy production; and
6. Partner with other organizations, companies, and government agencies to develop a variety of projects that achieve our vision.

(OREC 2015b, 2)

Beyond creating new opportunities for energy-system participation in principle, OREC boasts a general membership of over 700, each of whom has purchased a one-time membership share. It has also stated an ambitious target to have 5,000 members across Eastern Ontario by 2020. Given that members are also usually investors, the growth in OREC's base demonstrates considerable local interest in pursuing local investment opportunities and in 'greening' the electricity system to mitigate climate change. This interest also comes through in significant contributions of volunteer time: In 2016–2017, OREC recorded more than 2,000 hours of volunteer time donated by the board, and by members and supporters (OREC 2017b, 3). In addition, while membership in the Cooperative was originally limited to residents of the City of Ottawa, the decision was taken at a special members' meeting in May 2015 to expand the Cooperative's boundaries (both in terms of membership eligibility and project siting) to many other Eastern municipalities and townships. So, while the organization has in one sense limited public participation by imposing a local residency requirement, it has also demonstrated a willingness to shed those boundaries – even if for reasons of expedience as much as to demonstrate its adherence to democratic principles.

In terms of its internal governance, OREC operates according to a fairly conventional set of procedures for any incorporated cooperative entity as governed by Ontario's *Co-operative Corporations Act*. In practice, this restricts direct participation by most members to attending the AGM, selecting a board of directors, participating via investment opportunities, and volunteering opportunities promoting OREC's work. Thus, despite a strongly stated sense of democratic mission, in important respects OREC is still mostly confined to enabling only certain modes of public participation in RE projects – notably, the role of 'green investor'. Project participation is pursued mainly through ownership of shares or investment notes: Members are either part-owners or lenders but are otherwise mostly passive participants in project development. It is the board and the executive committee who oversee all major operational decisions and activities for the Cooperative, including applying for contracts, developing projects, identifying potential lease partnerships, administering unspent capital, distributing dividends, and borrowing from financial institutions. The main function of the general membership is to elect the board and to provide financing – financing that is for the most part dependent on expectations for healthy and low-risk returns. As one board member reflected (in a personal interview):

Membership doesn't play a big role in decision-making. The main role is the membership elects the board, and [after] that point in time, it's up to the board to make most if not all of the decisions. [pause] I'm not sure what the broader membership *would* be able to decide on … My personal view is, I don't think it makes sense to have the membership involved in what projects, for example, are approved. Solar, although it is a relatively simple technology, it can be very complicated [and] there are a number of different factors that go into the decision-making process, and so I think it would be confusing more than anything else if you're bringing the membership into those types of decisions. And [the question becomes] how would you go through that process, then?

But the participative/inclusive aspect of democracy is also about its external interactions. Here, the public/private question is not about how it is a hybrid of the two, as above, but about how in generating various sorts of relations across eastern Ontario, OREC contributes to the making of new public spheres and novel forms to democratic practice (Paterson 2014). These practices take a number of forms.

First, OREC has pursued its (self-set) mandates to educate the public and to collaborate with others to improve overall accessibility to and awareness of sustainable energy solutions (see goals 3 and 6 earlier in this section). While its periodic share offerings implicate increasing numbers of people in its mission, its professional communications manager organizes regular community outreach, including informational programming such as project tours and film screenings. This communications activity helps to build its organizational reputation and, according to proponents, its social license to build projects.

Second, OREC has self-consciously constructed a series of partnerships in developing its projects. It has partnered with an array of different communities, including schools (e.g. Maurice Lapointe, Franco-Ouest, Franco-Cité, Samuel-Genest), non-profit social housing complexes (e.g. Eileen Tallman, Better Living, Presland), and a housing cooperative (Co-opérative d'habitation LaFontaine), among others.

Its recently completed ground-mounted solar project in the municipality of Alfred and Plantagenet (around sixty kilometres to the east of Ottawa) provides a useful illustration. This is one of OREC's largest, and also one of OREC's more technologically advanced projects: A single-axis solar tracking system enables the solar modules to follow the sun throughout the day, thus maximizing energy production and expected revenue. The municipality is a partner because it leases the land, which was formerly the site of a pumping station for water treatment, as well as a dumping ground for snow removal services. The project itself is co-owned by OREC and the Keewaywin First Nation, a community located in a remote part of northern Ontario. Speaking on the day of the project launch, a representative from Keewaywin spoke first of some of the hardships that his home community had faced. He then remarked,

this partnership does mean a lot in our six communities that I represent, which means that, you know, just a little bit more money to spend on various things like recreation for kids, you know, looking after elders, and things like that. We don't receive anything from the government. So way back when, six years ago, we made a commitment to start looking outside for other sources of revenue so that our kids and our people and our First Nations can enjoy the same thing, the same things that the mainstream society enjoys, which is [a] better standard of living.

(personal observation)

OREC also contends that the Alfred installation represents a national milestone as the first solar project in Canada to be jointly owned by a cooperative and a First Nation. Certainly, by repurposing otherwise underused municipal land, and creating revenue for the township, OREC has demonstrated a commitment to using community solar as a vehicle for local development. And through the partnership with Keewaywin First Nation, it has also enabled a historically marginalized community not only to share in the benefits of RE development as a part-owner, but also to have been involved as an active participant in decision-making during earlier phases of the project development.

Other partnerships have been integral to OREC's activities. Beyond supporting jobs in the local renewables sector (i.e. installation/construction and operations/ maintenance, such as with companies like iSolara, a solar installer), the cooperative's emphasis on its projects' locality also embraced a desire to seek, where possible, economic benefits for others. 'Local ownership' in this sense implies not just a geographically bounded set of shareholders, but an approach to project development that cultivates alliances with neighbours and partners who come to have a stake – whether formal or informal – in the project's delivery. Thus, as noted, OREC successfully negotiated several property lease partnerships and joint venture (revenue-sharing) arrangements. In partnering with low-income housing cooperatives (e.g. Eileen Tallman and Better Living), schools, a First Nation, and a non-profit immigrant service provider (OCISO Non-Profit Housing Corporation, now Unity Non-Profit Housing Corporation Ottawa), OREC has pursued an expansive approach to the idea of local ownership – one in which traditionally marginalized communities beyond OREC's own membership are enabled to learn about and access the advantages of RE generation, and so to shape their own relationship to energy production and consumption.

Third, this ethos is also evident in OREC's engagement with other sustainability-minded local actors. Its practice of community-building involves regular interaction with (and cross-promotion of) other Ottawa-area businesses and social enterprises, including Impact HUB Ottawa, the local incubator/ accelerator and networking space; Terra20, an 'eco-products' retailer; Beau's, a prominent independent brewery; and VRTUCAR, a locally founded but now multi-city car-sharing service in Ontario. OREC members qualify for various benefits or discounts on these partners' product or service offerings. From their association with the cooperative, the partners reinforce their green *bona fides* and gain a measure of visibility amongst a likely, if small, customer base.

Engagement with likeminded small- and medium-sized enterprises expresses OREC's mission as a cooperative, independent of its mission as an agent of energy transition. However, from its beginnings through the present, board and general members have also identified OREC's capacity to offer individuals a way of materially connecting to that latter mission as another important factor in the cooperative's initial success and in its endurance over time. During a public 'e-dialogue' (webinar) on energy security and sustainable development, one board member emphasized the importance of how OREC's emergence helped satisfy 'eager residents who have been waiting a long time for this opportunity' (Dale and Foon 2013, 10). OREC created an outlet for those who lack the resources or technical know-how to build their own residential RE systems, but nonetheless remain committed to promoting the uptake of these new energy technologies, harvesting community benefits, and/or mitigating climate change.

Participation in OREC's version of 'energy democracy' is of course limited, notably by questions of class and income. The core set of member-investors is inevitably drawn from a more limited pool of people, namely those with disposable investable assets. Participation as a shareholder or lender requires a certain degree of privilege: In 2017, OREC reported that the average member investment was over $17,600 (OREC 2017b, 5). The need for individual members with financial means is also evident in some of OREC's promotional material, which states for example that an 'investment of $20,000 amounts to a 25% reduction of the average Ontarian's carbon footprint' (OREC 2017b, 4). The target audience is offered a chance to bolster their green virtue by means of the investment transaction. Once made, the investment is for most members a passive (and profitable) commitment that does not entail any of the behavioural changes that more direct action to lower one's individual carbon footprint would imply. However, as one director remarked:

Most people that are involved in community solar-type initiatives are likely more environmentally focused. The irony sometimes is [that] solar is not displacing fossil fuels in some situations; it depends on what the displaced fuel's source is. But, generally speaking, solar is obviously not bad for the environment ... And generally speaking [members] are more environmentally focused than the average individual.

(personal interview)

Thus, while OREC has demonstrated its capacity as an organization to involve new actors in the transition to renewable power, the scope of its own members' involvement is still influenced by the threshold of financial means.

Finally, in analysing OREC's participatory conduct and influence, it is worth considering what the geographic scope of its projects and the constraints on its membership reveal about its vision for community power. Here, Tarhan's distinction between 'communities-of-location' and 'communities-of-interest' in the RE sector is apt. The former type focuses on generating electricity for local consumption or in order to address local economic, social, and/or environmental need within a limited geographic zone (Tarhan 2015, 107). Conversely, the latter are not restricted by geographic boundaries, but are rather formed by individuals who assemble around a common subject of economic interest or environmental concern (Tarhan 2015). While we might think of each power project in its portfolio as a manifestation or blend of each type, at the organizational level OREC appears to embody a hybrid approach: It worked originally on behalf of members concentrated in Ottawa, and has maintained its geographic boundedness, even as it sought to attract new members by shifting to a more expansive residency requirement covering Eastern Ontario, and has engaged in partnerships with First Nations from far outside the region.

OREC thus can be seen to enact a fluid definition of community energy involving both its own members (as one community) as well as a multitude of external partners and beneficiaries, who may themselves be linked to other communities. This flexibility is only appropriate since in general communities are self-defined groups that may coalesce as a result of many possible factors and context-specific motives (e.g. geography, identity, issue-based concerns, local emergencies, and so forth) (Rogers et al. 2008). In the words of one board member:

One way to approach [OREC's definition] is: community solar is defined by whatever [the] community thinks. I would say, every community is different, they're going to have different values, so I think having that type of broad definition is probably fitting … I know people like to have very concrete definitions, but I think when it comes to people, and groups of people, it's very challenging to have those [ideas] very well defined.

(personal interview)

Viewed from this vantage, OREC's participatory character can be seen as a strategically managed asset that defines the organization's external relationships and public image, yet remains flexible enough to allow for relatively undemanding forms (democratically speaking) of non-board member participation.

9.5.2 Democratic Control and Accountability

The question of democratic control and accountability can also be thought of both internally and externally. Internally, OREC has a range of standard accountability mechanisms: A board of directors that makes key strategic decisions and oversees the management; a set of representative processes for members and constitutional processes governing decision-making; a preference for consensus decision-making with provision for majority voting; transparency mechanisms through reporting systems; and dispute resolution mechanisms (e.g. OREC 2015b). Most of these are governed by provincial or national rules regarding the operations of Cooperatives and/or businesses generally (as in the *Co-operative Corporations Act* in Ontario, see OREC 2015b, 8–9). However, OREC also engages in a series of communication strategies designed to demonstrate responsiveness to a range of broader community and social demands, reflecting the demand for 'horizontal' forms of accountability amongst its peers (Kronsell and Bäckstrand 2010, 41). Its 'Community Impact Report', for example, quantifies the Cooperative's effect on people, planet, and profit. Figures from this report state, for example, that there are 4,000 students attending schools that host an OREC project, that energy generated from its solar portfolio had mitigated 1,300 metric tonnes of greenhouse gases by 2017, and that $2.5 million (or nearly 80 per cent) of project profits have been used to pay local labour (OREC 2017b).

So, OREC remains accountable to its members by maintaining relatively transparent methods of decision-making and by proactively supplying access to information. Externally, however, questions of democratic control and account-ability become more paradoxical. It is questionable whether the background legislation enabling OREC's emergence has ultimately been conducive to greater local control over RE systems. As one board member remarked, 'there's kind of an ironic element here … so although [the Ontario government] set up these types of cooperatives that could invest in renewable energy, they actually took power away from the municipality in terms of the power to say yea or nay on a project' (personal interview). In fact, by curtailing the powers of Ontario's municipalities and many local distribution companies, the GEGEA has arguably suppressed more traditional state-centred modes of local democratic control over energy systems.

The Act did this in three principal ways: First, by exempting RE projects from the environmental assessment requirements of the *Environmental Assessment Act*; second, by streamlining multiple mandated permit applications under the *Environmental Protection Act* into a single 'Renewable Energy Approval'; and finally, by substantially limiting municipal powers previously accorded under the *Planning Act* (Kussner and Warren 2009; Manning and Vince 2010). Previously, RE developers had viewed municipalities as holding final approval powers for potential projects, through their general planning responsibilities. After the passage of the GEGEA, however, municipalities 'lost all of their powers to block, alter, or control renewable energy generation projects' (Manning and Vince 2010, 6), while local distribution companies faced a new regulatory mandate to connect all projects contracted via feed-in tariff to the local grid (Stokes 2013, 495). Furthermore, the Act's sweeping changes meant that the public 'lost a powerful forum in which to express concern and to influence development', including its third-party right of appeal against planning approvals (Manning and Vince 2010, 6).

The GEGEA's proponents generally saw the removal of municipal jurisdiction as key to eliminating one of the RE sector's most challenging non-economic barriers, and thus to increasing the speed of project deployment (Yatchew and Baziliauskas 2011; Stokes 2013). But the swift emergence of influential grassroots resistance groups, who contended that the accelerated approvals processes supporting the FIT programme were undemocratic, suggests a more equivocal democratic legacy for GEGEA. This scepticism is summed up in a protest sign, created for Wind Concerns Ontario (now Ontario Wind Resistance), which reads: 'Democracy: Gone with the wind' (Ontario Wind Resistance 2018). In reflecting on OREC's community energy model, one board member opined: 'Generally speaking they [the province] took power away from the communities. They said: You don't have a say, if the landowner wants to put solar or wind there, then they're allowed to do so' (personal interview). Overall, despite the individual success of OREC and other RE cooperatives, the GEGEA shows mixed results in enhancing Ontario communities' control over the energy systems that serve them – a reminder of the strength of the critique that questions the novelty of 'new modes' of environmental governance, which still 'operate in the shadow of the hierarchy, with background conditions of state authority, intervention, steering, and control' (Bäckstrand et al. 2010, 13).

9.5.3 Argumentative Practice and Deliberative Quality

The third aspect of the creation of novel public spheres is to do with the deliberative qualities of initiatives such as OREC. For the most part this is implicit in the practice of the organization. Amongst its peers, OREC is unusual for its open engagement with policy and politics. As one member noted, 'OREC does advocate politically probably to a greater degree than most coops do, and that's partly because we're in Ottawa, the nation's capital … We have MPs here, but also, the Ontario Minister of Energy [Bob Chiarelli], his riding was in Ottawa too, so that made him very accessible for us to communicate with' (personal interview). Not only did OREC gain visibility with sitting provincial Ministers of Energy, but it also counts another Ottawa-area politician – current federal Minister of the Environment and Climate Change, Catherine McKenna – among its members.

While the attention of influential politicians is only one indicator of successful democratic practice, OREC has embraced its advocacy and awareness mandate, and actively seeks opportunities to promote and defend its approach to RE development. In addition to readily interacting with local print, radio, and televised news media, its staff and directors have participated in policy discussions and direct advocacy at multiple levels of governing, from Ottawa City Council to the IESO to the provincial ministries of energy and environment. At the provincial level, OREC has submitted multiple briefs on community power to the energy minister; it has contributed detailed comments to the Ministry of Energy during its consultations on successive rounds of FIT procurement; and it argued strongly, if unsuccessfully, for a 1,000 MW procurement target (or 'set-aside') for community-owned power in the consultations for the province's 2013 Long-Term Energy Plan (OREC 2012, 2013). OREC members also serve as part of several standing public interest and industry groups, including the Environment and Sustainability Committee at the Ottawa Chamber of Commerce, the Net Metering Committee of the Ontario Sustainable Energy Association, and the IESO's Local Advisory Committee (OREC 2017b, 4). As windows on the policy priorities of other actors in the energy sector, these affiliations enhance the organization's public credibility and reputation while also affording it the opportunity to build coalitions of support for its own priorities.

At the local level, the cooperative has been especially active with respect to municipal RE issues and policy. For instance, in 2010, shortly after the GEGEA became law, Sustainable Ottawa (OREC's predecessor organization) had helped to found the 1,000 Solar Rooftops Network, a collection of local businesses, community organizations, academic institutions, and interested citizens. The Network 'work[ed] to engage, enlighten and enable the citizens of Ottawa to participate in the opportunities for solar power presented in the [GEGEA, and is] particularly interested in seeing communities get directly involved in the ownership of solar energy as it expands the awareness of sustainable energy issues' (Peters 2013, 2). Writing in frustration to the Minister of Energy on behalf of the Network, one board member criticized what he perceived to be the baseless rejections of most community energy projects under FIT 2. As he remarked,

The directive of the Ministry regarding the prioritization of projects that engage community members and municipalities as well as those . . . submitted to the FIT 1 program has not had the opportunity to be applied because all efforts were made to reject applications for any reason prior to the prioritization process. This has been an incredible waste of time, money, and good will in Ontario and is definitely not the way to build the world class green energy sector that is possible for [the province] . . . Unless something is done to salvage the situation . . . A large amount of goodwill will have been squandered!

(Peters 2013, 1)

Since OREC's inception, representatives from the Cooperative have also participated in many municipal forums related to energy and environmental policy, including the 'Beyond 2036' Sounding Board on revising the Official Plan and the City's consultations on its Climate Change Action Plan (Hamels and Shackleton 2014; OREC 2017b, 4). OREC has also testified before the City Council's Environment Committee and the Environmental Stewardship Advisory Committee (OREC 2014). In the latter forum, as well as in communications with Ward candidates during municipal elections, OREC has urged the City to pursue several key recommendations focused on enabling community-owned energy. While Ottawa's apparently exceptional permitting requirements for 'anti-seismic roof anchors' has been one source of concern (Hamels and Shackleton 2014), two other municipal policy proposals are notable from a deliberative perspective. First, OREC encouraged the city to leverage its position as a major building owner and sole shareholder in Energy Ottawa (Ontario's largest municipally-owned renewable power producer), to enable community investment in the city-owned utility's solar projects. Many of these were planned for installation on community complexes such as recreation and sports centres, but involved no other form of community engagement or benefit (OREC 2014). Second, OREC advocated that the City use local improvement charges (i.e. its local taxation powers) to remove barriers to capital that would otherwise prevent more homeowners from financing efficiency retrofits and residential solar projects (OREC 2014). Here again, OREC's emphasis on policies that serve its vision shows a deliberate and deliberative commitment to enabling greater individual and communal participation in the energy system.

Finally, it is possible to see a deliberative aspect in OREC's networking practices and organizational affiliations. For one, it has played an active role as part of the community of RE cooperatives in Ontario. It recently chaired the board of the Federation of Community Power Co-operatives (FCPC), an umbrella organization formed to represent and grow the provincial 'community power community' (OREC 2017b, 4). Much of the FCPC's work occurs in response to provincial policy developments (such as the consultations leading to the 2017 update to the Long-Term Energy Plan) that benefit from a coherent and coordinated voice from the RE cooperative sector. The Federation provides a single, unified voice for the sector. Further, OREC has developed a thoughtful set of organizational policies (in addition to its governing bylaws) that provide guidance on, for instance, how the organization should solicit non-member loans, or engage with other developers who propose partner projects. One of these, the Collaboration Policy, establishes firm criteria to govern OREC's decisions around working with potential partners. In particular, it requires that prospective partners must have at least two of nine favourable attributes (e.g. local ownership, non-profit status, environmental products or services, etc.). It also directs members to avoid working on OREC business with 'those using us for greenwashing purposes', those with links to political parties, and the fossil fuel and nuclear power industries (OREC 2015a).

9.6 Conclusions

OREC, and a broader movement towards pursuing RE transitions outside the traditional configuration of the electricity system dominated by large-scale generation plants and centralized distribution, represent an important part of the political landscape around climate change in Ottawa. It exemplifies the experimental character of initiatives on climate, but at the same time their structuring by multilevel forces – shifts in electricity regulation in the province, in particular, but perhaps more broadly by the private investment and property model that OREC's business model represents. Even when framed as 'energy democracy', this is expressed through individual ownership of shares and/or lending money to OREC to finance RE development, with an expectation and a guarantee of a (very solid) financial return. As with the gentrification associated with intensification projects (see Chapter 6), at one level at least OREC works within a neoliberal privatized logic that at the same time enables already relatively privileged citizens to pursue climate policy in ways that at least risk intensifying class inequalities.

For the members of OREC (and, we can imagine, for individuals belonging to other RE cooperatives), participation in a *community energy* or *community power* model has been prompted by different meanings and motivations, suggesting that the model is understood as a flexible, heterogeneous category or rallying point capable of accommodating a broad set of potentially competing visions for how RE futures might unfold. In this way, the community power model developed in Ontario and manifested in OREC can be thought of as possessing both the 'virtue' of being able to channel members' diverse (and perhaps often unstated) normative conceptions of long-term sustainability, as well as the 'vice' of potentially defusing some of the more radical political claims and social implications attached to the emerging energy democracy agenda.

But at the same time we should perhaps be cautious in dismissing the initiative. Along the lines of Connolly's (2013) argument outlined in Chapter 10, neoliberalism is only one of a number of systems in which we are enmeshed, not a single system determining everything. In particular, in this context, we should be mindful not to ascribe all of humanity's creativity and spontaneity to the entrepreneurial agents celebrated by neoliberal ideology. Organizations such as OREC mobilize citizen agency and are engaged in remaking the socio-technical systems of electricity provision in ways that are difficult to reduce solely to neoliberal dynamics, even if they express some of the logics of that form of political economy. As such, OREC's activity expresses nicely the 'purification vs. complexity' logic: OREC constitutes an intervention in a field that is critical to climate policy – the transformation of the electricity system away from fossil fuels – and in order to do so it builds partnerships with various organizations, schools, farms, and so on, in ways that reconstitute the field of electricity production. Sites that used to be only sites of electricity consumption now participate in its production, and in some cases this new source of value is also then integrated into other aspects of the operations of the building – into the curriculum for students for example. But at the same time OREC can be seen to be experimenting with novel forms of politics, articulating citizens to each other via joint ventures in RE, and constituting new sorts of publics, a new sort of demos if you like. Though it continues to express some of the logic of privatization and to operate within the broader dynamics of a neoliberal political economy, it goes well beyond mere entrepreneurialism in mobilizing citizen agency to intervene in the transition of electricity systems away from fossil fuels – a transition critical to effective climate policy. In so doing, it galvanizes the creativity of communities around projects of climate response and democratic renewal via renewables.

10

Conclusions

While I was finalizing the first draft of this book, in early 2019, the world saw an upsurge in radical protest activity over climate change. Extinction Rebellion, centred on the UK but spreading, the school strikes for climate initiated by Greta Thunberg but now occurring worldwide, the Sunrise Movement in the US, declarations of 'climate emergency' by municipalities worldwide and some national governments, and the radicalized vision of climate change (at least relative to previous incarnations) embodied in the Green New Deal (GND): All have *repoliticized* climate change in the terms I have been discussing, by bringing climate change squarely into the realm of public collective decision-making, articulating their activism as opposition to powerful forces destroying the climate, and emphasizing the conflictual qualities of climate change. This is of course against a background of recurrent activism that has similarly repoliticized climate change: At the United Nations Framework Convention on Climate Change (UNFCCC) Conferences of the Parties from the Hague in 2001 onwards; in organizations such as Plane Stupid and Climate Camp; over oil pipelines in Western Canada and elsewhere, coalmines in Australia, fracking in many places; over divestment from fossil fuels in universities and churches; and in new coalitions in international climate negotiations led by radical governments in Bolivia and Ecuador.

But even this renewed politicization of climate change is paradoxical. In one sense, Extinction Rebellion (XR) constitutes a radical challenge to political life by blocking bridges and roads, blockading the buildings of oil companies, and seeking to block up the courts and police stations through mass arrest as a deliberate strategy. But in many contexts the rhetoric of XR is anti-political: A prominent slogan used widely in coverage of recent climate protests (including XR) is of a woman (although not on an XR action but a more conventional march in Brussels) holding up a placard saying 'Climate First, Politics Second' (see e.g. PressFrom 2018). The trajectory of this rhetoric ended up in the rather absurd outcome of key XR founder Roger Hallam founding a 'Beyond Politics Party' whose website exhorts us to 'bring down the government' and 'support the revolution' (Beyond Politics Party n.d.). Presumably entailed here is the superficial account of politics alluded to in Chapter 1: The grubby struggles between self-serving politicians over the perks of political office. But nevertheless, it is paradoxical to say the least, if not simply incomprehensibly confused, to be against politics and to want to 'bring down the government'.

Students of global security will have had wry smiles about the spread of declarations of 'climate emergency'. Many of the debates over such things, at least since 9-11, have focused precisely on how such declarations seek to *de*politicize an issue in the sense of taking it outside the normal processes of democratic political decision-making and subject to 'exceptional' sorts of measures. In the post-9-11 era, this means camps such as Guantánamo or Sangatte, renditions, torture, and the like: What it entails in the climate change context is unclear. There has been a long debate about whether or not climate change is or should be 'securitized' in this way, from the Toronto Conference in 1988, which framed climate change as analogous to nuclear war in its implications, onwards, but mostly these efforts have been unsuccessful. Will climate emergency be different? It is hard to tell, but a recurrent dynamic of depoliticization as a strategy of political power is clearly being reproduced here, even if the specific purposes of the depoliticization are very different to those seeking to justify camps such as Guantánamo.

Responses to this upsurge in protest were similarly interesting in the light of the arguments I have been trying to make through this book. Regarding the XR protests, *The Guardian* reported that:

Claire Perry, the energy and climate change minister, also said that she 'got the science, motivation and passion driving climate emergency protests' but could not see that 'disrupting one of world's busiest transport systems ... blocking emergency routes and making life difficult for so many is going to *build consensus* and support for the changes we need'.

(Mason 2019, emphasis added)

Sadiq Khan, the Mayor of London, similarly argued that although he agreed with many of the aims of the protestors regarding the urgency of climate action, 'My message to all protestors today is clear: You must now let London return to business as usual' (Khan 2019). His choice of phrase of 'business as usual' brought considerable ridicule, given both the role of that phrase in debates about climate change indicating scenarios for emissions that go up as they have in the past, and that it is precisely 'business as usual' that the protestors sought to disrupt. More broadly, these responses illustrate that political elites (in the UK context, this is bi-partisan – Perry is Conservative, Khan is Labour) seek to reframe climate change as non-political in the sense of being consensual – something of common interest, where confrontational protest is likely to undermine the pursuit of that common interest. This is explicit in Perry's quote, but Khan's invocation of 'London' as a singular, socially homogenous place does much the same work to elide conflict as integral to climate change. But both also entailed a sense that climate change action and activism should still be subordinated to other issues: Khan's rhetorical device was to argue that the policing of the protests was affecting the ability to 'tackle issues like violent crime if they continue any longer' (Khan 2019).

But while Khan and Perry sought to depoliticize climate change, for reasons we can understand via the notion of cultural political economy, in order to undermine the protest activity, other responses recognized that some sort of antagonism is indeed integral to climate change. The *Financial Times'* cartoonist Ingram Pinn published a cartoon with the earth being pushed from both sides, on the top of a mound, with trucks and planes on one side belching the usual smoke, and myriad XR protestors on the other side (Pinn 2019). The title of the cartoon is 'Tipping Point', and the imagery presenting climate change as a purified struggle between two opposing forces.

But the idea of a tipping point of course also articulates climate change with the notion of complexity (presumably unconsciously so in Pinn's cartoon), discussed throughout this book. A tipping point, technically speaking, is not readily understood in simple terms of two opposing forces and the moment where the struggle tips one way or another. A tipping point arises out of the emergent causality within complex systems, it does not have simple agential causes.

10.1 System Change, Not Climate Change

This slogan has been a mainstay of climate change movements since the emergence of large-scale protests on climate change in the early 2000s. It has recurred in various incarnations of the movements, from climate justice and anti-carbon market protestors, to today's protests via XR and the school strikes. But the obvious questions then are 'what is the system?' and 'how does it, or might it, change?'

For most protestors, I suspect (although research on XR is in its infancy, see Doherty et al. 2018; Berglund and Schmidt 2020; Saunders et al. 2020; Wall 2020, chapter 6), and certainly for most left-leaning academics and writers commenting on movements that deploy the slogan, 'system' means capitalism (Bullard and Müller 2012; Kenis and Mathijs 2014; Foster 2015). As such it is understood rather differently to the meaning of system in complexity theory as it informs much scholarship on climate change, especially that invoking the notion of 'transitions' as outlined in Chapter 2.

This frame sits squarely on the pole of purification in the terms I have tried to develop in this book. Framing capitalism as *the* cause (emphasis on the singular) of climate change, where the necessary consequence is that capitalism must be transcended, abolished, ended, in order to deal with climate change, operates clearly in this way. Mann and Wainwright spell out how they see the consequences of this move very clearly and to my mind express its limits also very clearly. They frame climate politics as an insurrectionary moment. This is the character of Climate X, their preferred alternative to Climate Leviathan, Behemoth, or Mao.[1] The political moment in climate thus is limited to the heroic/tragic contestation of capital by revolutionary movements and indigenous/colonized peoples. Telling here is how they recognize that to be anti-capitalist is insufficient in relation to climate change:

Many peculiar qualities of climate change as an environmental problem – the importance of climate science for diagnosing the problem; the geographical unevenness and variation in its effects; the apparent urgency of coordinated response; the atmosphere's common pool character; and so on – can neither be explained nor overcome with an analysis limited to the dynamics of capital. Only a radical critique of capital *and* sovereignty can orient us today.

(Mann and Wainwright 2018, 170)

But nowhere here is a discussion of the complex particularities of decarbonization as a process. It is as if getting rid of capitalism (and sovereignty) is sufficient to the transformations involved by that process, so no attention needs to be paid to the political dynamics of shifting electricity systems, transport systems, buildings, urban planning, food systems, and the like: These are epiphenomena that can be reduced to the logic of capital, sovereignty, and their revolutionary antitheses. In Utah Phillips' words quoted in Chapter 2: 'The earth is not dying, it is being killed, and those who are killing it have names and addresses' (see e.g. Climate and Capitalism 2009). This even more sharply purifies climate politics to a question of the power and agency of specific individuals, powerful within a globally pervasive capitalism. As Malm (2018, 12) argues, the election of Donald Trump makes this particularly stark, dispelling 'the last lingering illusions that anything else other than organized collective militant resistance has at least a fighting chance of pushing the world anywhere else than head first, at maximum speed, into cataclysmic climate change'. Even without explicit anti-capitalist framings, it is a similar sort of purification we see in some of the literature focused on corporate power in

[1] They set up their account of different approaches to climate change in terms of an orientation to 'planetary sovereignty' and an orientation to capitalism, generating a straightforward two-by-two box with Climate Leviathan (capitalist, pro-planetary sovereignty), Climate Behemoth (anti-planetary sovereignty, pro-capitalist), Climate Mao (non-capitalist, pro-planetary sovereignty), and the enigmatically named Climate X (non-capitalist, anti-planetary sovereignty). See Mann and Wainwright (2018, 29).

climate politics discussed in Chapter 2 (e.g. Mildenberger 2020; Stokes 2020): Challenging the power of incumbent corporate actors – oil companies, electric utilities, and the like – is the principal, perhaps even sole, activity needed to pursue effective responses to climate change.

There are many ways to question this argument, but what I want to highlight is the strange abstraction (given the Marxist basis of many of these arguments) from the materiality of high carbon worlds and any plausible path to decarbonization that many such writers – perhaps most notably Swyngedouw, and Mann and Wainwright – engage in. The 'agonistic' accounts of climate change politics are similar in this regard, although they do not all share Mann and Wainwright's Marxist underpinnings. This way of thinking is for the most part rather divorced from the specificity of the 'devices and desires' associated with a high-carbon world or with shifts to a low carbon world. 'The political' is rather invoked as an abstract, general quality to be valued, and political agonism is rather devoid of material content: To McNay's (2014, 4) charge that this is 'socially weightless', we can add that it is ecologically weightless. We end up with politics as rather Manichean in quality – a struggle between forces for progress and 'the enemy'. At the same time, as Kenis and Mathijs (2014) demonstrate, the way that climate justice movements have internalized arguments about the need to oppose 'post-politics' itself, in order to open up political space for dealing with climate change, stands in tension with a desire to articulate new visions or imaginaries for the future. For at least some visions of politics as agonistic (which Kenis and Mathijs associate with Rancière), to even think about futures and alternatives is to engage in post-political activity – the political can only ever be about the present. The divestment movement serves here as an excellent example. While they have succeeded in very significant ways in repoliticizing climate change in the terms suggested here (see Mangat et al. 2018), they do so by articulating 'the fossil fuel industry', or 'the tar sands', etc., as 'the enemy'. Their pro-oil opponents respond often by a strategy that emphasizes the broad social embeddedness of energy, and often by accusing activists of hypocrisy – that because they drive, heat their homes, etc., they are compromised when they attack the oil companies (Gunster et al. 2018). While the charges of hypocrisy are of course self-serving, the point about the multidimensional nature of the incumbency of fossil energy is nevertheless surely correct, and we therefore need an account of such incumbency which is similarly multidimensional in order to be able to undo it (see e.g. Stirling 2019).

Rather, we need to think of politics-as-agonism where the material specificities of any particular intervention partially structure the qualities of the conflict around it. Barry's (2013) analysis of the politics surrounding the development of a pipeline from the Caspian Sea oilfields through to the Mediterranean is useful here. He manages to keep in play the sense of conflict and the 'big picture' issues around which that conflict is structured – geopolitical conflicts between Russia and other oil producers, the power of the oil companies involved, the local and global environmental dangers it produces – but at the same time show how various specificities, from the technical specifications of the pipe's joints to the financing arrangements in London, produce the particular sorts of conflicts and dynamics in the case. We also need to think of politics-as-agonism as everyday rather than heroic, where, in Williams (2012, 75) terms, 'we agonise over ordinary matters, including ... whether or not to venture out in bad weather unprotected by a raincoat, to engage others' passion for trains, or to continue with a panel process that challenges one's own beliefs'. Keeping these two elements in play is a useful corrective to the more abstract, 'socially weightless' notion of agonism from Mouffe. My intention at least has been to show in similar ways that the contestations over climate change in Ottawa have often involved the intertwining of 'macro' conflicts – 'developers vs. community' in the intensification case (Chapter 6), the 'keep the oil in the soil' rhetoric of divestment campaigners in the University of Ottawa (Chapter 8), for example, with agonizing over ordinary matters such as the detailed technicalities of the heights of buildings (Chapter 6), the design of heating systems (Chapter 8), the experience of time (Chapter 5), or the building of cooperative arrangements for renewable energy development (Chapter 9).

These cases also show that the 'us–them' agonistic politics needs to be understood as intertwined with a politics of subjectivity where it is precisely our ambivalence over the devices and practices of daily life that are the site of conflict. The debates over intensification (Chapter 6) showed this most strikingly, but it can also be seen in the broad history of the city's climate policy (Chapter 3), which can be read as a story where city councillors periodically announce their desire for a strong response to climate change by getting the city's emissions under control, but this is almost always heavily compromised when it comes to the shaping of the specific practices (mobility, housing, planning, and development) that are entailed by enacting such a desire.

This tension between desire and achievement is often understood as a question of hypocrisy. However, in media debates about 'climate hypocrisy', one of the interesting forms of that discussion is how it is used by people to open up conversations about their daily lives and the dilemmas produced by being embedded in high-carbon systems while seeking to contest them (Gunster et al. 2018). Connolly expresses this problem of the ambivalence entailed nicely:

Enhanced sensitivity to what is most fragile about ourselves and our place on the planet does not go smoothly with militancy. The combination may seem like carefully laying a mirror down on the ground and then trampling on it as you ride a horse into battle.

(Connolly 2013, 10)

Connolly's account of climate change in *Facing the Planetary* (2017, see also 2019) is couched fundamentally in what he calls 'entangled humanism' – a deep intertwining of human action with biological, geological, technological systems, or 'force fields' as he prefers. Nevertheless, his account of political action on climate change, which is rather similar to that of Mann and Wainwright in terms of being resolutely a strategic account – politics as a struggle of social forces for progressive futures – struggles to articulate this activist-oriented account with his various 'entanglements'. He focuses on a 'politics of swarming' – of generating myriad sorts of political interventions in different sites to build movements and momentum for transformative change, and a 'cross-regional general strike'. Both of these are thus oppositional and miss the sorts of politics of 'accomplishing' climate change governance, as in Bulkeley's (2016) account sketched in Chapter 2. This is in part perhaps because his accounts of the 'force fields' within which humanity is entangled are focused on questions of geology and biology and designed to disrupt 'human exceptionalism' or 'sociocentrism' by showing how for example the ocean conveyor belt, methane releases, or ocean acidification are means by which we have to face a world where even if we act 'successfully', there are a range of dynamics, both intrinsic to those planetary systems/forces, and unleashed by anthropogenic carbon emissions, that exceed our ability to control. But the socio-technical systems within which high carbon worlds are sustained and may be being disrupted can similarly be understood in his terms as force fields. There are hints, as in his discussion of Gandhi (Connolly 2017, 132) in relation to the notion of the general strike, where he emphasizes the way Gandhi wanted all Congress activists to spin once a day and to buy from local spinners. We get a sense from this of the rooting of political activism in daily material practices connected to a normative account of society. Connolly doesn't make a lot of this but could certainly articulate the swarming politics through connectedness to material practices (cycling, guerrilla or community gardening, etc.).

Nevertheless, Connolly's account is radically different in terms of his account of capitalism, compared to Swyngedouw, or Mann and Wainwright, in particular. Neoliberalism plays an important part of his analysis, as a specific form of capitalism, but capitalism is framed as simply one of many force fields within which human action occurs. And as a consequence, the sense of a single insurrectionary moment that can lead to a radically alternative society (Climate X, eco-socialism, degrowth, etc.) is refused, in favour of a more open-ended activism without knowing where it might end up: 'Today it is wise to scale back utopian images of human perfection while simultaneously upping the ante of militancy against extractive capitalism and the world order it promulgates' (Connolly 2017, 122).

Overall then, I have tried to argue that we need to understand the importance both of an overt agonistic, often directly confrontational, politics of climate change, and a subtler, messier, politics that works on the problem of shifting the enormously complex high carbon socio-technical system towards a low or zero carbon one. Each has its own logics that often appear to their participants or protagonists as opposed. In the University of Ottawa divestment campaigns, the campaigners saw the patient work of university engineers as minor tinkering where what was needed was to confront the fossil fuel companies, while many university managers saw divestment as a distraction from their focus on solving the problem via its intensive programme of energy management on campus. But it seems to me there is a necessary dynamic between the two – the confrontational activism of climate activists, while it will almost by definition never directly reduce carbon emissions, can radically change the conditions within which those operating in a variety of other political arenas operate, and might even change the character of those arenas and who gets to participate in them, as in the emergence of national climate assemblies, arising in part out of XR activists making claims for such institutions to be established (Howarth et al. 2020).

10.2 Beyond Ottawa

I have of course relied on what might seem to many as a rather specific, perhaps even idiosyncratic, site to explore and develop this set of arguments. There are two responses to this charge. One is to reiterate the point made in Chapter 1, and following many scholars of urban climate politics, that this is a scale where we can pick apart the forces that determine GHG emissions and therefore the political dynamics of trying to get rid of those emissions. This makes it easier to see the source of conflicts over climate change, which may be more obscure when we get to national or global scales, and perhaps why recent works emphasizing political conflict and interest group politics over climate change largely neglect these cultural dynamics (e.g. Mildenberger 2020; Stokes 2020). It is also the case, as Robinson (2006) argues, that all cities are 'ordinary', in the sense of having many core similarities across the world, despite their diversity. So I do hope that wherever in the world the reader find themselves, they will recognize initiatives, dilemmas, struggles, forces, and processes in the stories about Ottawa I have told, that are similar to those they see around them in their setting. But second, these forces are nevertheless the key drivers of political, and therefore policy, developments at those other scales, and that the dynamics of purification and complexity, and de- and repoliticization, play out there also. It is worth illustrating briefly these dynamics operating elsewhere in climate policy and politics, but the literature underscoring the empirical dynamics sketched here is vast.

The cultural political economy drivers of climate politics are not that difficult to find. Policies and strategies across the world have been shaped by the need to enable capital accumulation to continue. Governments and the experts who advise them both obsess about the GDP impacts of any policy they may wish to introduce, and are highly attentive to the interests of, and pressure from, key industries. This explains both the concerted opposition to those whose business model depends on continued fossil fuel exploitation and the ways that governments seeking low carbon transitions have done so. In the former, we have the strategies of large corporations, led by coal and oil but often joined by electricity producers, car manufacturers, and carbon-intensive industries such as steel and cement producers, to slow down UN negotiations, undermine efforts at national and subnational levels to promote renewable energy, and secure continued policy support for fossil fuels.[2] We see this most obviously and importantly in the recurrent success in shaping climate policy in the US, but also in other countries, notably Canada and Australia, and of course the oil-exporting Gulf States. But we also see its effects across many countries – subsidies to fossil fuel exploration and use continue in many countries, including those that otherwise have relatively advanced climate policies such as Germany or the UK. At local levels, we see it in business organization against restricting car use, in favour of sprawl, among other things, just as we saw in relation to Ottawa.

But low carbon strategies have also revolved around generating new sorts of business activity around which accumulation can be organized. In some instances, this entails entirely new commodities and markets – in the markets in carbon emissions generated by emissions trading systems and carbon offset schemes. These now cover around 13 per cent of global GHG emissions according to the World Bank.[3] But even without this sort of policy and economic innovation, policies to promote renewable energy have been shaped around generating patterns of investment and growth. There are multiple accumulation logics within the global development of renewable energy, notably those centred on IP development and the monopoly profits provided by patents, classic Fordist ones centred on low cost mass production of solar pV units, and those centred around the installation of solar and wind and the resulting sale of electricity into grids (Lachapelle et al. 2017). In other arenas, policy has focused on channelling investment into, among other things, new public transport infrastructure, building retrofits, smart grid technologies, electric vehicle charging infrastructure and battery technologies, new manufacturing processes for low or zero carbon steel or cement, 'climate smart agriculture', and the like. Private sector investors have at the same time had

---

[2] The literature demonstrating this is enormous. For a selection, see Newell and Paterson (1998), Newell (2000), Pinkse and Kolk (2009), Wright and Nyberg (2015), Mildenberger (2020) and Stokes (2020).

[3] See www.worldbank.org/en/programs/pricing-carbon, accessed 10 June 2019. This figure includes both carbon market and carbon taxes as ways to 'price' carbon. However, carbon markets provide the great majority of these systems in terms of coverage.

ongoing internal conversations about how climate change affects their activities and business models, from worries about extreme weather events by insurers, to attempting to use their investor power to shape corporate strategies on climate, to worrying about their 'stranded assets' if governments succeed (as they have not yet of course) in getting global emissions on a downward path. The design of these policies and strategies of course reflect locally-specific struggles and political imagination, but nevertheless the logic that holds them together is that they all seek to promote new sorts of economic activity. Implicitly at least, this is because of the systemic imperatives of capitalism, combined with the fact that any low carbon transition will entail shaking out large sectors of the existing global economy and 'stranding' their assets, and precisely why we see so much resistance, as for example Stokes (2020) shows in great detail for why electric utilities resist abandoning coal plants in the US, to prevent such assets being stranded, in processes reminiscent of Malm's demonstration of the specifically capitalist dynamics that triggered the shift from water to coal in the nineteenth century. This is also why perhaps the most recent framing amongst climate activists on the left has been that of the GND (e.g. Klein 2020) – a strategy specifically to generate new forms of investment, employment, and growth, allied to egalitarian political strategies, in order to build coalitions in favour of climate policy understood as a transformational logic. But as Klein also understands, as such it contains a series of its own contradictions: Invoking the original New Deal means that it can become something focused on infrastructure development in ways that could undermine a zero carbon future.

But these political economy dynamics are always at the same time cultural. The defence of fossil fuels has frequently been couched in terms of established ways of life, identities, and practices that have come to have deep value for many. From 'the American way of life is not negotiable' in 1992 (George W. H. Bush, as quoted in Vidal 2012), to 'the government wants to take away my SUV' as a campaign slogan against the Kyoto Protocol (Schneider 2002), to Australian Prime Minister Scott Morrison bringing a lump of coal into the House of Representatives to underscore his commitment to fossil fuels (Murphy 2017), symbolic politics of specific cultural attachments, intertwined with political economy questions of supporting specific incumbent industries, has very much been used to oppose action on climate change. These are widespread and if anything becoming more extreme in current right-wing populist orientations to climate change (e.g. Fraune and Knodt 2018). Daggett (2018) shows how many of the orientations of US right-wing populists are embedded in forms of masculinity that are more about climate refusal than climate denial – celebrating forms of fossil fuel culture through activities such as coal-rolling. Our 'three minutes more' example in Chapter 5 is more modest, but nevertheless contains a micro-level version of the same narrative as George Bush's claim. And it would be unwise to dismiss these as mere rhetorical flourishes or cheap gimmicks. As with the analysis in preceding chapters, such questions (the height of buildings, how long a journey car drivers might have to take, and so on) can often intrude powerfully into political deliberations over low carbon initiatives, and reflect deeply embedded normative visions of the good life.

Conversely, many seek to use cultural politics to attempt to accelerate low carbon transitions or otherwise intervene in climate politics (Bulkeley et al. 2016). Carbon markets have operated through the cultivation of an emotional enthusiasm for marrying financial innovation with normative purpose (Descheneau and Paterson 2011), similar to the dynamics we saw in relation to carbon accounting (Chapter 4). Technical interventions such as smart grids, solar pV, and electric vehicles (and not just cars - think of the recent take-off of electric bicycles in many places) often seek to mobilize a desire for novelty and gadgetry (e.g. Caprotti 2012), even while they produce novel cultural problems such as 'range anxiety' (Kester 2019). Other interventions seek to directly generate new subjectivities that articulate low carbon lives in varying ways – carbon footprinting, carbon dieting, personal carbon allowances, and so on (Paterson and Stripple 2010). More broadly, many climate imaginaries have focused on generating enthusiasm for imagining the social improvements entailed in a low or zero carbon world, from healthier food, to walkable cities, to clean air, and so on, just as we saw in Ottawa the struggles over intensification (Chapter 6) were often about competing imaginaries of the 'good city'. Witness for example the widely shared video written by Alexandria Ocasio-Cortez and Avi Lewis, and voiced by Ocasio-Cortez, on the US GND, which spoke from the point of view of a future where the GND had succeeded and narrated the process by which it was achieved, including notably the political fights involved (Ocasio-Cortez and Lewis 2019).

Attempts to depoliticize climate change, with corresponding repoliticizing reactions, are also omnipresent. The Kyoto Protocol's flexibility mechanisms – emissions trading, joint implementation, and the Clean Development Mechanism – have as one of their origins (they had multiple of course), the effort to detach questions about where emissions would be reduced, who would pay for that effort, and who would be seen to 'share the burden', from the actual political bargaining over the targets countries would take on. The market would be used as a depoliticizing mechanism. Indeed in the first proposal for emissions trading at the global level (Grubb 1989) this was explicit: One of his key arguments was that political bargaining over the targets each country might take on would be too complex or intractable that a market mechanism was necessary both to lower the overall costs of reducing emissions and to detach the question of the financial costs (who would pay) from that of the distribution of emissions reductions.

Climate has also been routinely framed as a question of technological innovation and breakthrough. While this can of course be defended as an argument in various ways, and there are certainly a number of aspects of decarbonization where it is still very unclear how the world will 'solve' the technical problems (flying most obviously, and the fantasy world of negative emissions technologies, but also a number of smaller but important questions about cement and steel manufacture, battery technologies, or methane from ruminant animals, for example). But the technofix strategy has also had an important depoliticizing dynamic: An attempt to reframe climate change in ways that avoid the apparent need for various changes in social practices with what most assume is a toxic political dynamic that would result ('the American way of life is not negotiable'). Electric vehicles to avoid having to shift to cycling, walking, and public transport, and reshaping cities to enable this, as we have seen in Ottawa. Changing cows' diets so we don't have to stop eating beef. As I argued of course in Chapter 1, this dichotomy of behaviour vs. technology makes very little sense as an account of social processes and social change, but it is a powerful rhetorical device to attempt to elide the real political conflicts involved in climate change.

Depoliticization can also be seen in the managerial strategies of governments. Perhaps the most elaborate of these is contained in the Climate Change Act 2007 in the UK, and the system it has created of rolling five-year carbon budgets, the Climate Change Committee as an arms-length agency both to advise the government on strategies for improving policy but also playing an auditing role in reporting on whether the government is on track, and a whole raft of more department-specific processes of implementation (e.g. Fankhauser et al. 2018). This institutional apparatus has as one of its features precisely to express a bi-partisan logic within the explicit political processes: That all political parties are committed to climate action and thus can outsource the real debates about how to get there to experts, with the parties competing solely on who is best placed to actually achieve decarbonization. Again, as in the account of the University of Ottawa I gave, a case can certainly be made (as Fankhauser et al. 2018 largely do) that this approach has in many ways been highly successful: Despite wavering commitment in the government to climate action since at least the Conservative's election as a single-party government in 2015, if not before, the institutional architecture is still in place and UK climate policy remains in that paradoxical situation as being simultaneously one of the strongest in the world and nevertheless far from adequate. Its depoliticization via this deep institutional 'mainstreaming' is part of the reason for this.

But this interpretation is deeply contested on two grounds (see variously Lockwood 2013; Kuzemko 2016; Gillard 2016). One is that the depoliticization has in many ways limited innovation in climate policy, precisely by insulating the decision-making process from a range of ideas and actors. This is resonant of Dryzek et al.'s (2003) argument about the importance of the State not crowding out all space for innovation and opposition by environmental NGOs: Green states are best served by a lively NGO / social movement sphere through which new ideas are generated but can get access to government if they push effectively. The other however is that it has failed in the end to succeed in depoliticizing climate change, in both the sense that partisan conflicts within parliament have produced shocks to the system which it was supposed to be insulated from, and that its various limits and weaknesses have caused eruptions of more confrontational politics over time, in similar ways as outlined by Barry (2002), as I discussed in Chapter 2. For example, one of the features of the carbon budgeting logic was to think over a relatively short time frame, and during the mid-2000s one of the decisions within this was to shift incentives to get more people to buy diesel vehicles, because of their greater fuel efficiency and thus lower carbon emissions than gasoline cars. A decade later, this generated a crisis in urban air quality in London in particular, which caused political eruptions and backlash. More broadly, we could usefully adapt Mouffe here to argue that the political eruptions of school strikes and XR are part of a repoliticizing dynamic that is a response to the limits of a consensual, depoliticized process.

In the discussion in Section 10.1 of purification amongst some recent literature on climate politics, I argued that they purify it to a political struggle, often centred on (anti)capitalism. This is not, however, the only way climate change is purified, simplified down to a singular logic at the expense of attention to its messy complexities. As discussed in Chapter 2, more common purifications in climate politics operate around technology, prices, and population. At times, they are about heroic individual agency ('Elon Musk will save us') along the lines generated (somewhat ironically perhaps) by Carbon 613 with their carbon accounting superhero (Chapter 4). The claim by many (not all) economists regarding the power of carbon pricing to generate a successful response to climate change has this characteristic even more obviously. The singular focus on technological breakthroughs, often even on a single magic bullet technology, has a similar logic. The key difference however between these and anti-capitalist purifications are that these of course purify by depoliticizing, while the anti-capitalist arguments are purifying while repoliticizing.

10.3 In Search of Climate Politics

If you read this book sceptical about whether climate change should be understood as a political problem, then I hope to have persuaded you that it is intrinsically so. But more than that, or if you already accepted this underlying premise, then I hope to have shown that we need to understand the plural qualities of politics as a concept and phenomenon – as sites or arenas of collective decision-making, as the question of power and authority, and as an intrinsically conflictual process – in order to make sense of climate change's politics. I also hope to have shown that climate politics has two recurring dynamics.

The dynamic between de- and re-politicization arises out of the tensions between the different aspects of politics itself: The strategies of those exerting authority seeking to take decision-making out of deliberative arenas, for example. Even with what appear to be explicit repoliticizations of climate change, existing political actors can be routinely expected to try to tame them. The GND is a case in point: It is not difficult to see how it becomes understood in the technocratic language of infrastructure funding, shifting tax systems, and so on, and abstracted from the sorts of political mobilization that have made it possible. As Klein (2020, 259–72) argues, it is sustained movement mobilization that will make the GND 'work' to achieve its radical potential. The dynamic between purification and complexity arises out of the qualities of politics with the specificities of climate change: The political desire to reduce conflict to simple stories, to render climate change both manageable politically and/or to motivate activists to keep up the pressure on decision-makers, colliding with the character of the hugely complex socio-technical systems through which GHG emissions are organized and mobilized, which resist being purified into single logics of pricing, technology, or capital.

With both of these dynamics, I have argued that it is not about choosing one side, but rather recognizing that both are necessary moments in the life of climate politics, expressing necessary aspects of thinking and acting on climate change politically. And underlying these, I have shown that the substantive driving forces of many of these dynamics have been conflicts over the pursuit of capital accumulation and the cultural questions of subjectivity that are integral to the practices of daily life through which such accumulation is pursued and contested.

This matters because politics will continue to intrude into humanity's ongoing efforts to address climate change, whether or not people wish it would go away. Understanding its dynamics is important to recognizing the limits of managerial projects focused on tracking carbon emissions, introducing carbon pricing, developing this or that technology, building new forms of infrastructure, designing a new international agreement, and so on. Each of these both express a particular logic of purification vs. complexity, de- and re-politicization, and cultural political economy. And each will generate specific reactions that will be expressed politically and disrupt the ability to roll out the particular intervention smoothly. These will have various specific triggers, from reactions by powerful industries, to conflicts over distributional impacts and thus questions of justice, to disruptions to daily life and practices, to the aesthetics of urban design. My approach clearly doesn't generate much by way of specific predictions, prognoses, or prescriptions, beyond the general arguments about the types of drivers of political conflicts over climate change, and to pay attention to the specifics as they unfold – to recognize that 'three minutes' of commute time, or the height of buildings, might really matter in climate politics.

It also matters in that, as I said I assumed in Chapter 1, but have not talked about throughout the book, the temporal constraints of dealing with climate change are becoming ever more acute. Invocations of 'climate emergency', with the logic of 'twelve years' (by the time you read this, more like eight) to get emissions solidly on a rapid downward path, express this very effectively. The politics of this could of course get very nasty. Emergencies are most commonly invoked to generate reactionary authoritarian politics, not emancipatory democratic ones. But the politics of societal collapse is also usually nasty. Perhaps the COVID-19 crisis will help avoid such possible collapse into authoritarian dynamics – showing that radical ruptures are possible, and can even generate broad public support. Indeed the COVID-19 crisis can be seen as opening up new possibilities, because variously: It showed a glimpse of a world with drastically lower carbon emissions; it disrupted daily practices at various scales, perhaps enabling more basic switches to occur from high carbon to low carbon ones in key areas (transport, food systems, most obviously); it prompted an inevitable question about how to pursue 'economic recovery', which in the context became immediately a set of high carbon (more roads, bailout the airlines, oil industry, relax regulations, and so on) or low carbon (embrace expanded cycle lanes, pursue local food security, embrace the 'care economy', recover through 'green jobs' in energy efficiency, electrification, and so on); and perhaps most palpably, showed that the idea of such a radical social disruption is 'unrealistic' is a lie that should 'never again … be given a hearing' (Malm 2020, 27). But as I am finalizing this book (September 2020), we have only faint glimmers of whether COVID-19 will be such a switch point, opening up space in this way.

Whatever the effects of COVID-19 on climate political dynamics, it seems to me indeed increasingly important to keep attention squarely on climate's politics in order to keep up pressure for rapid decarbonization, while the temporal nature of the crisis means that climate impacts will get progressively more severe. For example, how progressive, often anti-capitalist movements arguing for 'system change' manage to articulate that transformational vision with the messy complexity of decarbonizing is important to making the latter avoid becoming simply a new form of technocratic climate governance. Such technocratic governance would be likely to result in highly unequal outcomes and at the same time generate a reactionary authoritarian backlash. This would be a backlash that would either shore up the high carbon world and/or repress rebellions that contest the unequal impacts of such a form of decarbonization, such as the *gilets jaunes* in France. Conversely, how those developing governmental means of institutionalizing climate change as in the UK Climate Change Act manage to navigate the tension between thoroughly institutionalizing low carbon transitions (which inevitably depoliticizes), while leaving open sufficient political space for new ideas, expression of dissent, and so on, will be important to meaning that the repoliticization of climate change doesn't occur in ways that undermine action on climate *per se*, through climate denial or 'climate refusal'. What we can learn from these stories about Ottawa is that it is important that dissent is expressed as divestment activism, struggles to make cooperative renewable energy ownership less the preserve of the rich, and to create vibrant walkable and cyclable neighbourhoods in cities, rather than simply minimizing the commute time for car drivers or protecting the current 'character of the neighbourhood' against all forms of change. For those pushing for climate action, to recognize the intrinsically political qualities of that action is the starting point for shaping the politics in these positive ways.

References

Adam, Mohammed. 2012. Groups Slam Call for Bike Helmets; Cycling Advocates Say They Don't Help. *Ottawa Citizen*, 19 June, p. C1.

Agarwal, Anil, and Sunita Narain. 1991. *Global Warming in an Unequal World: A Case of Environmental Colonialism*. New Delhi: Centre for Science and the Environment.

Ala-Mantila, Sanna, Jukka Heinone, and Seppo Junnila. 2013. Greenhouse Gas Implications of Urban Sprawl in the Helsinki Metropolitan Area. *Sustainability* 5(10): 4461–78.

Andonova, Liliana, Michele Betsill, and Harriet Bulkeley. 2009. Transnational Climate Governance. *Global Environmental Politics* 9(2): 52–73.

Andrew, Caroline. 2007. Trying to Be World-Class: Ottawa and the Presentation of Self. In Timothy A. Gibson, and Mark Douglas Lowes, eds., *Urban Communication: Production, Text, Context*. Lanham, MD: Rowman & Littlefield, 127–40.

Angel, James. 2016. *Strategies of Energy Democracy*. Brussels: Rosa-Luxemburg-Stiftung.

Bäckstrand, Karin, Jamil Khan, Annica Kronsell, and Eva Lövbrand. 2010. The Promise of New Modes of Environmental Governance. In Karin Bäckstrand, Jamil Khan, Annica Kronsell, and Eva Lövbrand, eds., *Environmental Politics and Deliberative Democracy: Examining the Promise of New Modes of Governance*, Cheltenham, UK: Edward Elgar, 3–28.

Barry, Andrew. 2002. The Anti-Political Economy. *Economy and Society* 31(2): 268–84.
2013. *Material Politics: Disputes along the Pipeline*. Chichester: Wiley-Blackwell.

Bart, István László. 2010. Urban Sprawl and Climate Change: A Statistical Exploration of Cause and Effect, with Policy Options for the EU. *Land Use Policy* 27(2): 283–92.

Beer, M. 2018. Mayor Watson, Stop Turning Your Back on Climate Leadership. *Ottawa Citizen*, 5 January. Retrieved from: https://ottawacitizen.com/opinion/columnists/beer-mayor-watson-stop-turning-your-back-on-climate-leadership

Berglund, Oscar, and Daniel Schmidt. 2020. *Extinction Rebellion and Climate Change Activism: Breaking the Law to Change the World*. London: Palgrave.

Berman, Marshall. 1982. *All That Is Solid Melts into Air: The Experience of Modernity*. London: Verso.

Bernstein, Liz, and Mathieu Fleury. 2013. Streets That Work for Everyone. *Ottawa Citizen*, 5 October, p. B7.

Bernstein, Steven, and Matthew Hoffmann. 2018. The Politics of Decarbonization and the Catalytic Impact of Subnational Climate Experiments. *Policy Sciences* 51(2): 189–211.

Best, Jacqueline, and Matthew Paterson, eds. 2010. *Cultural Political Economy*. London: Routledge.

Beyond Politics Party. n.d. *Burning Pink*. https://burningpink.org/

Blythe, Jessica, Jennifer Silver, Louisa Evans, Derek Armitage, Nathan J. Bennett, Michele-Lee Moore, Tiffany H. Morrison, and Katrina Brown. 2018. The Dark Side of Transformation: Latent Risks in Contemporary Sustainability Discourse. *Antipode* 50(5): 1206–23.

Borgatti, Steve, Martin Everett, and Lin Freeman. 2002. *Ucinet for Windows: Software for Social Network Analysis*. Harvard, MA: Analytic Technologies.

Bouteligier, Sofie. 2012. *Cities, Networks, and Global Environmental Governance: Spaces of Innovation, Places of Leadership*. London: Routledge.

Boyle, Stewart, and John Ardill. 1989. *The Greenhouse Effect: A Practical Guide to the World's Changing Climate*. London: Hodder & Stoughton.

Brady, Sheila. 2014a. At the Heart of Main Street; Developers, Community Work Together to Create a Village Vision for Historic Oblate Lands. *Ottawa Citizen*, 22 November, p. G1.

2014b. The Fight for Height; Finding a Balance between the Needs of Community, City and Developer When It Comes to Intensification Is Not Easy. *Ottawa Citizen*, 14 June, p. G1.

Bratman, Eve, Kate Brunette, Deirdre C. Shelly, and Simon Nicholson. 2016. Justice Is the Goal: Divestment as Climate Change Resistance. *Journal of Environmental Studies and Sciences* 6(4): 677–90.

Breetz, Hanna, Matto Mildenberger, and Leah Stokes. 2018. The Political Logics of Clean Energy Transitions. *Business and Politics* 20(4): 492–522.

Buckingham, Susan, and Virginie Le Masson, eds. 2017. *Understanding Climate Change through Gender Relations*. London: Routledge.

Bulkeley, Harriet. 2013. *Cities and Climate Change*. London: Routledge.

2016. *Accomplishing Climate Governance*. Cambridge: Cambridge University Press.

2019. Navigating Climate's Human Geographies: Exploring the Whereabouts of Climate Politics. *Dialogues in Human Geography* 9(1): 3–17.

Bulkeley, Harriet, Liliana Andonova, Michele Betsill, Daniel Compagnon, Thomas Hale, Matthew Hoffmann, Peter Newell, Matthew Paterson, Charles Roger, and Stacy VanDeveer. 2014. *Transnational Climate Change Governance*. Cambridge: Cambridge University Press.

Bulkeley, Harriet, and Michele Betsill. 2003. *Cities and Climate Change: Urban Sustainability and Global Environmental Governance*. London: Routledge.

Bulkeley, Harriet, and Vanesa Castán Broto. 2013. Government by Experiment? Global Cities and the Governing of Climate Change. *Transactions of the Institute of British Geographers* 38(3): 361–75.

Bulkeley, Harriet, Vanesa Castán Broto, and Gareth Edwards. 2015. *An Urban Politics of Climate Change: Experimentation and the Governing of Socio-Technical Transitions*. London: Routledge.

Bulkeley, Harriet, Vanesa Castán Broto, Mike Hodson, and Simon Marvin. 2010. *Cities and Low Carbon Transitions*. London: Routledge.

Bulkeley, Harriet, Matthew Paterson, and Johannes Stripple. 2016. *Towards a Cultural Politics of Climate Change: Devices, Desires and Dissent*. Cambridge: Cambridge University Press.

Bullard, Nicola, and Tadzio Müller. 2012. Beyond the 'Green Economy': System Change, Not Climate Change? *Development* 55(1): 54–62.

Burke, Matthew J., and Jennie C. Stephens. 2018. Political Power and Renewable Energy Futures: A Critical Review. *Energy Research & Social Science*, Energy and the Future, 35(January): 78–93.

Campbell, Scott. 1996. Green Cities, Growing Cities, Just Cities?: Urban Planning and the Contradictions of Sustainable Development. *Journal of the American Planning Association* 62(3): 296–312.

Caprotti, Federico. 2012. The Cultural Economy of Cleantech: Environmental Discourse and the Emergence of a New Technology Sector. *Transactions of the Institute of British Geographers* 37(3): 370–85.

Carbon 613. 2016. *Sustainability Report 2016*. Ottawa: Carbon 613/Envirocentre.

   n.d. a. Carbon613 – Supporters. Retrieved from https://carbon613.ca/supporters/.

   n.d. b. Carbon613 – Membership. Retrieved from https://carbon613.ca/membership/.

Carleton University. 2018. Sustainability Energy Master Plan 2018. Retrieved from https://carleton.ca/fmp/wp-content/uploads/Sustainability-Energy-Master-Plan-2018-21.pdf.

Carr, Davis. 2017. Carbon 613 Celebrates Their Second Year on June 6th; Members Announce First Targets to Reduce Their Carbon Emissions. *EnviroCentre*. Retrieved from www.envirocentre.ca/carbon-613-second-evening-of-recognition/.

Castán Broto, Vanesa, and Harriet Bulkeley. 2013. A Survey of Urban Climate Change Experiments in 100 Cities. *Global Environmental Change* 23(1): 92–102.

Chernushenko, David. 2013. A Main Street for Everyone. *Ottawa Citizen*, 24 June, p. A1.

Chianello, Joanne. 2013. Get Set for the Battle on Main Street; Urban–Suburban Tiff Seems All but Inevitable. *Ottawa Citizen*, 11 June, p. C1.

   2014a. Infill Rules Not Easily Met by All; Conformity Can Be Challenging. *Ottawa Citizen*, 20 March, p. C1.

   2014b. Watson Likely Looking toward Next Election. *Ottawa Citizen*, 27 March, p. C1.

   2016. Ottawa Councillors Unrattled by Ban on Corporate Campaign Contributions. *CBC News online*, 5 July. Retrieved from www.cbc.ca/news/canada/ottawa/ottawa-council lor-corporate-campaign-funding-ban-1.3638660.

   2017. Critics Pan City's 'Inadequate' Environment Budget. CBC News. Retrieved from www.cbc.ca/news/canada/ottawa/environment-committee-2018-budget-energy-evo lution-1.4412022.

Ciplet, David, J. Timmons Roberts, and Mizan R. Khan. 2015. *Power in a Warming World: The New Global Politics of Climate Change and the Remaking of Environmental Inequality*. Cambridge, MA: MIT Press.

City of Ottawa. 1990a. Reduction of CO_2 Emissions. City of Ottawa Archives, Ottawa, Ontario, pp. 143–47.

   1990b. Environment As a Corporate Priority for 1991. Minutes of the City Council Meeting, 13 December, pp. 28–33.

   1992a. Reduction of Carbon Dioxide (CO2) Emissions. Ottawa City Council Minutes, 2 July. City of Ottawa Archives, Ottawa, Ontario, pp. 415–20.

   1992b. Reduction of Carbon Dioxide (CO2) Emissions. Ottawa City Council Minutes, 5 August. City of Ottawa Archives, Ottawa, Ontario, pp. 158–63.

   1994a. Taskforce on the Atmosphere Demonstration Report. Ottawa City Council Meeting Minutes, 29 June. Ottawa, pp. 113–16.

   1994b. Taskforce on the Atmosphere Demonstration Report. Ottawa City Council Meeting Minutes, 29 June. Ottawa. Supporting documentation, pp. 5–7.

   1995a. Opportunities for Energy Efficiency: A Call to Action. City of Ottawa Council Minutes, 4 October. Background Document 2. Ottawa, Ontario, pp. 63–131.

1995b. Environment – City of Ottawa Task Force on the Atmosphere Action Plan: Opportunities for Energy Efficiency: A Call to Action. City of Ottawa Council Minutes, 4 October. Ottawa, Ontario, pp. 53–61.

1996. City of Ottawa's Corporate Plan for Greenhouse Gas Reduction: First Annual Progress Report. Ottawa, Ontario.

1997. Corporate Plan for Greenhouse Gas Reduction: Second Annual Progress Report. Environmental Management Branch, Department of Engineering and Works, Ottawa.

1998. Greenhouse Gas Reduction Action Plan: Second Annual Progress Report. City of Ottawa Council Minutes, 6 May 1998, pp. 160–96.

1999. Third Annual Progress Report towards the City's 20% Greenhouse Gas Reduction Target. Department of Urban Planning and Public Works, Ottawa.

2000. Community Greenhouse Gas Reduction Action Plan: Third Annual Progress Report. ACS2000-PW-ENV-0001, Ottawa.

2003. Environmental Strategy for the City of Ottawa. Ottawa.

2004. Air Quality and Climate Change Management Plan. Ottawa, Ontario. Retrieved from http://ottawa.ca/cs/groups/content/@webottawa/documents/pdf/mdaw/mdc4/~edisp/cap078824.pdf

2009. Update – Choosing Our Future: an Integrated Approach to Building a Sustainable and Resilient National Capital Region. Report to Planning and Environment Committee, 20 April.

2011a. *Old Ottawa East Community Design Plan*. Ottawa: City of Ottawa, Planning and Growth Management Department.

2011b. *2011 Sustainability Baseline. Choosing our Future: 2011 Report on Sustainability.* Ottawa: City of Ottawa.

2013a. Transportation Master Plan. Ottawa. Retrieved from http://ottawa.ca/en/city-hall/planning-and-development/official-plan-and-master-plans/transportation-master-plan.

2013b. Main Street Renewal Project (Echo Drive to McIlraith Bridge), Environmental Assessment Study Recommendation. Report to Transportation Committee, 25 June. Ottawa.

2013c. GHG Roundtable: A Discussion Primer, March. Ottawa.

2014a. Ottawa's First Complete Street, Churchill Avenue, Opens Early and On Budget. City of Ottawa Press Release, 3 November.

2014b. 2014 Election Results. Retrieved from https://ottawa.ca/election/index_en.html

2014c. Main Street Renewal Project (Echo Drive to McIlraith Bridge), Environmental Assessment Study Recommendation. Transportation Committee Minutes, 5 July. Ottawa.

2014d. Air Quality and Climate Change Management Plan. Ottawa, Ontario. Retrieved from http://ottawa.ca/en/city-hall/planning-and-development/official-plan-and-master-plans/air-quality-and-climate-change.

2016. Ottawa's Population, 19 December. Retrieved from https://ottawa.ca/en/city-hall/get-know-your-city/statistics-and-economic-profile/statistics/ottawas-population.

2017. *Energy Evolution: Ottawa's Community Energy Transition Strategy – Phase 1.* Ottawa: City of Ottawa Planning, Infrastructure and Economic Development.

n.d. Community Design Plans. Retrieved from http://ottawa.ca/en/city-hall/planning-and-development/community-plans-and-design-guidelines/community-plans-and-0#what.

City of Ottawa Environment Committee. 2016. Document 3: Renewable Energy Strategy Update, 8 February 2016.

City of Toronto. 1989. *The Changing Atmosphere: A Call To Action*. Toronto: City of Toronto, Special Advisory Committee on the Environment, Report No. 1, 30 October.

Clark, Brett, and Richard York. 2005. Carbon Metabolism: Global Capitalism, Climate Change, and the Biospheric Rift. *Theory and Society* 34(4): 391–428.

Climate and Capitalism, 2009. Utah Phillips: Who Is Responsible? *Climate & Capitalism*. Retrieved from https://climateandcapitalism.com/2009/05/12/quotable/.

Climate Ottawa. 2013. GHG Roundtable Outcome, 25 March. Retrieved from http://climateottawa.ca/631/ghg-roundtable-outcome/.

Cockburn, Neco. 2012. 'Significant' changes proposed for Bronson Avenue near Carleton University. *Postmedia Breaking News*, 5 December.

Colgan, Jeff D., Jessica F. Green, and Thomas N. Hale. 2020. Asset Revaluation and the Existential Politics of Climate Change. *International Organization*, 1–25. Online first at: https://doi.org/10.1017/S0020818320000296.

Connolly, William E., 2013. *The Fragility of Things: Self-Organizing Processes, Neoliberal Fantasies, and Democratic Activism*. Durham, NC: Duke University Press.

2017. *Facing the Planetary: Entangled Humanism and the Politics of Swarming*. Durham, NC: Duke University Press.

2019. *Climate Machines, Fascist Drives, and Truth*. Durham, NC: Duke University Press.

Crawford, Blair. 2016. UOttawa to Seek Ways to 'Shift' Fossil Fuel Investments; Rejects Full Divestment. *Ottawa Citizen*. Retrieved from http://ottawacitizen.com/news/local-news/uottawa-commits-to-cutting-carbon-footprint-but-not-full-divestment-from-fossil-fuels.

Crick, Bernard. 2000. *In Defence of Politics*. London: Continuum.

Daggett, Cara. 2018. Petro-masculinity: Fossil Fuels and Authoritarian Desire. *Millennium* 47(1): 25–44.

Dale, Ann, and Rebecca Foon. 2013. Sustainable Energy Innovations: Series II of The Solutions Agenda. E-Dialogues for Sustainable Development, 15 March. Sustainability Solutions Group, Royal Roads University. Retrieved from: www.crcresearch.org/sites/default/files/u641/solutions_agenda_e-dialogue_series_ii_-_sustainable_energy_systems.pdf

Delcan. 2013. *Downtown Moves: Transforming Ottawa's Streets*. Ottawa: Delcan, The Planning Partnership, for the City of Ottawa.

Denley, Randall. 2010. Pity Doucet isn't Our Needed Antidote to the 'Twins'; A Cazy Quilt of Contradictions. *Ottawa Citizen*, 9 October, p. C1.

Descheneau, Philippe, and Matthew Paterson. 2011. Between Desire and Routine: Assembling Environment and Finance in Carbon Markets. *Antipode* 43(3): 662–81.

Doherty, Brian, Joost De Moor, and Graeme Hayes. 2018. The 'New' Climate Politics of Extinction Rebellion? *OpenDemocracy*. Retrieved from www.opendemocracy.net/joost-de-moor-brian-doherty-graeme-hayes/new-climate-politics-of-extinction-rebellion.

Dong, Changgui. 2012. Feed-in Tariff vs. Renewable Portfolio Standard: An Empirical Test of Their Relative Effectiveness in Promoting Wind Capacity Development. *Energy Policy*, 42: 476–85.

Doucet, Clive. 2004. Two Storeys Matter in a Livable City. *Ottawa Citizen*, 14 January, p. B4.

2007. *Urban Meltdown: Cities, Climate Change, and Politics-as-Usual*. Gabriola Island, BC: New Society Publishers.

Dowding, Keith. 2001. Explaining Urban Regimes. *International Journal of Urban and Regional Research* 25(1): 7–19.

Dryzek, John S. 1999. Transnational Democracy. *Journal of Political Philosophy*, 7(1): 30–51.

——— 2000. *Deliberative Democracy and Beyond: Liberals, Critics, Contestations*. Oxford: Oxford University Press.

Dryzek, John, David Downes, Christian Hunold, David Schlosberg, with Hans-Kristian Hernes. 2003. *Green States and Social Movements*. Oxford: Oxford University Press.

Dufresne, Jean-Marc. 2013. Living Off the Wall … Literally. *TABARET: uOttawa's Online Magazine*. Retrieved from http://web5.uottawa.ca/mcs-smc/tabaret/en/2013-02/living-off-the-wall.html.

Duggal, Sneh. 2011. Ottawa East Development Plan Receives Cautious Reaction: Area Residents Fear Potential Changes by Developer. *Ottawa Citizen*, 11 March, p. C3.

Ecology Ottawa. 2009. *Inching towards Sustainability, Striding towards Sprawl: An Ecology Ottawa Response to the City of Ottawa Draft Official Plan Amendments and Supporting Documents*. Ottawa: Ecology Ottawa.

——— 2014a. 'Complete Streets' Wins Overwhelming Approval. Ecology Ottawa, 17 October. Retrieved from https://ecologyottawa3.files.wordpress.com/2014/09/15-09-14-candi dates-election-survey-on-complete-streets-last-updated-september-15.pdf.

——— 2014b. Complete Streets Strategy Report, Draft. Ecology Ottawa. Retrieved from https:// ecologyottawa3.files.wordpress.com/2014/06/report1.pdf.

——— 2015. Community Groups, Citizens Mobilize to Voice Strong Support for Complete Streets. Ecology Ottawa. Retrieved from https://ecologyottawa.ca/2013/03/25/com munity-groups-citizens-mobilize-to-voice-strong-support-for-complete-streets/.

Evans, James, Ross Jones, Andrew Karvonen, Lucy Millard, and Jana Wendler. 2015. Living Labs and Co-Production: University Campuses as Platforms for Sustainability Science. *Current Opinion in Environmental Sustainability* 16: 1–6.

Fankhauser, Sam, Alina Averchenkova, and Jared Finnegan. 2018. *10 Years of the UK Climate Change Act*. London: Grantham Research Institute on Climate Change and the Environment, London School of Economics.

Federation of Canadian Municipalities. 2012. National Measures Report. Ottawa, Ontario. Retrieved from: www.fcm.ca/home/programs/partners-for-climate-protection/national-measures-report.html.

——— 2013. National Measures Report. Ottawa, Ontario. Retrieved from: www.fcm.ca/home/ programs/partners-for-climate-protection/national-measures-report.html.

——— 2015. Partners for Climate Protection. Get Started. Ottawa, Ontario. Retrieved from: www.fcm.ca/home/programs/partners-for-climate-protection/get-started.html.

——— 2016a. Partners in Climate Protection. Ottawa, Ontario. Retrieved from www.fcm.ca/ home/programs/partners-for-climate-protection.html.

——— 2016b. National Measures Report. Ottawa, Ontario. Retrieved from www.fcm.ca/home/ programs/partners-for-climate-protection/national-measures-report.html.

——— 2016c. Members: Partners for Climate Protection program. Ottawa, Ontario. Retrieved from www.fcm.ca/home/programs/partners-for-climate-protection/members-partners-for-climate-protection-program.htm.

——— 2016d. Green Municipal Fund. Ottawa, Ontario. Retrieved from www.fcm.ca/home/ programs/green-municipal-fund/funded-initiatives.htm?lang=en&project=aa7d8bfa-cd45-e111-968a-005056bc2614&srch=Ottawa.

Flyvbjerg, Bent. 1998. *Rationality and Power: Democracy in Practice*. Chicago: University of Chicago Press.

Foon, Rebecca, and Ann Dale. 2014. Interactive Case Studies in Sustainable Community Development: OREC, a Renewable Energy Co-operative Model. Community Research Connections: Sustainable Community Development. Retrieved from https://crcresearch.org/community-research-connections/crc-case-studies/orec-renew able-energy-co-operative-model

Fossil Free uOttawa. 2014. *The Case for Fossil Fuel Divestment at the University of Ottawa*. Ottawa: Fossil Free uOttawa. Retrieved from: http://350ottawa.org/wp-con tent/uploads/2014/02/Report-The-Case-for-Fossil-Fuel-Divestment-at-U-of-O_with-appendix.pdf.

n.d. To: The Board of Governors of the University of Ottawa – Le Bureau Des Gouverneurs de l'Université d'Ottawa. Divest the University of Ottawa from Fossil Fuels. Retrieved from: https://campaigns.gofossilfree.org/petitions/divest-ottawa-uni versity-from-fossil-fuels.

Foster, John Bellamy. 2015. The Great Capitalist Climacteric: Marxism and 'System Change Not Climate Change'. *Monthly Review* 67(6): 1–18.

Fraune, Cornelia, and Michèle Knodt. 2018. Sustainable Energy Transformations in an Age of Populism, Post-Truth Politics, and Local Resistance. *Energy Research & Social Science* 43: 1–7.

Friends of Lansdowne Inc. v. Ottawa (City). 2011. ONSC 4402 10-49352.

FSCO. 2017. Table of Registered Co-operatives in Ontario. Toronto: Financial Services Commission of Ontario. Retrieved from www5.fsco.gov.on.ca/co-op/default.aspx.

Furey, Anthony. 2011. Road Warriors: The Foes of Proposed Bronson Ave. Changes Up in Arms over Reasonable Alterations. *Ottawa Sun*, 26 November, p. 5.

Fyfe, Alice. 2014. How a Grocery Store Changed the Face of a Neighbourhood. *Kitchissippi Times*. Retrieved from: https://kitchissippi.com/2014/11/14/how-a-grocery-store-changed-the-face-of-a-neighbourhood/.

Gartman, David. 1994. *Auto Opium: A Social History of American Automobile Design*. London: Routledge.

Geels, Frank W. 2014. Regime Resistance against Low-Carbon Transitions: Introducing Politics and Power into the Multi-Level Perspective. *Theory, Culture & Society* 31(5): 21–40.

Gillard, Ross. 2016. Unravelling the United Kingdom's Climate Policy Consensus: The Power of Ideas, Discourse and Institutions. *Global Environmental Change* 40: 26–36.

Gillet, Brandon. 2017. UOttawa Surpasses Energy Goals. *Gazette*. Retrieved from: www .uottawa.ca/gazette/en/news/uottawa-surpasses-energy-goals.

Glaeser, Edward L. and Matthew E. Kahn. 2010. The Greenness of Cities: Carbon Dioxide Emissions and Urban Development. *Journal of Urban Economics* 67(3): 404–18.

Goeminne, Gert. 2013. Does the Climate Need Consensus?: The Politics of Climate Change Revisited. *Symploke* 21(1): 147–61.

Gordon, David J. 2013. Between Local Innovation and Global Impact: Cities, Networks, and the Governance of Climate Change. *Canadian Foreign Policy Journal* 19(3): 288–307.

2016a. Lament for a Network? Cities and Networked Climate Governance in Canada. *Environment and Planning C: Government and Policy* 34(3): 529–45.

2016b. The Politics of Accountability in Networked Urban Climate Governance. *Global Environmental Politics* 16(2): 82–100.

2020. *Cities on the World Stage: The Politics of Global Urban Climate Governance*. Cambridge: Cambridge University Press.

Gore, Christopher D. 2010. The Limits and Opportunities of Networks: Municipalities and Canadian Climate Change Policy. *Review of Policy Research* 27(1): 27–46.

Gorz, André. 1980. From Nuclear Electricity to Electric Fascism. In *Ecology as Politics.* London: Pluto Press, 102–13.

Government of Ontario. 2016. *Ontario's Five Year Climate Change Action Plan, 2016–2020.* Toronto: Queen's Printer for Ontario. Retrieved from www .applications.ene.gov.on.ca/ccap/products/CCAP_ENGLISH.pdf.
  2017. Minister's Climate Change Action Plan Progress Report 2017. Retrieved from www.ontario.ca/page/ministers-climate-change-action-plan-progress-report-2017.

Grady-Benson, Jessica, and Brinda Sarathy. 2016. Fossil Fuel Divestment in US Higher Education: Student-Led Organising for Climate Justice. *Local Environment* 21(6): 661–81.

Graham, Katherine A., Allan M. Maslove, and Susan D. Phillips. 2001. Learning from Experience? Ottawa as a Cautionary Tale of Reforming Urban Government. *Journal of Comparative Policy Analysis: Research and Practice* 3(3): 251–69.

Gray, Ken. 2011. Lessons from Lansdowne. *Ottawa Citizen*, 3 August, p. A11.

Green, Jessica. 2013. Order out of Chaos: Public and Private Rules for Managing Carbon. *Global Environmental Politics*, 13(2): 1–25.

Green Economy Canada. n.d. What We Do. *Green Economy Canada*. Retrieved from https://greeneconomy.ca/what-we-do/.

Greenspace Alliance of Canada's Capital. n.d. Choosing our Future Reports and Papers. Retrieved from http://greenspace-alliance.ca/index.php/archives/archives-ottawa-city-hall/choosing-our-future-reports-and-papers/.

Grubb, Michael. 1989. *The Greenhouse Effect: Negotiating Targets.* London: Royal Institute of International Affairs.

Gunster, Shane, Darren Fleet, Matthew Paterson, and Paul Saurette. 2018. 'Why Don't You Act Like You Believe It?': Competing Visions of Climate Hypocrisy. *Frontiers in Communication* 3. https://doi.org/10.3389/fcomm.2018.00049.

Hamels, Johan, and Keith Shackleton. 2014. Presentation to City of Ottawa Environment Committee – Consultation re Climate Change Action Plan, 20 May 2014. Retrieved from https://orec.ca/wp-content/uploads/2015/02/20140527-Climate-Change-Action-PlanOREC-submision.pdf.

Hay, Colin. 2002. *Political Analysis: A Critical Introduction.* London: Palgrave.
  2007. *Why We Hate Politics.* Cambridge: Polity Press.

Hodson, Mike, and Simon Marvin. 2010. *World Cities and Climate Change: Producing Urban Ecological Security.* Maidenhead: Open University Press.

Hoffmann, Matthew J. 2011. *Climate Governance at the Crossroads: Experimenting with a Global Response after Kyoto.* Oxford: Oxford University Press.

Hoornweg, Daniel, Lorraine Sugar, and Claudia Lorena Trejos Gómez. 2011. Cities and Greenhouse Gas Emissions: Moving Forward. *Environment and Urbanization* 20(10): 1–21.

Hopke, Jill E., and Luis E. Hestres. 2017. Fossil Fuel Divestment and Climate Change Communication. In *Oxford Research Encyclopedias: Climate Science.* Oxford: Oxford University Press. Retrieved from http://climatescience.oxfordre.com/view/10.1093/acrefore/9780190228620.001.0001/acrefore-9780190228620-e-566.

Howarth, Candice, Peter Bryant, Adam Corner, Sam Fankhauser, Andy Gouldson, Lorraine Whitmarsh, and Rebecca Willis. 2020. Building a Social Mandate for Climate Action: Lessons from COVID-19. *Environmental and Resource Economics*, 76(4): 1107–15.

Hulme, Mike. 2010. *Why We Disagree about Climate Change.* Cambridge: Cambridge University Press.

ICLEI-Local Governments for Sustainability. 2016. *Partners for Climate Protection*. Toronto. Canada. Retrieved from www.icleicanada.org/programs/mitigation/pcp.

Jackson, Emma. 2015. Ottawa's Planning Committee Greenlights Oblates Redevelopment. *Metro Ottawa*, 24 November.

Jacobs, Jane. 1961. *The Death and Life of Great American Cities*. New York: Vintage.

Jenkins, Phil. 2013. The Rise (and Rise) of Cars in Ottawa. *Ottawa Citizen*, 15 April, p. A10.

Jimenez, Benedict S., and Rebecca Hendrick. 2010. Is Government Consolidation the Answer? *State and Local Government Review* 42(3): 258–70.

Johnson, J. 2011. Residents Oppose Nepean Condo Development; Intensification Project in Line with City Mandate. *Ottawa Citizen*, 12 August, p. C5.

Kenis, Anneleen, and Erik Mathijs. 2014. Climate Change and Post-Politics: Repoliticizing the Present by Imagining the Future? *Geoforum* 52: 148–56.

Kenner, Dario. 2019. *Carbon Inequality: The Role of the Richest in Climate Change*. London: Routledge.

Kern, Kristine, and Harriet Bulkeley. 2009. Cities, Europeanization and Multi-Level Governance: Governing Climate Change through Transnational Municipal Networks. *Journal of Common Market Studies* 47(2): 309–32.

Kester, Johannes. 2019. Security in Transition(s): The Low-Level Security Politics of Electric Vehicle Range Anxiety. *Security Dialogue* 50(6): 547–63.

Khan, Sadiq. 2019. UPDATE: My Message to All the Climate Change Protestors Today Is Clear: Let London Return to Business as Usual. Pic.Twitter.Com/ 2o5jwbwLC2. *@sadiqkhan*. Retrieved from https://twitter.com/sadiqkhan/status/ 1119954442512629760?lang=en.

Klein, Naomi. 2014. *This Changes Everything: Capitalism Vs. The Climate*. Toronto: Knopf Canada.

———. 2020. *On Fire: The Burning Case for a Green New Deal*. London: Allen Lane.

Koch, Max. 2012. *Capitalism and Climate Change: Theoretical Discussion, Historical Development and Policy Responses*. London: Palgrave.

Kolk, Ans, David Levy, and Jonatan Pinkse. 2008. Corporate Responses in an Emerging Climate Regime: The Institutionalization and Commensuration of Carbon Disclosure. *European Accounting Review* 17(4): 719–45.

Kotyk, Alyse. 2016. University of Ottawa Becomes First Canadian University to Divest from Fossil Fuels. *Rabble*. Retrieved from http://rabble.ca/news/2016/04/university- ottawa-becomes-first-canadian-university-to-divest-fossil-fuels.

Kronsell, Annica, and Karin Bäckstrand. 2010. Rationalities and Forms of Governance: A Framework for Analysing the Legitimacy of New Modes of Governance. In Karin Bäckstrand, Jamil Khan, Annica Kronsell, and Eva Lövbrand, eds., *Environmental Politics and Deliberative Democracy: Examining the Promise of New Modes of Governance*. Cheltenham, UK: Edward Elgar, 28–46.

Kussner, Barnet, and Robert Warren. 2009. Proposed Green Energy Act Places Limits on Municipal Land Use Planning Powers. WeirFoulds LLP Government Update – Energy Bulletin, 4 March 2009. Retrieved from www.weirfoulds.com/proposed- green-energy-act-places-limits-on-municipal.

Kuzemko, Caroline. 2016. Energy Depoliticisation in the UK: Destroying Political Capacity. *The British Journal of Politics and International Relations* 18(1): 107–24.

Lachapelle, Erick, Robert MacNeil, and Matthew Paterson. 2017. The Political Economy of Decarbonisation: From Green Energy 'Race' to Green 'Division of Labour.' *New Political Economy* 22(3): 311–27.

Langston, P. 2011. Vanier: A New View; Slowly Moving away from its Troubled Past, the Neighbourhood Is Attracting Condos, Infill Housing and a Stronger Sense of Community. *Ottawa Citizen*, 6 August, p. I1.

⸻ 2013. 'A Milestone of Urbanization'; The Skyline around Carling and Preston Is about to Change Rapidly. *Ottawa Citizen*, 11 May, p. I4.

Lasswell, Harold. 1936. *Politics: Who Gets What, When, How*. New York: Whittlesey House.

Lee, Taedong. 2014. *Global Cities and Climate Change: The Translocal Relations of Environmental Governance*. London: Routledge.

Leffers, Donald. 2015a. Conflict in the Face of Planning? Power, Knowledge and Hegemony in Planning Practice. In Enrico Gualini, ed., *Planning and Conflict: Critical Perspectives on Contentious Urban Developments*. London: Routledge, 127–44.

⸻ 2015b. Urban Sustainability as a 'Boundary Object': Interrogating Discourses of Urban Intensification in Ottawa, Canada. In Cindy Isenhour, Gary McDonogh, and Melissa Checker, eds., *Sustainability in the Global City*. Cambridge: Cambridge University Press, 329–49.

Leffers, Donald, and Patricia Ballamingie. 2013. Governmentality, Environmental Subjectivity, and Urban Intensification. *Local Environment* 18(2): 134–51.

Leftwich, Adrian. 2004. Thinking Politically: On the Politics of Politics. In Adrian Leftwich, ed., *What Is Politics?*. Cambridge: Polity, 1–22.

Lévesque, Jean-François, Christopher Caners, Don MacLean, and Tony Vetter. 2010. *University Data Centres: Policy and Business Case for Reducing Greenhouse Gas Emissions*. Winnipeg: International Institute for Sustainable Development.

Levin, Kelly, Benjamin Cashore, Steven Bernstein, and Graeme Auld. 2012. Overcoming the Tragedy of Super Wicked Problems: Constraining Our Future Selves to Ameliorate Global Climate Change. *Policy Sciences* 45(2): 123–52.

Lipp, Judith, Mumtaz Derya Tarhan, and Alice Dixon. 2016. Accelerating Renewable Energy Co-operatives in Canada: A Review of Experiences and Lessons. Prepared by TREC Renewable Energy Co-operative for Co-operatives and Mutuals Canada (CMC), March. Retrieved from www.trec.on.ca/reports/.

Lockwood, Matthew. 2013. The Political Sustainability of Climate Policy: The Case of the UK Climate Change Act. *Global Environmental Change* 23(5): 1339–48.

Lohmann, Larry. 2006. Carbon Trading: A Critical Conversation on Climate Change, Privatization and Power. *Development Dialogue* 48: 1–356.

⸻ 2010. Commodity Fetishism in Climate Science and Policy. Presentation at Imperial College London.

Lövbrand, Eva, and Johannes Stripple. 2011. Making Climate Change Governable: Accounting for Carbon as Sinks, Credits and Personal Budgets. *Critical Policy Studies* 5(2): 187–200.

Lovell, Heather, and Donald MacKenzie. 2011. Accounting for Carbon: The Role of Accounting Professional Organisations in Governing Climate Change. *Antipode* 43(3): 704–30.

Lovins, Amory. 1977. *Soft Energy Paths: Toward a Durable Peace*. San Francisco: Harper and Row.

Luque-Ayala, Andrés, Harriet Bulkeley, and Simon Marvin. 2018. Rethinking Urban Transitions: An Analytical Framework. In Andrés Luque-Ayala, Harriet Bulkeley, and Simon Marvin, eds., *Rethinking Urban Transitions: Politics in the Low Carbon City*. London: Routledge, 13–36.

Mabee, Warren E., Justine Mannion, and Tom Carpenter. 2012. Comparing the Feed-in Tariff Incentives for Renewable Electricity in Ontario and Germany. *Energy Policy*, 40(January): 480–89.

MacGregor, Sherilyn. 2014. Only Resist: Feminist Ecological Citizenship and the Post-Politics of Climate Change. *Hypatia* 29(3): 617–33.

Machin, Amanda. 2013. *Negotiating Climate Change: Radical Democracy and the Illusion of Consensus*. London: Zed Books.

MacLeod, Gordon, Martin Jones, Andrew E. G. Jonas, David Gibbs, and Aidan While. 2011. The New Urban Politics as a Politics of Carbon Control. *Urban Studies* 48(12): 2537–54.

Malm, Andreas. 2015. *Fossil Capital: The Rise of Steam-Power and the Roots of Global Warming*. London: Verso.

  2018. *The Progress of This Storm: On the Dialectics of Society and Nature in a Warming World*. London: Verso.

  2020. *Corona, Climate, Chronic Emergency: War Communism in the Twenty-First Century*. London: Verso Books.

Mangat, Rupinder, Simon Dalby, and Matthew Paterson. 2018. Divestment Discourse: War, Justice, Morality and Money. *Environmental Politics* 27(2): 187–208.

Mann, Geoff, and Joel Wainwright. 2018. *Climate Leviathan: A Political Theory of Our Planetary Future*. London: Verso.

Manning, Paul and Joanna Vince. 2010. Municipalities and the Green Energy Act: Benefits, Burdens, and Loss of Power. *Municipal World*, January 2010. Retrieved from www.willmsshier.com/resources/details/municipalities-and-the-green-energy-act-article—municipal-world-january-2010.

Martin, Charles Francis James. 2007. Tinker, Tory, Wobbler, Why? The Political Economy of Electricity Restructuring in Ontario, 1995–2003. PhD thesis. Queen's University, Kingston, ON.

Mason, Rowena. 2019. Sajid Javid Calls for 'Full Force of Law' against Extinction Rebellion Protesters. *The Guardian*. Retrieved from www.theguardian.com/environment/2019/apr/18/sajid-javid-calls-for-full-force-of-law-against-extinction-rebellion-protesters.

McGuirk, Pauline, Harriet Bulkeley, and Robyn Dowling. 2014. Practices, Programs and Projects of Urban Carbon Governance: Perspectives from the Australian City. *Geoforum* 52: 137–47.

McKibben, Bill. 2012. Global Warming's Terrifying New Math. *Rolling Stone*. Available from www.rollingstone.com/politics/news/global-warmings-terrifying-new-math-20120719.

  2013. The Case for Fossil-Fuel Divestment. *Rolling Stone*. Available from www.rollingstone.com/politics/news/the-case-for-fossil-fuel-divestment-20130222.

McKinsey & Co. 2009. *Pathway to a Low-Carbon Economy: Version 2 of the Global GHG Abatement Cost Curve*. New York: McKinsey & Company.

McLeod, Jonathan. 2013. Cars Don't Own Main Street. *Ottawa Citizen*, 16 November, p. B6.

McNay, Lois. 2014. *The Misguided Search for the Political*. Cambridge: Polity.

Mert, Aysem. 2013. Discursive Interplay and Co-Constitution: Carbonification of Environmental Discourses. In Chris Methmann, Delf Rothe, and Benjamin Stephan, eds., *Interpretive Approaches to Global Climate Governance*. London: Routledge, 23–39.

Mildenberger, Matto. 2019. The Tragedy of the Tragedy of the Commons. *Scientific American Blog*, 23 April. Retrieved from: https://blogs.scientificamerican.com/voices/the-tragedy-of-the-tragedy-of-the-commons/

2020. *Carbon Captured: How Business and Labor Control Climate Politics*. Cambridge, MA: MIT Press.

Millyard, Kai. 1992. *A Preliminary Carbon Dioxide Inventory for the City of Ottawa*. Ottawa: Friends of the Earth Canada for the City of Ottawa, February.

Mitchell, Joni. 1970. Big Yellow Taxi. Reprise Records.

Mitchell, Timothy. 2013. *Carbon Democracy: Political Power in the Age of Oil*. London: Verso.

Molotch, Harvey. 1993. The Political Economy of Growth Machines. *Journal of Urban Affairs* 15(1): 29–53.

Moore, Aaron A. 2013. *Planning Politics in Toronto: The Ontario Municipal Board and Urban Development*. Toronto: University of Toronto Press.

Moreland-Russell, Sarah, Amy Eyler, Colleen Barbero, Aaron J. Hipp, and Heidi Walsh. 2013. Diffusion of Complete Streets Policies Across US Communities. *Journal of Public Health Management and Practice* 19(3): S89–S96.

Mouffe, Chantal. 2005. *On the Political*. London: Routledge.

Mueller, Laura. 2014a. Sandy Hill Student Resident Plan Rejected by Council; Appeal to OMB Likely after Proposal for 180-Unit Apartment Turned Down. *Ottawa West News*, 3 April. Retrieved from www.ottawacommunitynews.com/news-story/44466662-sandy-hill-student-residence-plan-rejected-by-council-appeal-to-omb-likely-after-proposal-for-180-u/.

2014b. Somerset Candidates Talk Issues at Forum. *Ottawa Community News*, 25 June. Retrieved from https://www.ottawacommunitynews.com/news-story/4597664-somerset-candidates-talk-issues-at-forum/.

Murphy, Katharine. 2017. Scott Morrison Brings Coal to Question Time: What Fresh Idiocy Is This? *The Guardian*. Retreived from www.theguardian.com/australia-news/2017/feb/09/scott-morrison-brings-coal-to-question-time-what-fresh-idiocy-is-this.

Natural Resources Canada (NRCan). 2017. Photovoltaic and Solar Resource Maps. Data Set. Last modified 20 March 2017. Retrieved from www.nrcan.gc.ca/18366.

Newell, Peter. 2000. *Climate for Change: Non-State Actors and the Global Politics of the Greenhouse*. Cambridge: Cambridge University Press.

2005. Race, Class and the Global Politics of Environmental Inequality. *Global Environmental Politics* 5(3): 70–94.

Newell, Peter, and Matthew Paterson. 1998. A Climate for Business: Global Warming, the State and Capital. *Review of International Political Economy* 5(4): 679–703.

2010. *Climate Capitalism: Global Warming and the Transformation of the Global Economy*. Cambridge: Cambridge University Press.

Newman, P., and J. Kenworthy. 1999. *Sustainability and Cities: Overcoming Auto-Mobile Dependence*. Washington, DC: Island Press.

Nishimura, Kensuke. 2012. Grassroots Action for Renewable Energy: How Did Ontario Succeed in the Implementation of a Feed-in Tariff System? *Energy, Sustainability and Society* 2(1): 6.

Nixon, Rob. 2013. *Slow Violence and the Environmentalism of the Poor*. Cambridge, MA: Harvard University Press.

Norgaard, Kari. 2011. *Living in Denial: Climate Change, Emotions, and Everyday Life*. Cambridge, MA: MIT Press.

Ocasio-Cortez, Alexandria, and Lewis, Avi. 2019. A Message From the Future with Alexandria Ocasio-Cortez, 17 April. Retrieved from www.youtube.com/watch?v=d9uTH0iprVQ

Oji, Chijioke, and Olaf Weber. 2017. Advancing Sustainable Energy in Ontario: The Case of Regional Renewable Energy Cooperatives. CIGI Papers No. 133. Centre

for International Governance Innovation. Retrieved from www.cigionline.org/pub
lications/advancing-sustainable-energy-ontario-case-regional-renewable-energy-
cooperatives.

Ontario Ministry of Municipal Affairs and Housing. 1996. *Provincial Policy Statement 1996 (amended in 1997)*. Toronto: Ontario Ministry of Municipal Affairs and Housing.

———. 2005. *Provincial Policy Statement 2005*. Toronto: Ontario Ministry of Municipal Affairs and Housing.

———. 2014. *Provincial Policy Statement 2014*. Toronto: Ontario Ministry of Municipal Affairs and Housing.

Ontario Ministry of the Environment and Climate Change. 2015. *Ontario's Climate Change: Discussion Paper 2015*. Toronto: Ontario Ministry of the Environment and Climate Change.

Ontario Wind Resistance. 2018. Stephana Johnston: Ontario Wind Resistance's Grandmother. Undated Image. Retrieved from http://ontario-wind-resistance.org/2018/01/11/stephana-johnston-ontario-wind-resistances-grandmother/#jp-carousel-57186.

OREC. 2012. The Future of the Ontario FIT Program. Letter from Roger Peters, OREC Board President, to Christopher Bentley, Ontario Minister of Energy, 12 April 2012. Retrieved from https://web.archive.org/web/20160202175650/http://www.ottawarenewableenergycoop.com:80/policy-suggestions/ [access no longer available on live OREC website].

———. 2013. Recommendations to the Ontario Ministry of Energy Consultation on Making Choices: Reviewing Ontario's Long-Term Energy Plan, 16 September 2013. Retrieved from https://orec.ca/wp-content/uploads/2013/09/20130916-OREC-submission-to-Making-Choices-Reviewing-Ontarios-LREP.pdf.

———. 2014. The Role of the City of Ottawa in Encouraging Community Solar Power. Powerpoint Presentation to the City of Ottawa Environmental Stewardship Advisory Committee, September. Retrieved from https://orec.ca/wp-content/uploads/2015/02/20140917-Improving-City-support-for-community-solar.pdf.

———. 2015a. Collaboration Policy. Approved by the OREC Board, 20 January 2015 (Revised 28 June 2015). Retrieved from www.orec.ca/wp-content/uploads/2018/04/20150628-OREC-Collaboration-Policy.pdf.

———. 2015b. Ottawa Renewable Energy Cooperative By-Laws, As Amended May 2015. Retrieved from https://orec.ca/wp-content/uploads/2015/05/20150525-Ottawa-Renewable-Energy-Co-op-Bylaws-amended-May-2015.pdf.

———. 2017a. $1.98 M Invested in New Solar Power Projects. Retrieved from www.orec.ca/fifth.

———. 2017b. Community Impact Report. Retrieved from www.orec.ca/wp-content/uploads/2018/03/Community-Impact-Report-2017-English-Web.pdf.

———. 2017c. Invest through a RRSP or TFSA. Retrieved from https://orec.ca/rrsp-tfsa/

———. 2018. About Us. Retrieved from Lwww.orec.ca/about-us/

Ottawa Citizen. 2010. Political animals. Editorial. *Ottawa Citizen*, 12 May, p. A12.

Ottawa Sun. 2012. Segregated lanes the Wrong Way. *Ottawa Sun*, 20 May, p. 18.

Paterson, Matthew. 1996. *Global Warming and Global Politics*. London: Routledge.

———. 2007. *Automobile Politics: Ecology and Cultural Political Economy*. Cambridge: Cambridge University Press.

———. 2010a. Legitimation and Accumulation in Climate Change Governance. *New Political Economy* 15(3): 345–68.

2010b. *Towards Sustainable Transport in Ottawa: An End to Road Construction.* Ottawa: Ecology Ottawa.

2014. Climate Re-public: Practicing Public Space in Conditions of Extreme Complexity. In Jacqueline Best, and Alexandra Gheciu, eds. *The Return of the Public in Global Governance.* Cambridge: Cambridge University Press, 149–73.

2016. The Sociological Imagination of Climate Futures. In Paul Wapner and Hilal Elver, eds., *Reimagining Climate Change.* London: Routledge, 14–28.

2020. 'The end of the fossil fuel age?' Discourse Politics and Climate Change Political Economy. *New Political Economy.* Online first at doi: 10.1080/13563467.2020.1810218.

Paterson, Matthew, and Johannes Stripple. 2010. My Space: Governing Individuals' Carbon Emissions. *Environment and Planning D: Society and Space* 28(2): 341–62.

2014. Governing Subjectivities in a Carbon Constrained World. In Deserai A. Crow and Maxwell T. Boykoff, eds., *Culture, Politics and Climate Change: How Information Shapes Our Common Future.* London: Routledge, 189–202.

Pearse, Rebecca. 2017. Gender and Climate Change. *Wiley Interdisciplinary Reviews: Climate Change* 8(2): e451.

Pearson, Matthew. 2014. Spend $20M on cycling annually, safe cycling group urges. *Postmedia Breaking News*, 15 September.

Pelling, Mark, David Manuel-Navarrette, and Michael Redclift, eds. 2011. *Climate Change and the Crisis of Capitalism: A Chance to Reclaim, Self, Society and Nature.* London: Routledge.

Pepermans, Yves, and Pieter Maeseele, P. 2016. The Politicization of Climate Change: Problem or Solution? *Wiley Interdisciplinary Reviews: Climate Change*, 7(4): 478–85.

Peters, Roger. 2013. Rejection of FIT 2.1 Project Applications in Ottawa. Letter on Behalf of 1000 Solar Rooftops Network to Minister Chiarelli, 29 May 2013. Retrieved from https://orec.ca/wp-content/uploads/2013/09/20130529_1000Solar-Letter-to-MinisterChiarelli.pdf.

2016. Leaps and Steps: Towards 100% Renewable Energy. Powerpoint Presentation. Wintergreen Retreat, 27 May 2016. Retrieved from http://sustainableeasternontario.ca/wp-content/uploads/2016/05/OREC.pdf.

Pilieci, V. 2014. Planning Is Still a big Civic Issue: Two Candidates Say Rising Housing Costs are Also a Concern. *Ottawa Citizen*, 8 October, p. A6.

Pinkse, Jonatan, and Ans Kolk. 2009. *International Business and Global Climate Change.* London: Routledge.

Pinn, Ingram. 2019. Ingram Pinn's Illustration of the Week: Tipping Point. *Financial Times*, 11 April. Retrieved from www.ft.com/content/80f3c5aa-6110-11e9-a27a-fdd51850994c.

Porter, K. 2018. CBC Ottawa Explains: How Would Watson and Doucet Tackle Climate Change? CBC, 21 October. Retrieved from www.cbc.ca/news/canada/ottawa/cbc-ottawa-explains-watson-doucet-climate-change-1.4869011.

PressFrom. 2018. Leaders Gather for Key UN Climate Talks in Poland. *PressFrom - US.* Retrieved from http://pressfrom.info/news/offbeat/-217836-leaders-gather-for-key-un-climate-talks-in-poland.html.

PRI. n.d. a. Montreal Carbon Pledge Signatories. Retrieved from http://montrealpledge.org/signatories/.

n.d. b. Why Would I Want to Measure My Portfolio's Carbon Footprint? Retrieved from http://montrealpledge.org/how-to/why-measure-my-portfolio-carbon-footprint/.

Princen, Thomas. 2003. Principles for Sustainability: From Cooperation and Efficiency to Sufficiency. *Global Environmental Politics* 3(1): 33–50.

2005. *The Logic of Sufficiency*. Cambridge, MA: MIT Press.

Princen, Thomas, Jack Manno, and Pamela L. Martin, eds. 2015. *Ending the Fossil Fuel Era*. Cambridge, MA: MIT Press.

Rausseo, Jonathan. 2016. *UOttawa: Greenhouse Gas Emissions Program*. Ottawa: University of Ottawa Office of Campus Sustainability.

Reese, Laura A. 2004. Same Governance, Different Day: Does Metropolitan Reorganization Make a Difference? *Review of Policy Research* 21(4): 595–611.

Reevely, David. 2013a. Car Space on Main Street to Be Cut after Split Vote; 'Complete Street' Will Have Wider Sidewalks and Bicycle Lanes. *Ottawa Citizen*, 6 July, p. C2.

2013b. Part of Main Street Cut from Four Lanes to Two; City to Build Bike Lanes, Widen Sidewalks. *Ottawa Citizen*, 6 July, p. E4.

Rice, Jennifer L. 2016. 'The Everyday Choices We Make Matter': Urban Climate Politics and the Postpolitics of Responsibility and Action. In Harriet Bulkeley, Matthew Paterson, and Johannes Stripple, eds., *Towards a Cultural Politics of Climate Change: Devices, Desires and Dissent*. Cambridge: Cambridge University Press, 110–26.

Robinson, Jennifer. 2006. *Ordinary Cities: Between Modernity and Development*. London: Routledge.

Rogers, J. C., E. A. Simmons, I. Convery, and A. Weatherall. 2008. Public Perceptions of Opportunities for Community-based Renewable Energy Projects. *Energy Policy*, 36(11): 4217–26.

Rosenbloom, Daniel and James Meadowcroft. 2014. The Journey towards Decarbonization: Exploring Socio-technical Transitions in the Electricity Sector in the Province of Ontario (1885–2013) and Potential Low-Carbon Pathways. *Energy Policy*, 65: 670–79.

Rosenbloom, Daniel, James Meadowcroft, and Benjamin Cashore. 2019. Stability and Climate Policy? Harnessing Insights on Path Dependence, Policy Feedback, and Transition Pathways. *Energy Research & Social Science*, 50: 168–78.

Rosenfeld, Raymond A., and Laura A. Reese. 2003. The Anatomy of an Amalgamation: The Case of Ottawa. *State and Local Government Review* 35(1): 57–69.

2004. Local Government Amalgamation from the Top Down. In Jered B. Carr and Richard C. Feiock, eds., *City-County Consolidation and Its Alternatives: Reshaping the Local Government Landscape*. London: Routledge, 219–45.

Rowe, James K., Jessica Dempsey, and Peter Gibbs. 2016. The Power of Fossil Fuel Divestment (and Its Secret). In William K. Carroll and Kanchan Sarker, eds., *A World to Win: Contemporary Social Movements and Counter-Hegemony*. Winnipeg, Canada: ARP Books, 233–49.

Rowlands, Ian H., 2007. The Development of Renewable Electricity Policy in the Province of Ontario: The Influence of Ideas and Timing. *Review of Policy Research*, 24(3): 185–207.

Sachs, Wolfgang. 1992. *For Love of the Automobile*. Berkeley: University of California Press.

Saunders, Clare, Brian Doherty, and Graeme Hayes. 2020. *Extinction Rebellion's Activists in Profile* (CUSP Working Paper no.25). Keele University. Retrieved from www .cusp.ac.uk/themes/p/xr-study/

Saurin, Julian. 1994. Global Environmental Degradation, Modernity and Environmental Knowledge. *Environmental Politics* 2(4): 46–64.

Schneider, William. 2002. America Keeps on Trucking. *The Atlantic* 1 March 2002. Retrieved from: www.theatlantic.com/politics/archive/2002/03/america-keeps-on-trucking/377774/.

Scott, Nick. 2010. Storied Infrastructure: Tracing Traffic, Place, and Power in Canada's Capital City. *ESC: English Studies in Canada* 36(1): 149–74.

Scrase, Ivan, and Adrian Smith. 2009. The (Non-)Politics of Managing Low Carbon Socio-Technical Transitions. *Environmental Politics* 18(5): 707–26.

Shewan, Ian D. and Larry Sadler. 2012. Canada: The 50% Rule And Ontario Co-operatives, 2 April (originally published March 2010). Retrieved from www.mondaq.com/canada/x/170962/Corporate+Company+Law/The+50+Rule+and+Ontario+Cooperatives.

Shove, Elizabeth. 2012. Energy Transitions in Practice: The Case of Global Indoor Climate Change. In Geert Verbong and Derk Loorbach, eds., *Governing the Energy Transition: Reality, Illusion or Necessity?* London: Routledge, 51–74.

Shue, Henry. 2014. *Climate Justice: Vulnerability and Protection.* Oxford: Oxford University Press.

Sovacool, Benjamin K., and Marie-Claire Brisbois. 2019. Elite Power in Low-Carbon Transitions: A Critical and Interdisciplinary Review. *Energy Research & Social Science*, 57: 101242.

Spalding, Derek. 2013a. Coalition Pushes for Improved Roadways. *Postmedia Breaking News*, 7 October.

   2013b. Council Adopts 'Complete Streets': Cyclists', Pedestrians' Needs Are to Be Focus of City's Road Designs. *Ottawa Citizen*, 11 October, p. C6.

Spears, Tom. 1992. Glowing Green Promises Go Unfulfilled: Governments are Quick to Set Pollution Goals, Slow to Meet Them. *Ottawa Citizen*, 5 May, p. A1.

   2000. Ottawa Turns Green into Gold: Federal Overseer Grants City Top Medal for Success in Fight against Emissions. *Ottawa Citizen*, 20 September, p. C3.

Stavins, Robert, Zou Ji, Mariana Conte Grand, Michel den Elzen, Michael Finus, Joyeeta Gupta, et al. 2014. International Cooperation: Agreements and Instruments. In Ottmar Edenhofer, Ramón Pichs-Madruga, Youba Sokona, Ellie Farahani, Susanne Kadner, Kristin Seyboth, et al., eds., *Climate Change 2014: Mitigation of Climate Change. Contribution of Working Group III to the Fifth Assessment Report of the Intergovernmental Panel on Climate Change.* Cambridge: Cambridge University Press, 1001–82.

Stephan, Benjamin. 2012. Bringing Discourse to the Market: The Commodification of Avoided Deforestation. *Environmental Politics* 21(4): 621–39.

Stern, Leonard. 2010. Growing Intense. *Ottawa Citizen*, 30 October, p. B6.

Stern, Nicholas. 2007. *The Economics of Climate Change: The Stern Review.* Cambridge: Cambridge University Press.

Stirling, Andy. 2019. How Deep Is Incumbency? A 'Configuring Fields' Approach to Redistributing and Reorienting Power in Socio-material Change. *Energy Research & Social Science*, 58: 101239.

Stokes, Leah C. 2013. The Politics of Renewable Energy Policies: The Case of Feed-in Tariffs in Ontario, Canada. *Energy Policy* 56(May): 490–500.

   2020. *Short Circuiting Policy: Interest Groups and the Battle Over Clean Energy and Climate Policy in the American States.* Oxford: Oxford University Press.

Strachan, Peter, David Lal, and David Toke, eds. 2010. *Wind Power and Power Politics: International Perspectives.* New York: Routledge.

Sum, Ngai-Lin, and Bob Jessop. 2013. *Towards a Cultural Political Economy.* Cheltenham: Edward Elgar.

Sustainable Ottawa. 2010. Sustainable Ottawa homepage. www.sustainableottawa.ca/.

Sweeney, Sean. 2014. Working Toward Energy Democracy. In Tom Prugh and Michael Renner, eds., *Governing for Sustainability*. Washington: The Worldwatch Institute/ Island Press, 215–27.

Swyngedouw, Erik. 2010. Apocalypse Forever? Post-Political Populism and the Spectre of Climate Change. *Theory, Culture & Society* 27(2–3): 213–32.

Tarhan, Mumtaz Derya. 2015. Renewable Energy Cooperatives: A Review of Demonstrated Impacts and Limitations. *The Journal of Entrepreneurial and Organizational Diversity* 4(1): 104–20.

Tencer, D. 2004. Breathing Life into Downtown. *Ottawa Citizen*, 21 October, p. C3.

Thistlethwaite, Jason, and Matthew Paterson. 2016. Private Governance and Accounting for Sustainability Networks. *Environment and Planning C: Government and Policy* 34(7): 1197–221.

Toronto Conference. 1989. The Changing Atmosphere: Implications for Global Security. In Dean Edwin Abrahamson, ed., *The Challenge of Global Warming*. Washington: Island Press, 44–63.

Torrie, Ralph. 2015. *Low Carbon Futures in Canada – The Role of Urban Climate Change Mitigation*. Seattle: Stockholm Environment Institute.

Torrie Smith Associates. 1994. *Amélioration de l'environnement par la gestion de l'énergie dans les villes*. Rapport de recherche. Montreal: Canada Mortgage and Housing Association.

Trencher, Gregory, Xuemei Bai, James Evans, Kes McCormick, and Masaru Yarime. 2014. University Partnerships for Co-Designing and Co-Producing Urban Sustainability. *Global Environmental Change* 28: 153–65.

Trencher, Gregory P., Masaru Yarime, and Ali Kharrazi. 2013. Co-Creating Sustainability: Cross-Sector University Collaborations for Driving Sustainable Urban Transformations. *Journal of Cleaner Production* 50: 40–55.

United Nations. 1992. *Framework Convention on Climate Change*. New York: United Nations.

University of Ottawa. 2015. *Report on Sustainable Development at the University of Ottawa*. Ottawa: University of Ottawa. Retrieved from http://sustainable.uottawa .ca/sites/sustainable.uottawa.ca/files/rapport_developpement_durable_2015_en_final_ accessible_0.pdf.

University of Ottawa. 2017. *Addressing Global Warming: First Annual UOttawa Progress Report*. Ottawa: University of Ottawa.

University of Ottawa. n.d. Destination 2020: The University of Ottawa's Strategic Plan. Retrieved from www.uottawa.ca/about/vision.

University of Ottawa Executive Committee of the Board of Governors. 2016. Response by the Executive Committee of the Board of Governors to the Report of the Finance and Treasury Committee: Addressing Global Warming. Retrieved from www.uottawa.ca/ administration-and-governance/response-executive-committee-report-finance-and-treasury-committee.

University of Ottawa Facilities. n.d. Power Plant. Retrieved from www.uottawa.ca/facil ities/sectors/operations-maintenance/power-plant.

University of Ottawa Faculty of Social Sciences. n.d. Social Sciences Building. Retrieved from https://socialsciences.uottawa.ca/about-faculty/fss-building.

University of Ottawa Finance and Treasury Committee. 2016. Addressing Global Warming: The UOttawa Response. A Report from the Finance and Treasury Committee to the Board of Governors of the University of Ottawa. Retrieved from www.uottawa.ca/ administration-and-governance/sites/www.uottawa.ca.administration-and-governance/ files/report_of_the_finance_and_treasury_committee_to_the_board.pdf.

University of Ottawa IRP. 2017. Quick Facts, Institutional Research and Planning. Retrieved from www.uottawa.ca/institutional-research-planning/resources/facts-fig ures/quick-facts.

University of Ottawa Office of Campus Sustainability. n.d. a. Energy. Retrieved from http://sustainable.uottawa.ca/energy.

University of Ottawa Office of Campus Sustainability. n.d. b. Green Reps. Office of Campus Sustainability. Retrieved from https://sustainable.uottawa.ca/green-reps.

University of Ottawa Office of Campus Sustainability. n.d. c. Sustainable Transportation. Office of Campus Sustainability. Retrieved from https://sustainable.uottawa.ca/sus tainable-transportation.

VandeWeghe, Jared and Christopher Kennedy. 2007. A Spatial Analysis of Residential Greenhouse Gas Emissions in the Toronto Census Metropolitan Area. *Journal of Industrial Ecology* 11(2): 133–44.

Victor, David G. 2004. *The Collapse of the Kyoto Protocol and the Struggle to Slow Global Warming*. Princeton, NJ: Princeton University Press.

Victor, David G. 2011. *Global Warming Gridlock: Creating More Effective Strategies for Protecting the Planet*. Cambridge: Cambridge University Press.

Vidal, John. 2012. Rio+20: Earth Summit Dawns with Stormier Clouds than in 1992. *The Guardian*. Retrieved from www.theguardian.com/environment/2012/jun/19/rio-20-earth-summit-1992-2012.

Viner Assets Inc. v. City of Ottawa. 2015. PL140348.

Walker, Gordon, and Noel Cass. 2007. Carbon Reduction, 'the Public' and Renewable Energy: Engaging with Socio-Technical Configurations. *Area* 39(4): 458–69.

Wall, Derek. 2020. *Climate Strike: The Practical Politics of the Climate Crisis*. Dagenham: Merlin Press.

Weber, Max. 2013/1919. Politics as a Vocation. In Max Weber, H. H. Gerth and C. Wright Mills, eds., *From Max Weber: Essays in Sociology*. London: Taylor & Francis, 77–128.

Wernick, Andrew. 1991. *Promotional Culture: Advertising, Ideology and Symbolic Expression*. London: Sage.

While, Aidan, Andrew E. G. Jonas, and David Gibbs. 2004. The Environment and the Entrepreneurial City: Searching for the Urban 'Sustainability Fix' in Manchester and Leeds. *International Journal of Urban and Regional Research* 28(3): 549–69.

Whitford, Jacques. 2002. Greenhouse Gas Inventory and Emission Reduction Strategies for the Transportation and Waste Sectors in the City of Ottawa. Report prepared for the City of Ottawa. Torrie Smith Associates.

Willems, Steph. 2014. Section of Churchill Ready to Reopen. *Ottawa Community News*, 31 July.

Williams, Stewart. 2012. Anoraks, Train Timetables, Bus Rides and Biscuits: Taking on the Impossible in the Politics of Climate Change. *Local–Global: Identity, Security, Community*, 10: 58–80.

Willing, Jon. 2013. Bike Lanes Here to Stay: Council OKs Strip of Laurier Ave. *Ottawa Sun*, 6 July, p. 6.

Willis, Rebecca. 2020. *Too Hot to Handle?: The Democratic Challenge of Climate Change*. Bristol: Policy Press.

Winfield, Mark, and Brett Dolter. 2014. Energy, Economic and Environmental Discourses and Their Policy Impact: The Case of Ontario's Green Energy and Green Economy Act. *Energy Policy* 68(May): 423–35.

Winner, Langdon. 1980. Do Artifacts Have Politics? *Daedalus*, 109(1): 121–36.

Woods, Michael. 2014. Neighbours Fail to Halt Student Housing: 'We Will Witness a Moral Decay of Society and Community Living', Opponent Says. *Ottawa Citizen*, 26 February, p. C3.

Wright, Christopher, and Daniel Nyberg. 2015. *Climate Change, Capitalism, and Corporations: Processes of Creative Self-Destruction*. Cambridge: Cambridge University Press.

Yatchew, Adonis, and Andy Baziliauskas. 2011. Ontario Feed-in-Tariff Programs. *Energy Policy, Special Section: Renewable Energy Policy and Development*, 39(7): 3885–93.

Yogaretnam, Shaamini. 2014. Implementation of 'Complete Streets' Policy a Matter of Steady Baby Steps, Panel of Councillors Say. *Postmedia Breaking News*, 29 March.

Zavestoski, Stephen, and Julian Agyeman, eds. 2015. *Incomplete Streets: Processes, Practices, and Possibilities*. London: Routledge.

Zeemering, Eric S. 2016. What Are the Challenges of Multilevel Governance for Urban Sustainability? Evidence from Ottawa and Canada's National Capital Region. *Canadian Public Administration* 59(2): 204–23.

Zielinski, Sue and Gavin Laird, eds. 1995. *Beyond the Car*. Toronto: Detour Press.

Index